CHRISTIAN ANARCHY

Jesus' Primacy over the Powers

by
Vernard Eller

WILLIAM B. EERDMANS PUBLISHING COMPANY
GRAND RAPIDS, MICHIGAN

Copyright © 1987 by William B. Eerdmans Publishing Company
255 Jefferson Ave. S.E., Grand Rapids, Mich. 49503

Library of Congress Cataloging-in-Publication Data

Eller, Vernard.
  Christian anarchy.

  1. Christianity and politics.
  2. Powers (Christian theology) I. Title.
BR115.P7E543   1987   261.7   87-6734

ISBN 0-8028-0227-3

CONTENTS

In appreciation of
JACQUES ELLUL

who has led me not only into Christian Anarchy
but into much more of God's truth as well.
Merci, mon ami!

PREFACE

I hope you find this book "important." But whether you do or don't, it is very important *to me*. More than thirty years into my writing career, I finally have my answer to the question "Who am I?"

From the outset, of course, I have been aware that my thought has been formed by the Anabaptist/Brethren tradition of my own church background—and that, it must be said, much more by its classic, historical manifestation than by any contemporary version. I knew then, too, who were the modern thinkers leading me further and further along this line of development. My doctoral dissertation had me exploring the convergence between the thought of Kierkegaard and that of early Brethrenism. Later, I discovered the Blumhardts and published a volume of excerpts from their work. I quickly caught on that Jacques Ellul was of this company and consequently have done studies of and had correspondence with him. More recently, I have had a growing appreciation of Karl Barth as being another representative of the school. My problem has never been that of floundering around. I have always known *where* I was—even if not quite sure *who*.

I even got this tradition identified (and I think accurately enough) as "Radical Christian Discipleship." However, although it worked for a time, that label didn't begin to explain the full distinction between this and other Christian traditions. And I regularly found myself at odds with other individuals and groups also claiming to represent Radical Christian Discipleship. This tradition, clearly, had made me a "pacifist"; yet I was entirely unhappy with the "pacifism" of contemporary Brethrenism. Why, I asked myself, did I always wind up on the wrong side of each of the Christian Left's enthusiasms—peace, justice, equality, liberation, feminism? After all, I was supposed to be *part* of that gang, not an *outsider*. Yet no matter what was said or implied about me, I knew I was not a "conservative" over against their "liberalism." I was every bit as unhappy with the positions of conservatism as with those of liberalism. So, being neither a radical, a liberal, nor a conservative, what under the sun was I? What other option could there be?

The chapters here following will recount my discovery of the rather easily identifiable but almost entirely subconscious and submerged tradition of "Christian Anarchy." And with that tradition I have found my home and am at peace. All of my battles of the past thirty years now fall into place and make sense. Now I can see a consistency throughout; I knew what I was doing but didn't have a name for it.

I really do believe the key was in coming up with the requisite terminology: "anarchy," with the derivatives "arky" and "arky faith." All along, of course, Scripture itself provided the terms that should have led us to this understanding but had not. Its talk of "the powers" would have done it—except that we automatically identified those only as the *evil* powers we were eager to combat and not at all including the *good* powers we embraced. Likewise, both with Jesus' "being not of the world" and Paul's "not being conformed to the world," we read them as counsels to separate ourselves only from the world's bad powers and certainly not from its good ones. Consequently, lacking an explicit terminology, even the greatest Christian anarchists—from Jesus on down—have not had themselves or their tradition identified in a way that would make possible explicit consideration, analysis, and debate.

Yet the material is there. In fact, even before I made my discovery of Christian Anarchy, several of the chapters of this book had been written as independent pieces. I now found that all I had to do was a bit of recasting into arky terminology in order to make them fit—and not only fit but also come alive with a clarity and relevance they had not had before. Indeed, I could now read any number of my earlier efforts and say, "Of course! If I had only had the concept 'anarchy,' I would have known what I was talking about." Actually, at one point I was right on the verge. In my book *The Promise* (New York: Doubleday, 1970), there was an untimely born, now-I-see-what-this-book-is-all-about chapter entitled "The Grand Irrelevancy of the Gospel," in which I spoke particularly of the grand irrelevancy of Jesus. That chapter can now be seen to be pure Christian Anarchy. But I didn't have the word for it and so had to wait another fifteen years to get the answer to "Who am I?" Sorry about that. Nevertheless, whether you find this book important or not, it is a most important one to me.

When it comes to acknowledging those who have aided in the creation of this book, I am in an impossible situation. In bits and pieces, the manuscript has circulated ever so widely. Some of the ideas and materials have been used in public presentation and discussion. I can't begin to recall who all contributed what helpful suggestions and criticisms. Therefore, I have decided here to list by name only those recognized scholars who have done the equivalent of a professional critique from their field of expertise. Most of these get mentioned within the book itself. And it must be emphasized that the appearance of a name here does not necessarily connote that person's approval of the book's thesis; in a couple of cases that definitely is not so.

But I here want to recognize my debt and express my gratitude to the following distinguished professors (all in the fields of theology and Bible except Jacques Ellul, who is distinguished in any number of fields, and James Stayer, who is a historian): Bernard Ramm (American Baptist Seminary of the West, Berkeley); Jacques Ellul (retired in Bordeaux, France); George Hunsinger (Bangor Theological Seminary); Warren Groff (Bethany Theological Seminary, Oak Brook, Illinois); Markus Barth (University of Basel, Switzerland); Martin Rumscheidt (Atlantic School of Theology, Halifax, Nova Scotia); James Stayer (Queen's University, Kingston, Ontario); Howard Clark Kee (Boston University).

The best I can do for all the other people who feel they have contributed to the book is this: I hereby want to express my heartfelt gratitude to all the other people who feel they have contributed to the book.

I do also want to give special thanks to the Wm. B. Eerdmans Publishing Company—in particular to Publisher Eerdmans and editors Gary Lee and Sandy Zeles. My relationship there has always been much more personal and precious than simply a business one.

As ever, I am deeply obligated to the members of my own family—some of whom made a direct contribution to this particular book; all of whom hold me up and keep me going through the labor of book-birthing.

Finally, regarding the typing and manuscript preparation, I have deep gratitude for my faithful TRS-80 Model I computer and its Allwrite word-processing program. It gets the job done right—and cheap.

VERNARD ELLER
La Verne, California
New Year 1986

BEFORE WE START

Enough of the manuscript already has been around enough that I can know for a surety what the major criticism of this book will be. It makes sense, then, for me to enter my rejoinder here—even before we start. This way, the readers can immediately be cognizant of the issue and thus prepared to weigh its pros and cons in the very process of their reading.

It already has been and will continue to be said that the position presented here has me essentially "apolitical"—and thus quietistic, unconcerned about the state of the world, irresponsible, and altogether deplorable.

For one thing, I would respond that the book is not exactly an arguing of "my position." Before it is that it is an effort to discover: (1) the position of *Scripture* (particularly Jesus and Paul); (2) in a major way, the positions of Jacques Ellul and Karl Barth; (3) in a lesser way, those of Søren Kierkegaard, J. C. and Christoph Blumhardt, and Dietrich Bonhoeffer; and (4) in a still lesser way, those of several contemporary New Testament scholars.

It is only out of these sources, then, I derive what might be called "my position." Accordingly, before denouncing Vernard Eller's "apoliticism" out of hand, any critic ought really to decide whether he means also to include Scripture and these other human authorities in that denunciation—or whether he is prepared to show that my interpretation of them is wrongheaded. I am ready to face the music either way; but I do think the critic needs to decide which is to be his tune.

However, regarding the issue itself, I would say that whether or not *our* position fairly can be charged as "apolitical" depends entirely upon how one defines "political." If "political" be taken in the narrow sense, as signifying those means and methods the world regularly accepts as normative for its doing of politics, then the position of me and mine clearly and admittedly is that of apoliticism.

If, however, "political" be understood in the broad, etymological sense, as identifying whatever actions have public effect upon the life of the "city" *(polis)*, then there are no grounds for accusing either "me" or any of "mine" of advocating apoliticism.

No, our position is meant precisely to challenge the assumption that the worldly way is the only way to be of ameliorative political effect. Consequently, we urge Christians to be as political as all get out, *in their own peculiarly Christian way*. Otherwise, if the gospel *must* simply accept and buy into the world's definition of politics, then as much as that gospel can hope to offer is counsel and instruction on how to play worldly power-politics effectively and well. And I can't see that as being much of a *gospel* at all. Anything expecting to be called "good news" just has to be better than that.

I propose, therefore, that the basic distinction between worldly politics and Christian politics lies in two assumptions that are fundamental to the worldly practice but absolutely rejected by the gospel.

In the first place, the exercise of worldly politics rests upon a quite unfounded confidence in the moral competency of human beings—and more particularly, upon a quite arrogant error in attributing categorical moral superiority to partisans of the one "true" ideology over against those of any party else. This proud claim extends not only to moral *wisdom* ("We know what is right as no one else does") but also to moral *authority* ("Because we are right, that justifies our use of propaganda, demonstration, boycott, and all such power tactics in imposing our 'right' upon those people we know to be wrong"). Worldly politics is built upon pretentious claims of moral superiority—of which the Christian gospel recognizes nary a one.

Second, it follows that a prime characteristic of worldly politics is its invariable forming of itself as "adversarial contest." There has to be a battle. One party, ideology, cause group, lobby, or power bloc which has designated itself as "The Good, the True, and the Beautiful" sets out to overbear, overwhelm, overcome, overpower, or otherwise impose itself on whatever opposing parties think *they* deserve the title. And if this power contest among the morally pretentious is what is meant by being "political," then Eller and company are indeed happy to be called "apolitical."

We claim, however, that there is another form of politics—another form of action affecting the *polis*—that the gospel can fully approve. In this form, rather than one worldly party setting itself in moral judgment over all others, our political action would be submission to *God's* moral judgment upon everything and everyone human (which judgment, it is clear, falls firstly and foremostly upon God's very own partisans). Rather than taking sides, this politics would be nonpartisanly critical of all adversary contest and power play. It would be a politics of servant ministry completely ignoring party lines—a politics intent on mediation and the reconciling of adversaries instead of supporting the triumph of one over another. It would be a political theology of liberation intent to liberate humanity from nothing so much as its enslavement to worldly politics.

Nobody anywhere in this book says anything remotely suggesting that Christians need have no concern regarding the grave social problems of our world. I don't think anyone cited would have difficulty with Karl Barth's "not of this world" politics—which we now undertake merely to suggest with a few quotations out of the later chapter dealing exclusively with him.

> He [Barth] thought that the church could neither prescribe a political decision nor leave it open (as though it were merely "a matter of discretion"); [the church's] task was to make the issues quite clear. [This "clarifying of the issues" I take to mean an open and objective presentation of all interpretations and points of view rather than the pushing of the one ideological line the pastor (or some other partisan) has already decided is the Christian one.]
>
> The [church's] proclamation [of justice to the world] is good when it presents the specific commandment of God, and is not good when it puts forward the abstract truth of a political ideology.
>
> [The church should exercise] an active and responsible participation in the state. [But] of course, the church's decisive service to the state was, in Barth's view, its preaching: "By proclaiming the divine justification, it performs the best service to the establishment and maintenance of human justice."
>
> The church best performs its service in the midst of political change when its attitude is so independent and . . . so sympathetic that it is able to summon the representatives of the old and new order alike [i.e., rightist supporters of the establishment and leftist supporters of the revolution] . . . to humility, to the praise of God, and to humanity, and can invite them all to trust in the great change (in the death and resurrection of Christ) and to hope in his revelation.

Obviously, there is a sense (the partisan power-contest sense) in which Barth's position very accurately could be called "apolitical"—especially when he starts inviting secular bureaucracies to accept Jesus and trust in his coming again (that's politics?). Yet, just as obviously, if "apolitical" has to mean "socially unconcerned," "hopeless about any possibility of change," "helpless that either God or the church might publicly act"—if "apolitical" has to carry these overtones, then it is the last word in the world that will apply to Karl Barth.

Consider that the "coming of Jesus" (even now underway) involves the greatest political change the world will ever see, namely, the disappearance of worldly politics with all its moral pretension and adversarial contest. And if this is what the coming of Jesus *portends,* then the first place this disappearance should be observable is among the members of Christ's body. Thus, God's indication is that the church should be moving *away* from hard-ball politics rather than (as we are doing) *baptizing* such politics—and this in complete disregard of what the hymnist knew almost a century ago: "For not with swords' loud clashing, / Nor roll of stirring drums, / But deeds of love and mercy, / The heavenly kingdom comes."

CHRISTIAN
ANARCHY

Chapter One

CHRISTIAN ANARCHY
—THE VERY IDEA!

Why don't we really get radical for once? Yes, I know it wasn't easy to get the word *radical* understood as an adjective appropriate to *discipleship*. And yes, it was even harder to get *revolution* and *revolutionary* so understood. But do you think it a bit more than the traffic can bear for me now to push on to *anarchy*? Do you see me going from bad to worse? Not so. I stand prepared to show that to go from *revolution* to *anarchy* is to go from wrong to right, from misunderstanding to understanding, from unbiblical to biblical, from world to gospel. And yes, it will take another transforming renewal of our minds to understand *anarchy* as the gospel, the good news it actually is.

The word is ANARCHY. The prefix ("an-") is the equivalent of the English "un-," meaning "not"; it does not particularly mean "anti-" or against. Thus, we are speaking of that which is more *not something* than it is opposed to or against something. The "-archy" root (which I have made into an English term spelled a-r-k-y) is a common Greek word that means "priority," "primacy," "primordial," "principal," "prince," and the like. (Look at that last sentence and realize that "pri-" is simply the Latin equivalent of the Greek "arky.") The most frequent appearance of "arky" in the New Testament is where it is translated as "beginning." Indeed, in Colossians 1:18 Paul actually identifies Jesus as "the beginning," "the prime," "THE ARKY." However, our particular concern with the word is in Paul's writings where it is translated "principalities." Clearly, the apostle assumes that we live in a world with arkys filled that threaten to undo us—and those constantly battling each other for primacy.

For us, then, "arky" identifies any principle of governance claiming to be of primal value for society. "Government" (that which is determined to *govern* human action and events) is a good synonym—as long as we are clear that political arkys are far from being

I

the only "governments" around. Not at all; churches, schools, philosophies, ideologies, social standards, peer pressures, fads and fashions, advertising, planning techniques, psychological and sociological theories—all are arkys out to govern us.

"Anarchy" ("unarkyness"), it follows, is simply the state of being unimpressed with, disinterested in, skeptical of, nonchalant toward, and uninfluenced by the highfalutin claims of any and all arkys. And "Christian Anarchy"—the special topic of this book—is a Christianly motivated "unarkyness." Precisely because Jesus is THE ARKY, the Prime of Creation, the Principal of All Good, the Prince of Peace and Everything Else, Christians dare never grant a human arky the primacy it claims for itself. Precisely because *God* is the Lord of History we dare never grant that it is in the outcome of the human arky contest that the determination of history lies.

Obviously, the idea of "power" goes hand in hand with "arky"; the two are inseparable. Indeed, every time Paul uses "arky" in the sense of "principalities," he couples it with one of the Greek "power" words. Yet regarding both "power" and "arky" we must make a crucial specification: we are always supposing a power or a government that is *imposed* upon its constituency. It is, of course, proper to speak of, say, "the power of love." Yet this is power in an entirely different sense of the word in that it carries no hint of imposition at all. Looking only at the phrase itself, "the kingdom of God" would appear to be an "arky" no different from the others. Yet we will come to see that this is not so. When Jesus said "My kingdom is not of this world," he was saying that, although all worldly arkys *have* to be impositional, his is radically different in that it does not have to be—and in fact is not.

This matter of an arky's being *imposed* leads us to the helpful term "heteronomy"—namely, that law or rule which is "different from," "other than," or "extraneous to" whomever it would govern. All worldly arkys are by nature heteronomous—each is out to impose *its* idea of what is right upon whoever has any different idea.

Consequently, for *secular* anarchists the solution is "autonomy"—the self being a law unto itself (which is what we customarily have understood "anarchy" to be). However, Christianity contends that autonomy is simply another form of heteronomy, that to use my own self-image as the arky governing my self is actually to impose a heteronomous arky upon me. The assumption that I am the one who best knows myself and knows what is best for myself is to forget that I am a creature (a sinful creature, even) and that there is a Creator who, being my Creator (and also being somewhat smarter than I am), knows me much better than I ever can know myself.

For Christian anarchists, then, the goal of anarchy is "theonomy"—the rule, the ordering, the arky of *God*. At this idea, of course, the world rises up to insist that the arky of God is just as impositional as (if not more so than) any other arky that might be named. But Christians say No—and that on two counts. First, particularly as God has been revealed in Jesus Christ, the style of his arky is not that of imposition but of the opposite, namely, that of the cross, the self-givingness of agape-love. And second, God's arky, his will for us, is never anything extraneous to ourselves but precisely that which is most germane to our true destiny and being. Anarchist Søren Kierkegaard hammered this one home with his analysis of the Danish word for "duty"—which, in our context, would represent "God's arky for us." Kierkegaard writes: "For duty is not an *imposition* [in Danish, *paalaeg,* lit. "that which *is laid* upon"] but rather 'duty' is something which is *incumbent* [in Danish, *paaliger,* lit. "that which *lies* upon"]." Rather than a heteronomous imposition, God's arky spells the discovery of that which is truest to myself and my world.

The contention of Christian Anarchy, then, is that worldly arkys are of the "all" that "in Adam" dies and are no part of the "all" that "in Christ" is made alive (1 Cor. 15:22). Consequently, worldly arkys must die (and we must die to them) in order that the Arky of God (his kingdom) might be made alive in us (and us in it).

At this point of definition, then, we should note that the idea of "revolution" is not anarchical in any sense of the word. Revolutionists *are* very strongly opposed to certain arkys that they know to be "bad" and to be the work of "bad people." However, they are just as strongly in favor of what they know to be "good" arkys that are the work of themselves and other good people like them. For instance, these revolutionists might seem to be superanarchical, finding nothing good to say about the establishment U.S. arky; but they turn out to be very proarchical, finding nothing *but* good to say about a revolutionary Sandinista arky. Indeed, the regular procedure of "revolution" is to form a (good) power-arky that can either overthrow and displace or else radically transform the (bad) arky currently in power. This selectivity amounts to a passionate faith in the power of arkys for human good and the farthest thing possible from a truly anarchical suspicion and mistrust of every human arky. Thus "anarchical" is a synonym for "nonpartisan"; and "anarchy" and "partisanship" are direct opposites.

This book was written in a way no other of mine has been written. Some books I have been asked to do, some I have thought up on my own, some I have seen coming, some I have stumbled into— but into this one I was *enticed* by a serpent too innocent to know what he was doing. My old friend Bernard Ramm, evangelical beyond fundamentalism and professor at American Baptist Seminary of the West, simply wrote me a brief note:

> I would appreciate a letter from you on "passive anarchism." The bulk of the material on the subject is devoted to the various Russian or revolutionary views. But I suspect that there is a "passive Christian anarchism" ("all states are created equally wicked"). One review just mentioned Blumhardt—and if my memory serves me okay, you have a book on the father/son.

Now that poor man certainly wrote to me without the intention of starting anything. Nevertheless, I gave him just what he was asking for—beginning with a long letter, which I intended to use also as an article, but which wound up as the very chapter you are now reading.

However, my first reaction to Ramm's note was, "What on earth is he talking about? I don't know anything about 'anarchism period'—let alone 'passive Christian anarchism.' And I haven't the foggiest as to what all that has to do with the Blumhardts. Coming to me, he's got him the wrong boy."

Yet, if I was to have any chance of keeping Bernie bluffed regarding my scholarly reputation, I would have to come up with something. And the something I did come up with was the recollection that Ellul had had an article on the topic some years back. I must have been feeling tired or ornery when I originally read it, because I had entirely dismissed it as one of his less successful efforts. All I could remember is that he had set out to demonstrate the agreement between his personal version of Christianity (which he called "anarchism") and the secular anarchism of what Ramm calls "the various Russian or revolutionary views." It had been my impression that, in the process, Ellul had so qualified his Christian anarchism as to lose any real concept of "anarchy" entirely.

Yet, for Ramm's sake, I had to dig up that old article, "Anarchism and Christianity" (*KATALLAGETE* [Fall 1980]; hereafter: *Anarchism*). In the process, of course, I reread it—no, truly read it for the first time: "Oh, that's what you meant by 'Christian anarchism.' Right on, Friar Jacques! And sure, if that's what anarchism is, then, that's exactly where the Blumhardts belong, too."

So now, as "the oracle of the man whose eye is opened (finally)," I propose here to enlarge Ellul's insight into a thesis regarding Christian history itself. To my mind, Ellul demonstrates decisively that a particular version of "anarchism" (Ramm's adjective "passive" is not quite the right modifier) is the sociopolitical stance of the entire Bible in general and the New Testament in particular. I would add that, from there, the understanding was picked up by that church tradition perhaps most often identified with "radical discipleship"—through which it came even to Ellul himself.

In very broad strokes, I would trace that somewhat amorphous (anarchical, of course) tradition thus: Although there are scattered flashes within earlier church history, the thread first establishes itself in the Radical Reformation of the sixteenth century. There it is found in the Anabaptists, predecessors of the Mennonites and other groups. My own Church of the Brethren was born out of this tradition in the eighteenth century. And there are other denominations that show more or less of the influence since. Not necessarily the term "anarchism" but the spirit and idea could be cited out of the early thought and life of all these bodies.

As we move from institutional groupings to individual thinkers, the anarchism is even easier to spot. The title of the published version of my doctoral dissertation was "Kierkegaard and Radical Discipleship" (perhaps the first time the phrase "radical discipleship" had appeared in print). And it doesn't require much effort to show that, in attitude, S. K. was quite anarchistic toward church, state, and society.

I didn't know where Ramm had found the word *anarchy* in connection with the Blumhardts; but the identification is accurate. The one explicit use of the word I find is in the younger Blumhardt's statement:

> Of course, thought cannot go too far in this direction before we come upon a word which is very much forbidden today. Yet there is something to be said for it. I will state it right out: "Anarchy!" Regarding the inhabitants of earth, a certain freedom, a veritable rulelessness, would almost be better than this nailed-up-tight business which as much as turns individual peoples into herds of animals closed to every great thought. (*Thy Kingdom Come* [Eerdmans, 1980], p. 21)

And the idea, if not the word, comes through in the following remarks—which could be multiplied at length:

All [the arkydom] we have had up to this point is on its last run downwards. Our theology is moving down with the rapidity of a lowering storm. Our ecclesiastical perceptions are rapidly becoming political perceptions. Our worship services are being accommodated to the world. And thus it is necessary that all that has been should cease, should come to its end, making room again for something new, namely, the kingdom of God.

Again:

People are afraid of the collapse of the world. I am looking forward to it. I wish it would begin right now to crash and break apart. For this world of the humanly great is and remains the cause of all misery. They cannot do anything about it, these well-intentioned people, these good kings and ministers, these excellent prelates and popes. However much they try, they cannot. I would like to tell all of them, "You cannot do it!"

In this next quote, Blumhardt makes clear that it is only because of the *eschatological* character of the faith we can afford to be *anarchical* regarding this world:

"Lo, I am with you always, to the close of the age" (Matt. 28:20). The Savior's being with us has reference to the end of the world, not to its continuance. . . . Jesus is not *with* a person who spends his days for the sole purpose of sustaining earthly life. The Lord does not wish to spend too much effort on the continuance of the world. After all, it is corruptible; there is nothing left to be done but to await the wearing out of the decaying structure and the creating of a new one.

For the time being, we must do the best we can with what we have. . . . [But] in all our work, then, let us be careful to fix our eyes, not on the continuance of the world, but on its end. (Pp. 121-22)

Subsequent to the Blumhardts, then, Karl Barth and Dietrich Bonhoeffer have shown more-or-less anarchistic tendencies—in that order. In his second edition of the commentary on Romans, Barth wrote:

What is true of the generality of men is true also of the men of God. As men they do not differ from other men. . . . There are no saints in the midst of a company of sinners. . . . Their criticism and invective and indictment of the world inevitably

place them—unless they be themselves its object—within the
course of this world and betray that they too are of it. . . .
This is as true of Paul, the prophet and apostle of the Kingdom
of God, and of Jeremiah, as it is of Luther, Kierkegaard, and
Blumhardt! (P. 57)

Goodness knows the thought expressed here is anarchical
enough of itself. Yet it is the accident of that final sentence which
is so telling for our purpose. Undoubtedly in a quite offhand way,
without even stopping to think, Barth nominates *his* Christian saints
(who he knows, of course, would be the very last people to claim
sainthood for themselves). Nevertheless, with the exception of Jeremiah, our study will, in a greater or lesser way, tie each of these
thinkers into the tradition of Christian Anarchy. Whether con-
sciously or only subconsciously, Barth knew himself to stand in the
very succession we have in mind for him.

Finally, along comes Jacques Ellul to crystallize the idea and
give it what is probably the most self-conscious and explicit exposition the tradition has produced. Now, for the first time, it is out
where we can talk about it.

Probably the most typical and conspicuous model of the radical-discipleship tradition of our day is *Sojourners* magazine, although the current intellectual and theological leadership of the
Brethren and Mennonite churches, plus all the recent converts of
the new evangelicalism, belong there as well. Yet the concept of
Christian Anarchy is so very crucial today because it enables us to
see that what commonly passes as the radical-discipleship tradition
has slipped a cog that actually puts it clear outside the biblical and
historical tradition we have just traced. As Ellul says: "The Christians
who are engaged in the theological overhaul to which we have al-
luded are politically Leftist, even extreme Left. But they do not
really know what anarchism is" (*Anarchism*, p. 15).

More recently, Ellul has published an autobiography, in interview form, entitled *In Season, Out of Season* (Harper & Row, 1982;
hereafter: *Season*). In it, he uses the term *anarchy* only infrequently—
and the term or concept *Christian anarchy*, never. Yet wide-flung
passages are germane. For example, in response to the question "Do
you consider yourself an anarchist?" he says:

The anarchist milieu is the only one in which I often feel
perfectly at ease. I am myself there. On the other hand, I am
not at ease either in the right-wing milieu, which doesn't in-

terest me, or in the left-wing milieu, for whom I am not overtly
a socialist and even less a communist. And I am not at all,
really not at all at ease in the milieu of the Christian left. . . .

[The interviewer asks:] Aren't you nevertheless a partisan of
a more rational society?

Oh, no, not at all. On the contrary, I believe that the greatest
good that could happen to society today is an increasing disorder. . . . I am in no way pleading in favor of a different social
order. I am pleading for the regression of all the powers of
order. (Pp. 195-96)

Ellul's "anarchism" has him most markedly distinguished from
and opposed to those intent on creating "a new, Christian social
order." That is the group he identifies as "the Christian Left." And
what we have here called "the contemporary version of radical discipleship" clearly constitutes at least one segment of that Christian
Left. The problem (as shall become clear) is that these people are
totally dedicated to "revolution" where Ellul sees Christianity dedicated to "anarchy." The two ideas are not simply different but ac-
· tually opposed to each other. And it is to this point we will return
time and again throughout the treatment that follows.

Ellul grounds his concept of Christian Anarchy with a quick survey
of the Bible, focusing upon its opinion of that particular (and perhaps prototypical) arky, the civil government, or state. I shall do an
even quicker survey of his survey, centering upon those places where
I want to say something of my own.

As key and theme statement, Ellul naturally uses God's and
Samuel's warnings about what will be the harvest of Israel's bright
dreams for a "mono-arky." Right out of the gate, then, King Saul
demonstrates the truth of what God and Samuel had said. Ellul next
calls David's reign "an exception" and proceeds to recount the sad
history of the remainder of the monarchy. But I want to insist that
David is not the exception but actually the heart of the pattern. (I
do not like to hear it said that I automatically accept whatever Ellul
says as being gospel truth; that is not [quite] true.)

Until the time of David's adultery with Bathsheba and the
murder of her husband, it is indeed the case that he was brilliantly
successful in forming a strong arky that accomplished all sorts of
good for Israel. Yet upon the discovery of that sin, God tells the
king, "I anointed you king over Israel [and did all these fine things

through you and for you]. . . . And if this were too little, I would add to you as much more. Why have you despised the word of the Lord, to do what is evil in his sight?" (2 Sam. 12:7-9).

None of David's accomplishments actually should be credited to the power of his arky. They were manifestations of God's arky working through him. David's sin, then, was precisely the claiming of that arky power as his own, proposing that his kingly arky gave him executive privilege even over God's moral arky that prohibits adultery and murder. And if, even with so good and dedicated a believer as David, power-arky inevitably goes pretentious, then what hope is there that other human arkys can ever do better? Hear the word of Blumhardt to these well-intentioned people, these good kings and ministers, these excellent prelates and popes (these zealous Christian revolutionaries): "You cannot do it!"

Far from being the exception, David is our one best argument for anarchy. With his arkycal pretension (even though repented), his career goes into the skid that runs right on through the breakup of the kingdom under Solomon and into the disaster of the kings that followed. Indeed, in the process of recounting the gosh-awfulness of the arky of one King Jehoram, the writer says, "Yet the Lord would not destroy Judah, for the sake of David his servant, since he promised to give a lamp to him and to his sons for ever" (2 Kings 8:19). God's covenantal promise was the only thing keeping the Davidic arky afloat. And of course, even that sad ship sank once for all, with the destruction of Jerusalem and the Babylonian exile.

Does this mean, then, that God's covenant with David came to *nothing?* Not at all. By this time, prophets had come to see that the track of God's promise was never meant to be that of the human arky of David; that was a false lead. No, the actual track of the covenant was that pointing to the coming Messiah, the one true Son of David. And that Jesus, of course, turned out to be King of the one truly anarchist, nonimpositional, nonheteronomous, not-of-this-worldly kingdom. Ellul is right that the Bible's mainline tradition regarding politics is most "unarkycal," can be deemed as nothing but "anarchist."

In the New Testament (our discussion of which will not always rely on Ellul) Jesus is being presented as history's Arch-Anarchist (if that oxymoron be allowed). Quite in passing (this not from Ellul), the German New Testament scholar Joachim Jeremias (in *Rediscovering the Parables* [Scribner, 1966], pp. 96-97) makes an observation that is most supportive of our argument. He opines, first, regarding the Gospel accounts of the temptation of Jesus, that it is likely the Master, perhaps on different occasions, used three different "parables" (stones into bread; leap from the temple; and worship the devil) to recount to his disciples what was actually one temptation experience rather than three separate ones. Then Jeremias suggests, "He told his disciples about his victory over the temptation to present himself as a political messiah—perhaps in order to warn them against a similiar temptation."

Yet, "political messiah" is precisely what a good many Christian leftists would now make of Jesus—namely, sponsor of the particular revolutionary arky *they* have in mind for bringing peace and justice to the world. As much as any word in Scripture, Jesus' condemning of arky-messiahship as a *temptation* places him distinctly in "anarchy" over against any and all who, instead, hold that there are indeed good human arkys elected and sponsored by God.

Another picture of Jesus' anarchism (again, of my choice rather than Ellul's) is his appearance before Pilate, particularly as it is recounted in John 18:33–19:11. Let me try a paraphrase that—admittedly far from Jesus in its language—may nevertheless catch the "feel" of the incident:

> Please, fella, don't bother yourself to tell me how great is this Roman Empire of yours and how great the fact that *you* are a governor of it. I've heard that stuff all my life and know it already. Yet I also happen to know that the one, real, true kingdom isn't even *of* this world. I know, too, that you guys couldn't as much as lift a finger if my Father didn't let you do it. Sure, you can crucify me—*if he lets you.* But there is no way you can *eliminate* me. So just can it, Pilate. I don't want to talk to you, because nothing you say makes one bit of difference anyhow. Let's get on with this crucifixion; and I'll see you day after tomorrow, in church at the Easter Sunrise Service, OK?

Would it not be fair to characterize that attitude as "anarchistic"? Jesus will grant not one bit of weight to Pilate and his Empire.

Another such picture (chosen by Ellul rather than Eller) is that of Jesus and the tribute money (Mark 12:13-17). There Jesus' questioners face him with the political choice they consider all-decisive: "Are you going to be a rightist who supports the civil establishment with your taxes; or are you going to be a leftist revolutionary who opposes that evil establishment by withholding them?" To which Jesus comes back as perfect anarchist: *"I'm* not going to be either

one. That's a fake choice. Whether a person chooses God or not is
the only real issue—and one's political preference has nothing to do
with it. Give God what belongs to God."

As Ellul puts it:

"Render unto Caesar . . ." in no way divides the exercise of
authority into two realms. . . . [Those words] were said in response to another matter: the payment of taxes, and the coin.
The mark on the coin is that of Caesar; it is the mark of his
property. Therefore give Caesar this money; it is his. It is not
a question of legitimizing taxes! It means that Caesar, having
created money, is its master. That's all. Let us not forget that
money, for Jesus, is the domain of Mammon, a satanic domain.
(*Anarchism,* p. 20)

As noted, the above has been only somewhat dependent upon
Ellul. When he comes to Romans 13, however, Ellul really shines.
The passage, of course, is the first a person normally would go to
in order to *rebut* our "anarchism" argument. But Ellul won't let such
people have it; he wants it as a key to *his* argument. His contention
is that there is nothing here lending one bit of legitimacy to human
arky, Roman or otherwise. Rather, what Paul actually is about is
deliberately citing and following Jesus, in the effort to protect "anarchy" from being confused with, and misread as, "revolution."

Thus, "there is no authority except from God," etc. (v. 1) says
nothing different from what we just heard Jesus say in John 19:11.
If I may help him a bit, Paul is saying: "Be clear, any of those human
arkys are where they are only because God is allowing them to be
there. They exist only at his sufferance. And if God is willing to put
up with a stinker like the Roman Empire, you ought to be willing
to put up with it, too. There is no indication God has called *you* to
clear it out of the way or get it converted for him. You can't fight
the Roman Empire without becoming *like* the Roman Empire; so
you had better leave such matters in God's hands where they belong."

Then, in verses 6-7, Paul in effect joins Jesus in warning against
the withholding of taxes. Such action smacks of fighting the empire.
The proper name for it is "tax revolt"—and that signifies the pitting
of a "good" revolutionary arky against the "bad" establishment one.
Otherwise, letting Caesar take his coin—as Jesus would have it—is
the "anarchy" of going so completely with God's arky that any and
all human arkys (along with their tax coins) become as nothing. Just
the opposite, withholding the coin is the "revolution" that stakes
everything upon the contest of human arkys—supposedly to insure

the victory of the good, Christian arky that will spell the salvation of the race.

Finally, Ellul picks up on the fact that Paul explicitly does *not* name military service as something owed to the government. He takes this to indicate that Paul, again, understood himself to be following Jesus in seeing that the logic of tax payment does not apply regarding military service. A human being is anything but the "nothing" a few tax coins are. And the human being bears the image of God, not of the emperor. A true anarchist will never grant that any worldly arky (including the church) owns *people*.

With this, we come to some basic principles of Christian Anarchy (several of them straight out of Ellul):

1. For Christians, "anarchy" is never an end and goal in itself. The dying-off of arky (or our dying to arky) is of value only as a making of room for the Arky of God.

2. Christian anarchists have no opinion as to whether secular society would be better off with anarchy than it is with all its present hierarchies. We can say only as much as Blumhardt said: "There is no way anarchy could be much *worse* than the nailed-up-tight business we have now."

3. Christian anarchists do not even argue that anarchy is a viable option for secular society. Ellul: "Political authority and organization are necessities of *social life* but *nothing more than necessities*. They are constantly tempted to take the place of God" (*Anarchism*, p. 22).

4. The threat of the arkys is not so much their *existence* as it is our granting that existence reality and weight—our giving ourselves to them, attaching importance to them, putting faith in them, making idols of them. Revolutionists fall into this trap in their intention of using good arkys to oppose and displace the bad ones—thus granting much more power and being to the arkys (both evil power to the bad ones and righteous power to the good ones) than is the truth of the matter.

5. Christian anarchists do not hold that arkys, by nature, are "of the devil." Such absolutist, damning talk is rather the mark of revolutionists concerned to make an enemy arky look as bad as possible in the process of making their own arky look good. No, for Christian anarchists the problem with arkys is, rather, that they are "of the *human*"—i.e., they are creaturely, weak, ineffectual, not very smart, while at the same time they are extravagantly pretentious.

They pose as so much more important (or fearsome) than they actually are. There is no intent to deny that this "human fleshliness" does indeed provide entrée for the devil—but that as much into good arkys as into bad ones. The only thing more devilish than a "bad" arky is a "holy" one.

6. Christian anarchists would not buy Ramm's clever characterization that "all states are created equally wicked." They would agree that all are equally *human* and none the least bit *divine*. But my Brethren anarchist ancestors, for instance, were well aware that when they fled the persecuting arkys of Germany for the (comparatively) free arky of William Penn, they were trading a bad arky for a better one. And they were appropriately grateful to God for the change. But that from which their anarchy did preserve them was the confusing of Penn's arky with the kingdom of God. An arky is an "arky" for all that. None is as good as it thinks it is or gives itself out to be, and there is no guarantee that even a good one will stay good. The particular Brethren turf within Penn's arky is now a Philadelphia slum.

So, good arky or not, those anarchists retained a healthy biblical suspicion of arkys in general and *en toto*. There is no denying that, as he chooses, God can and does make positive use of the arkys—bad ones as well as good ones. It does not follow that we dare ever accept any as being select instruments of his goodness and grace.

And it was none other than anarchist Ellul who once chided the Christian *revolutionists* for their inability to see any moral distinction between the arky of the U.S. government and those of Hitler and Stalin. Christian Anarchy *does* allow room for the relative moral distinctions between arky and arky—and real appreciation for the same.

7. It is no part of Christian Anarchy to want to attack, subvert, unseat, or try to bring down any of the world's arkys. (It is here that Ramm's adjective "passive" makes sense, although it will not do so regarding points to follow.) To fight arkys, we have seen, is to form counterarkys, is to enter the contest of power (precisely that which Christian Anarchy rejects in principle), is to introduce arky in the very attempt to eliminate it. To undertake a fight against evil on its own terms (to pit power against power) is the first step in becoming like the evil one opposes.

8. Speaking of anarchy's model, Ellul says: "Jesus does not represent a-politicism or spiritualism. His is a fundamental attack

upon [he would better have said, 'refusal to conform to'] political authority. . . . He challenges every attempt to validate the political realm and rejects its authority because it does not conform to the will of God" (*Anarchism,* p. 20). With this and what follows, Christian Anarchy can no longer be called "passive."

9. Regarding Jeremiah's command that the exiles are to "seek the welfare of the city where I have sent you into exile, and pray to the Lord on its behalf" (Jer. 29:7), Ellul points out that such is not at all the same thing as approving and supporting the Babylonian arky. Just so, the radical-discipleship churches that have been most anarchist toward the state and the world may have the best track records regarding the loving of neighbors near and far and the serving of human need. Anarchism is no bar to social *service.* Whether the ends of political *justice* truly are served by our power-manipulation of the arkys is another question.

10. Christian anarchists occasionally are willing to work through and even use worldly arkys when they see a chance to accomplish some immediate human good thereby. This is an admittedly risky business; the regular pattern is to make a quick entrance and just as quick an exit.

For example, the civil arky of Christoph Blumhardt's day was really putting it to the working classes, and anarchist Blumhardt saw the revolutionary arky of the Social Democrats as a vehicle for helping those people get their rights. He joined the party, spoke for it, ran for office, and won a six-year term in the Württemberg legislature. But it didn't take a whole lot of arky red tape and politicking before he lost not only his interest but his cool: "I am proud to stand before you as a man; and if politics cannot tolerate a human being, then let politics be damned." That, my friends, is pure Essence of Anarchy: "Human beings, yes; politicians, never!" Blumhardt got out as soon as he graciously could.

Quick-in-and-quick-out is a proper anarchist maneuver but certainly not any moral obligation. Neither Blumhardt nor Ellul would claim his arky-adventures as the greatest contribution he has made. In fact, Ellul—who has been into as many of these as anyone—is inclined to deny that they ever accomplished anything:

> I had seen the failure of the Popular Front in 1936; the failure of the personalist movement, which we intended to be revolutionary and which we tried to start on a modest scale; the failure of the Spanish revolution, which had great importance for Charbonneau and me; and the failure of the liberation [of

France at the close of World War II]. All of this formed an accumulation of ruined revolutionary possibilities. After this, I never believed anything could be changed by this route. (*Season,* p. 56)

This attitude surely is poles away from the current revolutionist idea that the truest (if not "only true") Christian actions are those having political, arky relevance.

The anarchist maneuver, though proper, actually holds a very real danger—the danger of getting caught. Caught, first: The only members wanted by an arky are true believers. Spies, subversives, and heretics are likely to be shot on sight. Caught, second: Even the strongest anarchist runs the risk of losing his anarchism—his good, honest skepticism—in the surroundings of arky propaganda. He so easily can get to thinking that politicians actually do have more power in determining the future than the rest of us mere mortals do. He can so easily get caught up in the idea that what we in fact are doing is making the world safe for democracy, winning the world for Christ, building a just social order, reversing the arms race, or (as a well-known hymn has it) pushing through God's long-tarrying kingdom by bringing in the day of brotherhood and ending the night of wrong—when all that actually is happening is that an arky is becoming more and more impressed by its own importance in the scheme of things. And, of course, once such an anarchist starts "believing" in what he is doing, he is done for.

Ellul again: "As a Christian one must participate in the world of politics and of action. But one must do so to reject it, to confront it with . . . refusal that alone can call into question, or even prevent, the unchecked growth of power" (*Anarchism,* p. 22).

11. Ellul's critique of "Christian revolutionism" is perhaps best summed up as "a lack of *realism.*" And that, in turn, can be spelled out under four heads—namely, the revolutionary faith in (a) activism; (b) utopianism; (c) what we shall call "the trigger effect"; and (d) dramatization. Although, obviously, Ellul finds the Christian Left to be the opposite case, he believes that "Christians can be, among other things, more realistic and less ideological than others" (*Season,* p. 91).

a. *Activism.* Ellul, certainly, is not opposed to Christians being *active,* whether on the political, social, or ecclesiastical scenes or wherever. He does reject the activist presupposition that people's public, arky actions are the only true test of their Christian faith. Given Ellul's personal temperament, this one came hard for him:

"Because I have a realistic and active nature, meaning lay in action. But it is obvious that, for me, action itself does not embody meaning. Action more or less gives witness to meaning, expresses it to me or others. But the most basic meaning is beyond all action" (*Season,* p. 83). Ellul would not be one to say that as long as your actions are good (i.e., Christian) your theological beliefs aren't very important.

In fact, churchly activism regularly works just contrary to truly Christian action: "When we see Jesus Christ or the Holy Spirit act, a tremendous number of things come out of very little: look at the feeding of the five thousand. In the church we observe just the opposite: we put excellent men into action and we mount gigantic efforts that produce almost nothing. So I say to myself, 'This means that the Holy Spirit is not working' " (*Season,* p. 94). Human activism can represent an actual blockage of the Spirit's work.

Ellul makes a more fundamental point which, in a succeeding chapter, we will find even more strongly pressed by Karl Barth:

> There is no possible continuity between man's actions on earth and God's establishment of his kingdom. . . . Man can't achieve good on his own. And I again have to clarify here. The good of which Scripture speaks is not the equivalent of moral goodness but a condition of conformity to God's will. And the good that any moral philosophy describes to us may not necessarily coincide with God's will as it is shown to us in the revelation. In other words, when we say that man can't do good on his own, it means that man can't do God's will without God. (*Season,* p. 59)

This brings Ellul to a conclusion that will have his followers from the Christian Left accusing him of having deserted the faith:

> I was hostile to the politicization of the church, the primacy of politics; I was violently [he means "strongly," of course] against a well-known slogan: "Seek first the political kingdom, and all these things will be added unto you." . . . The popular opinion held that Christianity should be expressed above all in service. . . . I maintained that service means nothing if there is not an explicit proclamation of the message of Jesus Christ as Lord and Savior. (*Season,* p. 96).

Obviously, Ellul does not see the gospel as centering in Christian activism.

As a result, Ellul is very leery of today's common assumption

that Christians can magnify their power for good by joining forces
with secular arkys that are pursuing the same social goals:

> Should Christians join existing movements, those that are most
> just; should they, for example, side with the poor man; or does
> Christianity have something really specific and unique that
> should not be mixed up with anything else? Does God want
> to carry out a different action in history through Christians,
> who consequently don't need to adopt ready-made plans and
> doctrines? I am totally in favor of the second perspective. . . .
> [So] it is not a matter of founding a party or a Christian labor
> union or of uniting Christians around a social doctrine of the
> church. Nor is it that Christians should join any particular
> political party. (*Season*, p. 90)

When we get to that succeeding chapter, we will find Karl
Barth strongly "Amening" this point. The ideology of Christian
activism has us humans pushing in to take over and do God's work
for him—with what cannot be anything but disastrous results. Our
Christian anarchists, on the other hand, are with Jesus in wanting
to put the stopper on the activist obsession to serve God by being
out there pulling up tares (Matt. 13:24-30).

b. *Utopianism*. Ellul lays it out. "I have already said how much
all utopias irritate me, both for their lack of realism and their au-
thoritarianism" (*Season*, p. 219).

And is not the revolutionary rhetoric of the Christian Left—
whether in talking about "unilateral disarmament," "a world without war," "a truly just society," "the disappearance of the distinction
between males and females," "an economic equality," "a clean environment," and whatever—invariably and essentially utopian? And,
as Ellul would have it, does not this utopianism show a complete
disregard for pragmatic political possibility and, likewise, an impe-
rious decree in telling the world what order it should be getting
itself into?

Consider that "the kingdom of God" (according to the scriptural definition) cannot be considered a utopia—because in no way
is it a projection of what *we* propose to create, an order *we* are
undertaking to impose on things. Ellul, then, observes:

> Every program founded on our [human] analysis can only be
> a utopia. Now, I am violently opposed to any utopia because
> it is the epitome of illusory satisfactions. . . . Utopia is the final
> blow in humanity's death. And it is a very concrete death: the

last two great utopias were those visions of idealism and the
future known as Nazism and Stalinism. Now, motivated by a
desire to transform society globally, anyone who makes a pan-
oramic and *final* description of this transformation can only
be proposing a utopia. (*Season,* p. 198)

c. *"The Trigger Effect."* With this I have in mind the common
arky assumption that, by bringing our power to bear and working
a change at "the top," we can trigger a revolution of the entire
system. Ellul thinks differently:

> I have arrived at this maxim: "Think globally, act locally." This
> represents the exact opposite of the present spontaneous [i.e.,
> that which comes naturally to us] procedure. . . . We have the
> spontaneous tendency to demand centralized action, through
> the state, through a decision center that sends down the de-
> crees from above; but this can no longer have *any* success. The
> human facts are too complex and the bureaucracy will become
> heavier and heavier. (*Season,* pp. 199-200)

Consider, also, first, that "local action"—having a much shorter
linkage between "act" and "result"—has a much greater chance of
success than does "top-down action." Second, there is a great deal
of local action that won't have to include arky involvement at all.
And third, locally, even where political action is required, the arkys
are smaller, weaker, and more responsive. They will not call for the
same sort of bloc pressure and power plays that high-level politics
would. It is local action that is most appropriate to Christian Anarchy.

Yet consider how regularly our Christian revolutionaries—with
their anti-nuclear demonstrations, their tax revolts, their Equal Rights
Amendments, their getting the U.S. military out of Central America—prefer to try for the high-up jugular. Christian Anarchy (Ellul)
and the Christian Left plainly are of two quite different minds in
this matter. (Of course, this dream of changing things from the top
is just as characteristic of the Right as of the Left—and Ellul would
find it equally objectionable there.)

d. *Dramatization.* The term is Ellul's—or rather his interviewer's—but it intends "playing up," "exaggerating," or perhaps
what we later will call "zealotism" or "absolutizing." Ellul confesses
that in his earlier writings he tended to dramatize the threat of
particular evils "in order to back people into a corner, because I had
the conviction that human beings are so negligent, so lazy, that if
they are not driven to defend themselves, they will do everything

possible to avoid commitment" (*Season*, p. 223). But then he goes on to say,

> I do not write in quite the same way now, because the incred-ibly frivolous and thoughtless world of my youth has given way to a general conviction in people that the situation is hopeless. People today are afraid. Thus I will not tell them, in regard to the atomic bomb: "It is appalling, we will all be blown away." I think, on the contrary, that I should say: "There are ninety-nine chances in a hundred that it will never ex-plode." (*Season*, p. 224)

Because Christian Anarchy doesn't always have to be trying for "results," it can afford to be *realistic* and thus also more *honest*. And because it can be honest (speaking the truth in love), Christian Anarchy also can be less manipulatively authoritarian. It isn't trying to *make* anybody do anything.

Ellul's last word—only for the *Season* book, of course, though it would also serve well in the other sense—perhaps best shows the extent of the gap between himself and our social revolutionists:

> I was mistaken in my hope of triggering the beginning of a transformation of society.
>
> [The interviewer asks:] Do you think you were speaking to deaf ears?
>
> I don't pass judgments. I said what I thought, and it was not heard. I probably said it badly. But much more important, I may have had the opportunity at times to bear witness to Jesus Christ. Perhaps through my words or my writing, someone met this savior, the only one, the unique one, beside whom all human projects are childishness; then, if this has happened, I will be fulfilled, and for that, glory to God alone. (*Season*, pp. 232-33)

12. The nonconformity of Christian Anarchy—the refusal to recognize or accept the authority of the arkys of this world—is done in the name of human "freedom." And this is not at all the same thing as "autonomy"—that being the secular name for freedom, not the Christian. No human arky can create or grant freedom; the idea of "government," of "imposed arky," is essentially contradictory to that of "freedom." Yet, just as truly, the simple elimination of arky creates, not freedom, but only "anarchy"—which is not the same thing. No, Ellul suggests that there is for us no once-for-all libera-tion, but that our freedom is to be found only in the act of wresting

it from the powers. "It exists when we shake an edifice, produce a fissure, a gap in the structure" (*Anarchism,* p. 23).

That fissure may be as small (or as great) as Jesus' disinclination to respond to Pilate. What really gets in among the ribs of an arky is when anyone, upon being spoken to, fails to snap to attention, salute, and say, "Yes, sir" (or what is more likely, regarding a big arky of our day, "Yes, ma'am!"). Arkys don't really care whether you love them or fear them; what they can't stand is being ignored. Another fissure may be as small (or as great) as laughing in the face of arky pretentiousness—which is just what God did through the resurrection of Jesus. That gives big-shots as much trouble as being ignored—or anything else threatening their sense of self-importance. True, as with Jesus, showing disrespect toward an arky is the best way of getting yourself crucified (only *verbally,* of course, in our day of "loquacious damnation"). But anarchists are used to that.

Yet even with this fissure making, it is not as though we were creating freedom for ourselves. No, it is, rather, as the Blumhardts put it, that we have made a space for something new: the Arky of God—the God whose service is perfect freedom through Jesus Christ our Lord. Amen.

Regarding the tradition of my own Church of the Brethren, it is easy to see that ours was indeed a truly biblical anarchism up to the halfway point of this century—when we converted to revolutionism. Perhaps an illustration can best show the nature and magnitude of the switch. Two Christian men were involved in the Spanish Civil War (1936-39) in two quite different ways, for quite different purposes, seeking quite different goals. Both were intent to help "the poor"—but had quite different ideas as to who the poor were and how they could best be helped.

Earlier in this chapter we saw how Jacques Ellul, the first of these two, was involved as a political *partisan*—which means, of course, an "adherent of a particular *party* line." So for him "the poor" identified that particular ideological, class-distinguished social bloc arrayed against the oppressing powers of General Franco. Ellul's faith was that, if properly conducted, the political contest could be directed so as to bring justice to the "poor" side of the alignment.

Our other Christian activist was a Brethren leader named Dan West, in Spain as a Brethren Service Commission representative doing relief work. Just the opposite of Ellul, the approach of Dan West and his church was carefully *nonpartisan*. Thus they did not identify "the poor" with any sort of ideological grouping but simply as whatever individuals had needs the church was in position to serve. "Poverty" didn't even have to be understood sheerly as an *economic* category. And the church kept its involvement strictly nonpartisan precisely so it could be free to serve any and all kinds of poor people without distinction.

One of Dan West's jobs in Spain was distributing dried milk— and it was while so involved he got the better idea of persuading the Brethren farmers back home to donate live animals to replenish the herds, flocks, hutches, cotes, and hives of the devastated areas of the world. That idea gradually took form to become, today, Heifer Project International—a large-scale, long-lived, massively effective interdenominational service agency—which has been able to do its work only by sticking to the rule of political nonpartisanship. Jacques Ellul, of course, is quick to say that his Spanish adventure accomplished nothing at all. Neither Dan West nor anyone else would have said the same about his.

Yet here is the two-way switch: Jacques Ellul on the one hand and our current Brethren equivalents of Dan West on the other have traded places. Completely disillusioned about finding possibilities for good in political revolution and rapid social change, Ellul became a Christian anarchist. Theoretically, I suppose, he would agree that *if* we could in fact engineer a revolution that would create a just social order, that *might* mark a higher accomplishment than simply feeding hungry people. The trouble, of course, is that he has never found any indication that arky revolution can be trusted to deliver on its promises. Human beings just aren't morally capable of controlling arky power and making it work to beneficial ends. Power *corrupts*—as someone other than Ellul has said.

That is Ellul's switch. Now, switching the other direction, we have a Mennonite scholar's study, distributed by the Peace Section of the Mennonite Central Committee (the counterpart of Dan West's Brethren Service Commission). The locus now is Nicaragua rather than Spain, but the church's historic nonpartisanship is belittled as "quietism"—with the call that it be replaced by an ideological partisanship of the strongest order. Now, rather than a nondiscriminating concern for poor individuals of whatever political persuasion and whatever variety of "poverty," the formula runs: "the poor" = the Nicaraguan "people" = the partisans of the Sandinista Revolution. (And I don't see how this can avoid the implication that any dissenters from or critics of the revolution are "nonpeople.")

What I find most frightening about the Mennonite article is that the Christian gospel is equated directly with left-wing politics. Biblical-anarchical Mennonites and Brethren are now encouraged to enter the worldly arky contest with such completely partisan power plays as tax-withholding, the sanctuary movement's organized and advertised defiance of the government, civil disobedience, vengeful denunciation, *anything*—just as long as it stops short of physical brutality and so can still be justified as "nonviolence." That, if I may say so, marks one very long move away from Dan West—and one regarding which Jacques Ellul (having been there) can tell us what the harvest must be.

My guess is that it was the Social Gospel movement that tipped us into the faith that the world could be saved (or at least vastly improved) through our inspired arky actions of revolution and reform. Now our ancient anarchism has become an object of scorn: "Look at how much more actual good we have accomplished by *using* arky power rather than shying from it!" . . . I wonder.

I wonder. . . . It certainly proved right for Jesus not to let himself be associated with the just and righteous revolution of the tax-withholding Zealots; Rome saw to it that that godly effort came to nothing but a great big minus. Yet, of course, that revolution *was* violent. So let me now tell the story of the most successful Christian, nonviolent revolution in history—involving that same Roman establishment, would you believe?

You see, once upon a time there was this little anarchist church—in fact, the very one we've been talking about—that of Jesus, Paul, and the other New Testament Christians. And it—in its rather weak, unorganized, anarchical way (following the pattern of its anarchical apostle)—went bumbling about the empire, evangelizing handfuls of individuals here and there and leaving them in little anarchical house-groups.

Actually, in comparison to some other churches of other eras, its church-growth statistics weren't all that bad. Nevertheless, in time, some strategic planners came along who said, "Folks, this old, anarchical way of going at things is stupid. We'll never get the world won for Christ this way. Why, people are being born faster than we're set up to convert them (infant baptism not yet having been invented); we'll never catch up. We've got to start thinking big and quit being so leery about using a bit of organization and power. We need to operate from strength. What we really ought to do is go for the Arky—go for the Big One. God wants his church to grow. And just think of how much more good we can accomplish by using arky power rather than shying from it!"

And wouldn't you know, it worked! They went for the emperor and got him—and he brought the whole of the Big Arky over with him. Christianity was proclaimed the official religion of the Roman Empire—and the world was won for Christ. You know, you have to smile a bit at the Old Anarchy, thinking that three thousand in one day was pretty big stuff. I don't know just how long it took to get the changeover recorded; but I do know the Vatican computers were jammed trying to move names across from the PAGAN column to the CHRISTIAN column—until somebody realized it would be easier just to switch the headings.

At one fell swoop we now had a whole empireful of Christians; the church was finally in a position to do some real good for humanity and bring in the truly just society. Talk about *revolution!* The church praised God from whom all blessings flow . . . and the emperor snickered all the way to the bank. His empire had found the Lord and become "Christian" without having to make any changes at all; Christianity had done all the changing. Indeed, the conversion would probably qualify as "forensic justification": all it took was a word from God (or at least his official representatives) and we now had "The HOLY Roman Empire." Pretty neat, wouldn't you say?

But just look at what actually happened in this Christian revolutionizing of the empire. The church became the Biggest Arky of All, graciously taking unto itself every evil the empire had ever represented. It sacrificed all understanding and appreciation of its God-given anarchy in its zeal to make the world good and do good for it. It lost the beautiful anarchy of its house-churches of human beings to build cathedrals of politicians. (Remember that *cathedral* means "the *throne* of a bishop.") It lost the anarchical refusal of military service to mount armies bearing the banner of the cross and in this sign conquering. It lost its anarchical Jesus whose kingdom was not of this world to paint for itself an icon that needed a label before you could tell whether it was a picture of Christ or the Emperor (a sad, sad confusion). It lost its "holiness" in bestowing that title upon the empire instead. The trading of anarchy for Christian arky was the deflowering of the church.

So, my great fear about today's Christian revolution, out to transform and save the world for God, is not that it might fail but that it might succeed. As for me and my house, give me anarchy or give me the last laugh—which may come to the same thing.

Chapter Two

IN THIS CORNER
Arky Faith

In Chapter One we established the concept of Christian Anarchy.
In this chapter we will turn to its opposite, what I call "Arky Faith."
Arky faith is that enthusiastic human self-confidence which is convinced that Christian piety can generate the holy causes, programs,
and ideologies that will effect the social reformation of society. Differing only as to which actually *are* the holy causes, arky faith characterizes the Christian Right just as much as it does the Christian
Left. In either case, the true believer has no doubt at all as to which
arkys are the elect instruments for God's will being done on earth
as it is in heaven.

The dichotomy between Christian Anarchy and arky faith may
be as essential in defining true Christianity as any rubric ever proposed. Of course, the distinction won't begin to correlate with the
common *theological* one of "liberal" and "conservative." None of the
classic creeds or confessions is of any help in determining which—
"anarchy" or "arky faith"—is orthodox and which heretical. Our
study cuts in at a different level, addressing a new issue. The Bible
(we have seen and will see) very definitely does speak to the matter,
though Christian tradition as a whole has largely ignored it.

The issue at stake has to do with the ways and means of God's
work in history—rather than predominantly with God's own nature.
But arky faith is broad enough to include almost any concept of
deity; the following list is representative:

1. As with the Christian Right, arky faith may hold an entirely
orthodox view of God, positing only that it knows which of the
arkys God considers his chosen instruments.

2. As with many theological liberals of the Christian Left, the
"God" of arky faith may be simply a mytho-symbolic expression of
its utopian vision, set up to inspire the efforts of its adherents.

3. Arky faith may go beyond Christianity to base itself in the

universal religiousness of humanity. Now, rather than speaking of a particularistic "God," the preference is for "the spiritual [read: *cultural*] progress of the race"—as that is defined and directed by the elected arkys, of course.

4. Arky faith may be expressed in purely secular, humanist terms, with no transcendent reference at all.

Obviously, any and all these options qualify under our definition of arky faith, although because of our present interest we will treat only those claiming in some sense to be "Christian." But the point is that the crux of arky faith lies nearer its concept of "the human" than its concept of "God." Granted, the two are never completely separable; and Ellul did say of the arkys that "they are constantly tempted to take the place of God." That, of course, would be idolatry—though we are going to argue more closely that the sin of arky faith lies fundamentally in its adherents' seeing their chosen arkys as indubitably *messianic*, as being God's anointed agents of social redemption. The sin, then, is that which Jesus warns against as "chasing after false messiahs."

So, an arky's problem lies more in its self-image than in its image of God. The pretentiousness of that self-image has perhaps nowhere been more tellingly exposed than in the line Tennyson gives to Sir Galahad: "My strength is as the strength of ten, because my heart is pure." Contrast this to Jesus' statement: "So you also, when you have done all that is commanded you, say, 'We are unworthy servants; we have only done what was our duty' " (Luke 17:10).

There would seem to be no mystery as to why arky faith holds such appeal for us. Given the unquestioned certainty that *our* arkys are right, good, and dedicated to the service of God, three great advantages would seem to accrue:

1. Arky faith greatly simplifies moral decision making. One escapes the ambiguity and terrible complexity of dealing with actual individuals who always are very much a mixture of good and evil, actual forces and situations that are very much the same way. Now one can think in terms of homogenous arky power-blocs that clearly classify into either good or bad; moralizing can be done sheerly by knee-jerk reflexing. So "pacifism" (of whatever character) is good and anything that is not pacifism is "evil warmaking." A capitalist U.S. government is bad; a socialist Sandinista government is good. "Masculinity" is bad; "femininity" is good. The Moral Majority is bad; the National Council of Churches is good. Multinational cor-

porations are bad; cottage industries are good. Moral choice becomes wonderfully uncomplicated when human affairs are understood
simply in terms of a contest between the arkys wearing white hats
and those wearing black. The trouble, of course, is that this way of
doing morality bears no relationship to moral reality.

2. Perfectly confident that our own commitments are to the
"good," we cannot see why it should be anything other than good
that our power for good be "magnified" through the collective solidarities of good arkys. Nevertheless, the hard truth is that you, at
most, are one—one individual—and no matter how pure you know
your heart to be, you have no *right* to the strength of ten. That
excess strength belongs to nine other individuals—even if their hearts
are not nearly as pure as yours. You have no right to lecture at a
volume of "ten." Those other nine people are to be allowed to speak
for themselves, even if you know that what they have to say is
hogwash. The rule is "one person, one voice, one vote." And it is
every bit as wrong for piety to try to steamroller its "justice" into
place as for perversity its "injustice."

I am convinced there are many Christians (of both the left and
right) who, as individuals, are quite modest, humble, and of realistic
self-image—but who, then, proceed to satisfy their lust for power,
their delusions of grandeur, and their sense of self-righteousness
through the holy arkys with which they identify. Asserting their
"just cause" becomes a psychological disguise for asserting *themselves;* thus they find Christian justification for the sense of power
by which all of us are tempted.

3. Finally, one of the most alluring aspects of arky faith is what
we have called "the trigger effect" and now call "the David and
Goliath effect." Still completely confident about the justice of our
own cause, we dream about the possibility that, judiciously applied
to the right spot, the power even of a small pebble from our weak
sling will bring down the Goliath of Evil. The rock slinger may be
a minority of one righteous individual, namely *me* ("God and one
make a majority," you know—for those of us bold enough to claim
that where we *are* marks the spot where *God* is). Or the rock slinger
may be the minority of our own small but holy cause group. Yet
our faith (our arky faith) is that even a small power play at a key
point in the dam can trigger the flood in which "justice will roll
down like waters, and righteousness like an everflowing stream." Yet
Amos (whose words these are [5:24]) was making a point the precise
opposite of that of arky faith. It is very wide the mark to consider

that our "justice" is congruent enough with God's for the one to be the trigger of the other. No, Amos is saying, "Get out of there with your arky justice, religion, and piety. Your holy efforts are blocking God out, not helping him in. So step back and *let* justice (real justice) roll down like waters."

There is no doubt that the trigger effect does operate on the human scene. And it is indeed a sweet dream that we might be able to accomplish "so much good" just through our little holy-arky effort. Wouldn't God be delighted with us if we rose up, O men, women, and children of God, to trigger the day of brotherhood and end the night of wrong? In truth, is it not upon this trigger effect that all revolutionary action is premised—so much good, a sweeping reversal from evil to good, through our one holy pebble? "One person—namely, you—*can* make the difference!"

The hitch, of course, is that he who triggers the flood is going to have to take whatever flooding his triggering brings down. Once he has triggered his flood, he has no power to dictate its nature or even direct its course; "this thing is bigger than both of us." And so, what the Maccabean revolutionaries triggered *did* accomplish religious freedom and the liberation of the temple. But then, out of control, the waters swept on to devastate the moral character of both the triggerers and their Jewish state. There was nothing wrong, either, with the Zealot plan: if they could trigger as much as a general uprising against the Empire of Evil, then, they were certain, God's Messiah would come rolling down with his flood of justice to eliminate the Romans, set up Israel as the first of the nations, and introduce the promised Day of the Lord. But, sad to say, the flood they actually got was only more, more, and more of Rome. Nothing wrong, again, with the plan to convert the emperor and thus revolutionize the empire. The plan worked, but the resultant flood went its own way—to the detriment of everything Christianity stood for.

The dream that *our* "justice" might trigger the rolling waters of God's justice is indeed a sweet one—and one we will always find enticing. The pause is that any person presuming to use his power to *trigger* floods better also have at hand the power to *control* them— and that person, sad but true, is none of *us*.

The history of Christianity traces out rather clearly as a continuing contest to determine which arkys, at any given time, are actually the holy agents of God.

As we saw in the previous chapter, Christian arky faith got its start in the absolute conviction that the elected arkys of God were two—the Holy Catholic Church and the Holy Roman Empire. Any arkys else (be they churches or states; be they pagan, heretical Christian, or whatever) were enemies of God to be ruthlessly conquered and exterminated.

(In the earlier stages of Christian history, all arky power apparently was perceived as being institutionalized in either the form of churches or states. Only recently have we come to see that there are a whole host of other institutions—education, business, the media, etc.—that are just as intent to govern human thought and behavior.)

The split-up of the empire, with its division of the Western church from the Eastern, did not change the character of arky faith. But now, within Christendom, we had two sets of Christian arkys— each absolutely certain that it was of God and that the other was of Evil. From this point forward (or backward, depending upon God's opinion as to which way his church is going), the contest of arky election will take place as much or more *within* the church as between the church and the world.

The Protestant Reformation (i.e., the Magisterial Reformation, excluding the Anabaptists who played no part in this development) again fails to mark any significant change. The word *magisterial* betrays how strongly arky oriented that reformation was. The only thing new is that we now have a plethora of Christian church-state combines in actual military combat with each other for confirmation of their election by God. Not too nice a picture.

It is, then, only as we move into denominational pluralism, the advent of secularism, the development of democratic government, and a breakup of the unholy union between church and state, that we see any significant change in the picture. Yet in no sense is that change a move away from arky faith toward Christian Anarchy. It is simply arky faith taking on its modern form.

Ecclesiastical monopoly within a society no longer being an option, each church had to learn to tolerate intermixture—even while retaining the secret (or not so secret) conviction that it was elect in a way the others were not. A given state could no longer sport its churchly consort as proof of its own divine election. But that was no bar to civil governments claiming election on their own merits (like, say, "this nation under God").

However, with the new, democratic pluralism now making the ecclesiastical government of an entire populace an impossibility, the

denominations had to reformulate the nature and purpose of their
arky power. No longer could it be domination by decree but now
by propaganda. No longer could it be the power to grant whole
populations salvation through the holy sacraments or the preaching
of the holy word (or else, if they refuse it, damn them to hell). Now
it had to be the power of institutional programs of evangelization,
Christian nurture, moral instruction, and social reform that could
more subtly but just as powerfully get God's will done on earth (or
else, if people refuse it, let them go to nuclear hell). There is here
no less confidence than before as to whose arky is appointed of
God—and no less confidence than before that that arky carries the
power that can save the world.

There is evidence in our day that given denominations are
beginning to lose out as being the popular choice for "God's
anointed." Some Christians see ecumenical councils and agencies as
being the bigger and better arkys (more powerful and more effective) and so are pegging their hope and allegiance there. Some Christians see parachurch organizations and cause groups (anything from
Youth for Christ to Sojourners) as being the arkys of God's future.
And some Christians believe that, for our day, different ones of our
wholly secular movements, causes, and parties represent the most
truly elected arkys. What it adds up to is that, from Constantine
until NOW (that acronymic capitalization is not accidental), churchly
arky faith has completely carried the day.

Regarding the arky of civil government, the picture is no different. Though it is true that the Constantinian holy tandem of
church and state has largely disappeared, that was far from marking
the end of faith in the divine election of government. Many German
Christians, obviously, accepted the arky of the Third Reich as being
of God. Today, many American Christians see the United States of
America the same way (or else as that still-elect arky we are now in
process of re-Christianizing).

Of course, there are also a great many Christians who laugh
at this phenomenon, but that does not at all mean they have deserted
arky faith. They deride the idea that any establishment, rightist governments are elect of God—because they know that election already
belongs to whatever revolutionary, leftist government *talks* social
justice and reform. I say "talks," because, by the time one can get
around to making an evaluation on the basis of *performance,* the true
believer has already committed himself and has no option but to
defend his choice. Yet, whether of the Right or the Left, the nature

of arky faith is the same—the difference being only as to *which* arkys are of God and which of the devil.

My first inclination was to spot this as a modern development by citing Walter Rauschenbusch's at-the-time opinion that the government of the Russian Revolution was God's gift to the world as its best model of peace and brotherhood. Then I realized that the phenomenon has been with us as good as forever. In a succeeding chapter, we will see how devout Jews of the second century B.C. embraced the Maccabean Revolt on the basis of its talk about social justice (equality, liberty, brotherhood, and peace) and how their compatriots of the first Christian century embraced the Zealot Revolution on the same basis.

Certainly, on the basis of its sweet talk, many Christians accepted the American Revolution as being of God. The French Revolution probably won the same sort of Christian blessing in its turn. Malcolm Muggeridge has given us a fine account of how British Christians went ga-ga over the Russian Revolution, just as Rauschenbusch did. The Viet-Cong/North Vietnam "revolution" had its Christian following. There are still Christians affirming the godliness of the Cuban revolution, although people have become rather quiet about the Iranian revolution that unseated the Shah. And of course, the current favorite as "Christian arky" is the Sandinista revolution in Nicaragua—as on the Right it is that of the Reagan administration—each probably just as Christianly wrong as the other.

It is interesting that Christian proponents of revolutionary arky faith don't particularly care whether a regime is pro-church or anti-church as long as it talks peace and justice. Obviously, some of these revolutions actually have produced more of what they talked about than have others. That is not the point. There is no reason even to argue whether those Christians are wiser or more stupid who are plumping the divine election of the Sandinista revolution than those who plumped the divine election of the Holy Roman Empire. It is the same mistake either way. The only question is whether there ever has been any human arky—church, state, cause group, or whatever—that has merited recognition as God's chosen instrument of human salvation.

Accordingly, about the entire history we have just traced, true Christian anarchists feel nothing but incredulity as to how we got so far off base. Who can say whether that sequence marks a progression or a retrogression, when its heading is so far off the gospel in any case? And there is no point in bringing accusations of villainy, because obviously there were no particular villains involved. "All we, (exactly) like sheep, have gone astray-ay-ay-ay-ay-ay." And there is nothing to do about it but weep—or perhaps, better, laugh at the ridiculousness of it all . . . as a cover-up for our tears.

Within the foregoing history of Christendom, there are two churches, two Christian groupings in particular, that stand out as different. They are the New Testament church and the Anabaptists of the Protestant Reformation. I am not arguing that these are the only instances of true Christian Anarchy; yet my own interest and study brings them to focus. The New Testament already has been and will continue to be at the center of our attention, so it seems appropriate, here, to consider the Anabaptists.

Regarding the Christian Anarchy of that movement, the definitive study would seem to be James M. Stayer's *Anabaptism and the Sword* (Coronado Press, 1976). Stayer never uses the term "anarchism" except in the political, "anti-arky" sense; but "Christian Anarchy" probably would have served him better than the terminology he does use. On page 1, he points out that, in the theological disputations of the sixteenth century, the term "the Sword" (from Rom. 13:4) regularly identified "all temporal force." Stayer himself tends to narrow the reference to physical violence either by or against the civil state. His Anabaptist sources would be a bit more concerned also to keep the established church in the picture. Yet the theological issue itself invites us to broaden the term to cover the whole of what we have called "impositional pressure"—and so translate "the Sword" as "arky power."

Stayer sets out to challenge "classic Anabaptist historiography" for its assumptions: (a) that Anabaptism, from the outset, consistently represented "Christian Anarchy" (now to use our terminology in place of Stayer's); and (b) that the movement as a whole was indeed homogenous in its anarchical theology. There is no question that he makes his case; yet, to my mind, he fails to recognize how close he also came to proving the "classic interpretation" in the process.

Regarding (a), if "Anabaptism" be identified by the practice of believer baptism, then the movement's origin came in 1525. Stayer's research clearly establishes that, *no more than five years later,* out of the loose mix of Anabaptist fellowships, there were a goodly number that were self-consciously "anarchist" and who knew themselves to be in general agreement with each other (even if differing slightly in their theological rationales). Just as important, it is this growing consensus (and no other) that will survive as "the Anabaptist tradition" continuing down to the present day. Technically, I suppose, "five years later" is not the same as "from the outset"; but in the overall sweep of history, they come to as much as the same thing. My guess is that Anabaptism congealed into Christian Anarchy at least as quickly as, say, Lutherans or Calvinists congealed into their distinctive theological positions.

Regarding (b), Stayer shows that, at points in the early history, there were Anabaptist factions which held to a revolutionist arky faith rather than to Christian Anarchy. Some of these, apparently, were eager to take the sword as God's instrument for overthrowing the powers and establishing the kingdom. Others would take it up much more reluctantly, hoping that God's revolution could be accomplished more peaceably, by less violent means, and with a more limited use of power.

What Stayer (unknowingly) here has discovered is the economy we already have noted in Jesus and Paul and in moderns like Ellul. In a succeeding chapter we will find the pattern strongly enforced by Karl Barth. But Christian anarchists—who normally are under the gun, or facing the cross, of establishment power—hardly find themselves tempted to legitimize, or collaborate with, that establishment. Quite the contrary, they are forever tempted to legitimize—and must continually struggle to differentiate themselves from—the leftist arkys of just revolution.

Indeed, Christian anarchists do tend to come from the ranks of disillusioned revolutionaries—or those who, were they not anarchists, surely would be revolutionaries. With these revolutionists of the Left, Christian anarchists share the passion for justice and righteousness which insists that the present order of our human establishment must be radically changed. However, the anarchists have no faith at all that the powers of human piety and wisdom are in any way competent to effect or control such change. That change must come from *God*. On this point, then, they show affinity with the conservative Right where, of course, emphasis upon the sovereignty of God is strong. Yet the anarchists are not at home there, either—because they can't buy the conservative thesis that the present order of society *is* the one God wills for us. So, although Christian Anarchy does seem most often to be born out of the Left, it cannot be understood as a variety of either liberal or conservative Christianity. It is its own thing. And I, for one, would be just as happy to have the matter explained thusly: both the Left and the Right are corrupted versions of the original Christian Anarchy. Why not?

However, what Stayer's account *shows* but never quite *says* is that any sort of Anabaptist "revolutionism" always turns out to be short-lived and aberrational. Also, by far the greater part of movement *within* Anabaptism is one-way: revolutionaries and their parties either die out or else move into true Christian Anarchy. Stayer finds very few instances of the reverse movement of anarchical Anabaptists going revolutionary. Out of the earliest ambiguity, only Christian Anarchy survives as the virtually unanimous consensus of Anabaptism.

Now, what Stayer does also show is that, within this mainline anarchist consensus, different Anabaptists had somewhat different opinions as to just how much and what sort of political involvement were permissible to Christians. Yet, because none of these people come close to putting their "faith" in the possibilities of arky accomplishment, they all can be understood as falling well within Christian Anarchy. What it comes to, then, is that—in spite of all Stayer's emphasis on diversity—his study still shows that it is every bit as proper to make generalized statements about "Anabaptism and Christian Anarchy" as about "Lutheranism and Justification by Faith," or any other Christian tradition and its particular doctrine. "Generalized" does not have to mean "unanimous."

Where we use the term "Christian Anarchy," Stayer calls it "apoliticism." He divides the category into "moderate apoliticism" and "radical apoliticism." That distinction is real, of course. However, it does not affect the more fundamental theological distinction between those who see holy arkys as the means of our social salvation and the anarchists who reject the view. At some points (particularly p. 122) Stayer also uses the term "separatist nonresistance." "Separatist"—which he defines as "separation from the majority society"—seems to be the exact equivalent of his "apolitical" (and will come under our critique of that term). "Nonresistance" he defines as "refusal to use physical force"—and needs only to be opened out to include the rejection of all forms of impositional arky power.

Recall, then, that Ellul objected strenuously to Jesus' anarchism being called "apolitical." It all depends, of course, upon what one means by "political." If the term identifies only such action as is *deliberately calculated* to have an express effect in impositionally manipulating and directing public affairs to a desired end, then neither Jesus nor the Anabaptists were political. If, on the other hand, the term identifies whatever actions *do* in actuality have an effect on public affairs, then Jesus and the Anabaptists were as political as can be. So, if "apolitical" suggests people isolated and withdrawn from the life of society, or those whose actions have no effect upon the world around them, then the term is wrong for the Anabaptists.

Does it make sense to characterize the Anabaptists essentially as "apolitical" in a day when, by rights, the term would be just as applicable to over ninety percent of the population who were given no civic roles or responsibilities? How can it be right to call the Anabaptists "apolitical" when, at perhaps a higher percentage than any other church in history, their names are preserved in the *political* records, the court proceedings of their trials and executions? Granted, they didn't go to court *in order* to practice politics in the customary sense; but they were active right out in the midst of the political process, and their action of getting themselves executed could not happen without having considerable political consequence.

Further, there is no doubt that—over against the established concept of state-church, folk-church, territorial-church—it was the Anabaptists who introduced into Christendom the concept of a be-liever-, voluntary-, gathered-church. That concept, of course, has since carried the day—to the point that the papacy recently made formal acknowledgment that Italy itself is a secular state and not a Christian Catholic one, thus leaving even Roman Catholicism as a gathered church there. Now the Anabaptists obviously did not work this sea-change by means of impositional pressures toward arky re-form. There may be those who would argue that the change would have happened even without the Anabaptists. Nevertheless, "apo-litical" can't be quite the right term for a people in whose wake such changes of the *polis* do take place.

Again, it seems that the descendants of the Anabaptists were among the first to understand that the calling of the church includes a ministry of material service to the poor and desolate of the world. Today, that obligation is as much as universally recognized among the churches. In this case, again, there was never any arky effort to sell or impose the idea. Yet the *polis* of Christendom was transformed in any case. Indeed, an examination of their respective track records across Christian history might show that "apolitical" anarchists have had a more constructive political effect on the world than have the revolutionists who were *trying* to manipulate the political process for good. So if, as customarily used, "apolitical" is meant to imply "irrelevant to the real world," it is a poor synonym for Anabaptism's or any other form of Christian Anarchy. (Stayer, by the way, now agrees that "apolitical" is the wrong word and explains that he simply borrowed it from a Mennonite historian.)

Aside from its fine presentation of primary sources regarding the position of different Anabaptist leaders on "the Sword," Stayer's book is most helpful by including similar material regarding different ones of the non-Anabaptist reformers. Thus, he can help us clarify the distinctions between Christian Anarchy and differing types of arky faith. In the following, therefore, Stayer provides most of the information, although the interpretation and application are mine:

MARTIN LUTHER (Stayer, pp. 33-44): Surprisingly enough, on the basis of Luther's *published* position on "the Sword" (and particularly his exposition of Romans 13), Stayer finds him to be closer to the anarchical Anabaptists than is any other of the Reformers. Luther comes off sounding not completely unlike what we already have heard from the Blumhardts and Ellul and what we will hear from Karl Barth and Dietrich Bonhoeffer.

> See, these people [the Christians] need no worldly Sword or law. And if the whole world were true Christians—genuine believers, I mean—no prince, king, lord, Sword, or law would be necessary or useful. (P. 37)
>
> The temporal authority does not at all belong to the charge of Christ but is an external thing, like all other offices and estates. (P. 38)
>
> Follow the gospel and suffer injustice to yourself and your possessions as befits true Christians. (P. 42)
>
> [Stayer quotes Luther:] Since "the worldly power is a very small thing in the eyes of God," it was not worthwhile to undertake active resistance against its abuse. "Such an order we must have, but it is not a way to get to heaven and the world will not be saved because of it, but it is necessary exactly to keep the world from getting worse." (P. 43)
>
> Dominion and Kingship shall remain to the Last Day, but then all official powers will be abolished, both the temporal and the spiritual. (P. 44)

This, of course, is not the whole picture of Luther on the Sword. It is, however, enough to show a truly anarchistic skepticism that anything of God's good can ever be expected from human arkys. Consequently, Stayer awards Luther the label "moderate apoliticism," as against the "radical apoliticism" of the Anabaptists. But what Stayer fails to consider is Luther's *praxis* along with his *theory*. Do this once and, I contend, Luther is forever removed from consideration as a Christian anarchist. Quite the contrary, he takes on an arky faith of specific coloring.

Luther was of a staunchly *conservative* turn of mind and so shows up as regularly legitimizing the power of establishment arkys. In praxis, he is not "apolitical" in any sense of the term. He turns to the "princes" and their Sword to have them gain for him legal standing for his Protestant church and protect it from its enemies (clearly a case of using worldly arky to forward what he is convinced is God's work in the world). Although he knows very well that anarchical *ekklesia* represents the truly Christian form of the church (admitting this in so many words in his *The German Mass and Order of Worship*), for prudential reasons he opts to retain the structures of state-church arky. He preaches the priesthood of all believers but practices a hard-and-fast arky-power distinction between clergy and laity. He fears anything that smells of revolution and so blesses the princes in their brutal putting down of peasant revolutionaries— and the Anabaptist "fanatics" whom he perceives as being of the same spirit. Luther clearly does believe that conservative, establishment arkys actually do play a vital role in God's plan for humanity.

There is an entirely true and praiseworthy concern behind this conservative arky faith of Luther's. He cares about what happens to people. For instance, in that *German Mass* passage, he rejects the anarchical New Testament concept of a gathered ekklesia explicitly because he realizes that only a few people ever would choose to join such groups and, in effect, this would be to leave the masses outside the salvation of the church. For Luther, the stability of a powerful established order was the only thing holding human sin in check and thus making possible a liveable society. Whether he was right or wrong in this, his conservative, legitimizing arky faith is credible and deserving of all respect.

THOMAS MÜNTZER (Stayer, pp. 73-90): Müntzer's is an arky faith the polar opposite of Luther's. He is the sixteenth-century representative of today's "theology of liberation." For him, revolution *against* establishment arky in behalf of the poor and oppressed *is* God's Sword manifesting itself in history. It is true that the Peasants

War supported by Müntzer came to the same sorry end as the pre-Jesus Maccabean Revolt and the post-Jesus Zealot Revolt. Yet it is indubitable that all three of these were totally "just" revolutions, turning to violence only because there was no other alternative. Müntzer was every bit as sincere and religious as Luther—and had just as credible an argument for his position.

DESIDERIUS ERASMUS (Stayer, pp. 52-56): Erasmus had considerable influence on Ulrich Zwingli (our next case), but his thought is different enough to constitute a separate category. Erasmus can be understood as the first proponent of twentieth-century America's Social Gospel. Although it is not immediately apparent as such, his is another form of revolutionary arky faith (not entirely unlike Müntzer's). What Erasmus advocated was a "nonviolent, pacifist revolution." Consequently, the arky upon which his faith centered was what might be called Jesus-Piety. Jesus was to be followed as the perfect teacher and exemplar of the way of love. And Erasmus's faith, then, was the conviction that the arky of such pacifistic humanism is God's chosen vehicle for making the world right.

To the present day, it is undoubtedly this form of arky faith that is most tempting to the Christian Left and most easily confused with Christian Anarchy. Yet the difference between them is as fundamental as this: Christian Anarchy is based on the conviction that *no* human arky can serve God's ultimate will for humanity, that only God's own not-of-this-world arky will do. Erasmianism, on the contrary, places its ultimate faith in the conviction that, for the bringing in of his kingdom, God has committed himself to the political arky power of human pacifistic piety. However, even with that distinction, there is no question about the sincerity and truly Christian dedication of an Erasmus.

ULRICH ZWINGLI (Stayer, pp. 49-69): Zwingli is the reformer with whom the Anabaptists had the most direct contact and within whose Zurich church Anabaptism originated. He is the Reinhold Niebuhr to Erasmus's Social-Gospel liberalism. Appropriately, then, Stayer titles his Zwingli chapter, "From Erasmian Pacifism to Christian Realpolitik." Zwingli's, too, is a faith in the arky of Christian piety; but he believes Erasmus's ideas to be too naive and simplistic to succeed within the hard realities of a sinful world. So, Zwingli's is still the somewhat Erasmian vision of Christian piety gradually revolutionizing the world for good. Yet he knows this will take the combined arky efforts of his Zurich established church and the Zurich city council—and that with some well-directed political clout. He hopes he can keep the process peaceful but is prepared to go beyond peaceful means where that proves necessary. He is not a Müntzer who *welcomes* the Sword as the instrument of God's justice—yet neither is he an Erasmus who *renounces* it in the conviction that human lovingness is capable of winning its own way. Zwingli is realistic enough to know that his goal is not the bringing in of the kingdom but only the Christianizing of Zurich. So, as with the others, there is no doubt about the credibility and authentic Christian conviction of Zwingli's pragmatic arky faith.

Of the four we have presented, Luther's vision is obviously the most *pessimistic*—although, perhaps by the same token, also the most *realistic*. His legitimized establishment has held society together (sort of), which is as much as he ever hoped from it. Zwingli's is the most *optimistic/realistic*—although I don't know that Zurich has ever had a viable claim to being a "Christian" city. The visions of Müntzer and Erasmus, though apparently poles apart, are equally *idealistic*—each counting not so much upon the amassing of real power as upon the David-and-Goliath "triggering" effect and the purity of heart that magnifies strength tenfold.

Each of the four positions has a valid rationale. It could be debated at length as to which scheme is the most workable. I don't believe it is possible to determine which is the most "Christian"— any of the four having difficulty developing a *biblical* basis. Yet, in spite of all their obvious differences, the four *do* have in common the conviction that there is a human arky (better: a particular type of arky) which is "holy," which God has elected as the means through which his will shall be done on earth (and for earth) as it is in heaven.

ANABAPTISM: Not particularly in its being "apolitical" but in its being "anarchical" (i.e., lacking the faith that any human arky has a select role to play in God's plan of salvation), Anabaptism is radically distinguished from any and all of the visions above. It stands outside the spectrum of arky faith.

A more recent work of Stayer's throws further light on the matter. The title of his article, "The Revolutionary Origins of the 'Peace Churches'" (*Brethren Life & Thought*, Spring 1985), could just as accurately have read, "The *Anti*-Revolutionary Origins. . . ." For the thesis he so convincingly argues is that both sixteenth-century Anabaptism and seventeenth-century Quakerism represent the Christian, theological *rebound* following a gross failure of justice in a political revolution that had been seen as holding great promise. These "rebounders," then, wind up in a quite anti-revolutionary stance of anarchism and nonresistance, i.e., in what Stayer, from the 1527 Schleitheim Confession, typifies as "shunning all established churches and all governments [which is to say, the powers of both Right and Left, Establishment and Revolution]—all their worship services and their 'diabolical weapons of violence.' "

The completely proper and biblical conclusion drawn by these people was this: It has become apparent that no program of human power politics can be the method of social justice—in that sinful humanity is simply incapable of exercising impositional power without being corrupted by it. Therefore, we must look away from the powers of this world and turn to God as the one true source and hope of justice. With the Anabaptists, of course, the revolutionary disillusionment was that of the Peasants' War in Germany. With the Quakers, it was the Puritan Revolution. But I think Stayer is onto a pattern that shows up all over the place.

I don't know that there was involved a party that could be called "revolutionary," but the justice-barren futility of the Thirty Years' War certainly was sufficient to trigger the rebound of German Pietism and the anarchical shunning of the powers by its radical wing (from which came the Church of the Brethren). The original Christian Anarchy of the New Testament perhaps ought not be called a "rebound," as though triggered by the collapse of the Zealot liberation effort against Rome; that anarchism was in the works even before it became evident that the Zealot revolt was a disaster. Yet the biblical evidence is clear that Christian Anarchy developed precisely as the positive theological alternative (a different option) standing counter to negative Zealot revolutionism.

In so many words, Jacques Ellul tells us that it was the profound disillusionment of his own revolutionary involvements that turned him to the biblical position of Christian Anarchy. In Karl Barth's case, the term "revolution" is perhaps not as appropriate; nevertheless, with the onset of World War I, it was the "collapse by capitulation" of the peace-and-justice forces of Neo-Protestant theology and religious socialism that "rebounded" him *out* of his faith in the politics of human piety and *into* his powers-shunning hope of the kingdom of God. It might be said that Christian Anarchy exists to no other purpose than to rebound people toward *God's* justice once their hope has been shattered by the discovery of how treacherous and untrustworthy is any attempt at imposing our human justice upon the world.

However, in response to this analysis, Stayer still finds it important to stress that, nonetheless, all these Christian anarchists *had been* or *were very close to being* revolutionists; there is considerable affinity. Of course he is right; I have been as ready to grant the point as he is to make it. Yet that point has the precise effect of strengthening—rather than weakening—the conclusion that will perhaps best be drawn by Karl Barth in a chapter ahead of us.

In Romans 13, Barth finds the apostle Paul refusing to give divine legitimization to either the Roman establishment or the Zealot revolution against that establishment. Paul will not allow the gospel to be identified with either the Right or the Left—yet he comes down much harder against *leftist* revolution than he does against rightist establishment. Why?

> The revolutionary Titan is far more godless, far more dangerous, than his reactionary counterpart—because he is so much nearer the truth. To us, the *reactionary* [my italics—VE] presents little danger; with his Red brother [the then-current Bolshevik Revolution, of course] it is far otherwise. . . . Far more than the conservative, the revolutionary is "overcome of evil," because with his "No" he stands so strangely near to God.

Amen. It is precisely the undeniable "political" *resemblance* (the commitment to peace, justice, freedom, and human welfare) between leftist revolutionism and true Christian Anarchy that makes it so very crucial for us to spot the radical "theological" *opposition* between the two. Christian anarchists are not secret revolutionists, quasi-revolutionists, incipient revolutionists, or even toned-down, quietist comrades of the revolutionists; at the very least, they are disillusioned revolutionists who have made a theological, quantum-jump rebound out of revolutionism.

Yet goodness knows, in our time, we have seen enough of blasted revolutionary hopes—beginning, if you wish, with the Russian Revolution and running up through the Cuban and Nicaraguan ones (including such social and nonviolent examples as the Student Free Speech Movement and the Sexual Revolution)—to rebound the entire church of Jesus Christ into Christian Anarchy. Thus, what gives me such great concern is, in *that* situation, to find the leadership of my own Anabaptist-Brethren-Mennonite tradition moving in an exactly perverse direction: out of its time-tested anarchism and into today's dead-end revolutionism. Therefore, I hereby dedicate this book to hastening the inevitable revolutionary disillusionment that might bring these people back to the Christian Anarchy in which they belong.

The New Testament church and the Anabaptists of the sixteenth century display five basic characteristics in common and in contrast to all forms of arky faith:

a. Neither gives a hint of wanting to *legitimize* any of the powers that be. Those all exist by God's *sufferance;* none can boast his *blessing*.

b. Neither shows any inclination to fight the arkys (even those perceived as most wicked) nor to compete with them (whether physically or verbally). There is no felt need to be knocking heads with them or trying to get power over them. It is not in any such contest that the future of the race is being decided.

c. Neither shows any interest in making something of itself in the eyes of the world—getting its power consolidated, finding the organizational structures that will make it most effective and influential. Both are content to be quite weak and, shall we say, anarchistic.

d. Neither makes any big claims (or even small promises) about what it intends to do in the way of governing, saving, correcting, or even improving a lost and wrong world. Neither makes the sounds of a candidate for office.

e. Most of all, both show complete confidence that God can and will accomplish whatever he has in mind for his world, with or without their help. At his pleasure, God can use either arkys or anarchys, arkyists or anarchists. But he needs neither and, most definitely, licenses none.

I had it in mind now to use the book of Revelation as a depiction of the early church's understanding of Christian Anarchy and a means of documenting the five points just made. Yet surely, many people would think this book so revealing of arky battle to be the very last place one would expect to find any hint of anarchism. So perhaps the best way of making this transition is to meet the problem head-on, by addressing the comparison between Romans 13 and Revelation 13 that is found with some regularity in the literature of the Christian Left.

That comparison most often is done to establish the *contextualist* nature of the Christian relationship to the state: when a state is behaving well, then Christians *should* respect, obey, and honor it;

when it is nasty, then Christians are obligated to denounce, resist, and try to revolutionize it. The Christian response to government all depends upon how the government of the moment is comporting itself.

From this point of view, Romans 13 is read as quite legitimizing. The explanation is that, at the time of Paul's writing, the Roman Empire was in one of its more benevolent phases, making it natural for him to tell the Roman Christians that they should obey the authorities, pay their taxes, and all. Revelation 13, then, is seen to be the opposite case. There the empire is portrayed as the Beast from the Abyss—which is taken to indicate that, at the time of the Revelator's writing, the empire's behavior was quite different from what it had been in Paul's day. I will leave it for the reader to guess whether it is a Romans-13 or a Revelation-13 phase these interpreters presently find the U.S. Government to be in.

Yet truth to tell, the evidence won't begin to support this interpretation at either end of the comparison. First, the Romans-13 end: (1) We have already found Jacques Ellul—and in succeeding chapters will find both Karl Barth and Dietrich Bonhoeffer—strongly denying that Paul here either expresses or implies any sort of legitimizing, any sort of approval, any recognition of merit on the part of the secular state. (2) All three agree—Bonhoeffer the most emphatically—that the relative goodness or badness of the state is absolutely no factor in Paul's argument. (3) For my own part (as will be developed more fully later) it is incredible that Paul ever could have looked upon the Roman Empire as "benevolent." There is nothing in his Jewish background, his personal history, or the political situation of his time that would hint at his intending Romans 13 so.

Moving, then, to the Revelation-13 end of the comparison will also have the effect of getting us into the book we want to talk about. First, there is no evidence that the Beast described in Revelation 13 is to be identified as the Roman Empire. Clearly, the Revelator is here in process of introducing the three members of the Evil Trinity that are the negative spiritual counterparts of the three members of the Holy Trinity. The Beast, then, is Anti-Christ, the negative of God the Son. John's imagery throughout the book rather easily sorts out into that representing spiritual, heavenly entities and that representing earthly reality. With his dual trinitys, he is plainly on the spiritual level—and it is to make John break all his own rules to try to equate this Beast with the historical, earthly actuality of Rome.

Scholars who presume to read Revelation essentially as an anti-Roman tract are making an assumption they do not have textual evidence to support. As just suggested, the greater part of John's imagery has reference to spiritual powers that have no inherent correlation with earthly entities at all. In the first three chapters of the book, where the author is speaking directly of historical situations and events, Rome gets neither named nor implied. John's churches are troubled primarily by heresies from within. A couple are being persecuted from without—but *Jews* (not Romans) are designated as the persecutors. John tells us that, in Pergamum, "where Satan's throne is" (much more likely a reference to pagan shrines than to Roman political authority), a Christian named Antipas had been killed—yet without any hint that Rome was responsible. Regarding his own situation, John states it in the passive: "I was on the island called Patmos on account of the word of God and the testimony of Jesus" (1:9). Now if this author was intent upon writing an anti-Roman tract—and if, as is usually conjectured, Patmos was a Roman penal colony where presumably the Roman authorities had sentenced John to hard labor—then he sure doesn't know much about writing anti-Roman tracts, deliberately wording his way around first-rate opportunities for pointing the finger.

The one place where Rome stands a chance of figuring directly into the book of Revelation is in the passage (Chapters 17–18) built upon the woman/city imagery of the great whore, Babylon. My own opinion is that John, here as always, is speaking in quite general terms and meaning the woman/city as representative of "worldliness" (of whatever time or place), as the sum of all human arkydom, if you will. Yet my guess is that, if you were to have asked John what present entity best exemplified what he had in mind, he, without hesitation, would have pointed to Rome. Nevertheless, the book itself is a high-level theological discourse and anything but a time-bound political harangue against Rome.

However, the real argument against the contextualist Romans-13/Revelation-13 comparison is that—have him call Rome whatever names you will—the Revelator simply does not go on to suggest that Christians should therefore resist, withhold their taxes, or do anything else in opposition to this monster. There is nothing of that sort in the book anywhere. Actually, John's counsel as to what Christians should do in their situation takes two parts. Firstly (and repeatedly), they are asked to bear patiently whatever injustice and suffering comes upon them *by keeping faithful to Jesus*. There is certainly no hint of revolution there.

Secondly, in the midst of the fall of the Babylon-whore, there comes the counsel, "Come out of her, my people, lest you take part in her sins" (18:4). My understanding, based upon John's ways of thinking throughout the book, is that this is not a historical-point-in-time command regarding some group's making a geographical move. It is, rather, God's everyday command to every one of his people: "Today, come out from the arkys; separate yourself (spiritually and psychologically) lest you get yourself entangled and go down with them. Their fall takes place every day (which is not to deny that there will also be a final fall of the final day), and your coming-out must also take place every day."

Turn that one any way you will and, again, it can't be made to spell anything like "revolution." In fact, what those two counsels *do* add up to is Christian Anarchy: "Be entirely unarkycal by continually coming out from the arkys—and the only way to keep yourself clear is by sticking close, remaining ever faithful, to Jesus."

What it comes to is that the texts themselves simply can't be made to produce any sort of tension or disagreement between Romans and Revelation. There is no evidence that Paul felt good and John felt bad about the empire. Let John speak of the empire as he will; the evidence is that Paul would be the first to agree. Paul says that Christians should pay their taxes, but John certainly never suggests that they should withhold them. Paul discourages revolution, but John certainly never encourages it. Paul says, "Christian Anarchy is where it's at," and John says, "Amen, brother!"

So, back to Revelation and its big picture of Christian Anarchy. Therein, Babylon—the symbolic total of arkydom—falls time and again. That is, presumably it falls once (one continuous fall that has caught up every arky thus far), but that one fall is announced or described two or three times. (See both the passages [14:8; 17:1–18:24] and an interpretation of them in my volume *The Most Revealing Book of the Bible* [Eerdmans], pp. 139-40, 153-71.) Yet this Babylonian arky falls in a very anarchical way: it is never attacked by anyone or by any force—not even by the arky of God, let alone the arky of the church or that of any holy revolution. It simply collapses under the weight of its own evil—just as Christian Anarchy would suggest it should.

Then the Revelator wants to portray Jesus' final victory over all evil—God's arky over Satan's arky, as it were. He hasn't much choice except to use arky battle imagery, but he manages to do it without involving any actual arky contest at all. In his first go at it (16:12-17 on pp. 149-52), the arkys of evil are mustered at Armageddon, ready to take on the Lord God himself. Yet without any godly arkys so much as taking the field, the bullhorn from the squad car announces, "OK, boys! It's over!" And it is. Again, the day is carried anarchically. God's arky is not of this world—which means he can take out evil without the help of worldly arkys or without even using his own arky in a worldly way. And the reason the Revelator won't portray Jesus as going into battle at this point is that he knows Jesus has already won it all at Calvary, the most anarchical battle of all.

In his second go at the scene (19:11–20:3 on pp. 173-79), the Revelator presents Jesus as the Warrior King on a white horse (arky imagery, for sure). His forces take the field. The arkys of evil come on to face him—and promptly are taken prisoner and fed to the vultures without any battle being recounted at all. Apparently, the arkys of the world recognize that the Warrior King's bloody garments identify him as the Lamb who, in letting himself be bloodied at Calvary, had, once and for all, whipped them on the spot. And with that, all the fight immediately goes out of them. Consistently, John shows God's victory for the world as taking place *without any assistance from our holy human arky efforts.* And if God does not want or need such, we can afford to be the little anarchists he has called us to be.

Once more, in his finale, the Revelator as much as bends over backward to dispute the prophet Ezekiel. "I've been there since you were," he says, "and I saw NO temple in the New Jerusalem" (21:22 on p. 199). And why so great a "no"? Because John knows that temples and the whole apparatus of institutional religion are human arkys claiming to be able to put worshipers in touch with God. Now, in John's picture, the whole of the New Jerusalem *is* the church; so he is not equating "church" (gathered people) with the "temple" of arky apparatus. We are the ones so confused as to think that you can't have one without the other. Yet, where God himself is present, who needs it? He can be his own temple; human arkys are the last thing wanted.

So the book of Revelation knows all about the principalities and powers of arkydom—yet it knows *nothing* of the common arky-faith alignment that divides human arkys into two categories (the "good" ones sponsored by God and the "bad" ones by Satan) which are then pitted against each other in determining humanity's future. No, in Revelation, all human arkys are of a kind (showing only very relative moral distinction); it is this *totality* of human arkydom the Arky of God finally will overcome by ways and means of his own loving and redemptive discipline.

Humanity's blessed end is to be total anarchy—the escape from damned arky rather than the victory of any portion of it. Arkys have no ultimate significance or even lasting function. And, the New Testament tells us, if our final end is Christian Anarchy, it can't be wrong to start exercising and enjoying a bit of it now—by ever and always "coming out of her, my people!"

Chapter Three

CHURCHLY ARKYDOM
It's Unreal!

Would it be correct to say that, given his status as Creator and Lord, God's definition of reality (of what is real and what is unreal) is truer than ours? Could we say, even, that it is not for us to decide whether God is for real but for him to decide whether we are?

Therefore, having discovered that God is Primal Anarchist, the first and best around, it should come as no surprise that his is a most anarchical view of the human scene, one not at all inclined to deal with humanity in terms of its arky structures. Regarding this human race of ours, we can be certain he sees its essential reality as residing in the existence of the individual—human individuals who are every bit as real as the individual sparrows he watches, the very hairs of whose heads (the humans, of course, not the sparrows) are numbered. That "he careth for [each and every] *you*" (1 Pet. 5:7) is indisputable. That he careth a hoot about—or even recognizeth the reality of—any arky arrangement superior to individual existence is never said.

We will proceed, now, to speak only of the arkys of church-liness, although the argument could apply to any and all secular arkys as well. However, right off the bat it must be insisted that what we are calling God's concept of "individualistic reality" does in no way deny or even threaten the social concept of "church"—as long as "church" be properly defined.

When it is the *church* with which we are dealing, there is a complicating factor that can always confuse our analysis. I mean to focus on the two major components of the church that come "from below" to constitute its "human" side. The first of these is the *ek-klesia,* the "gathering" of the individual saints (better: the sainted individuals) into community. The second is all the institutional, cul-tic arky structure of house of worship, priesthood, ritual, organi-zation, polity, and what all.

What dare not be overlooked is that, being the church *of God*, it also involves a third, transcendent, "from above" component that takes priority over the other two. However, for us now to try to track down, identify, and define this "divine" component and then detail how it relates to and operates within the human two—such an investigation would lead us far from our intended track and undoubtedly bog us down in complete disagreement. So, in the effort simply to set that issue to one side rather than even try to settle it, let us, without prejudice, call that third component "the Holy Spirit in our midst" and move on to our analysis of the human side of the church.

My personal (and I think "biblical") opinion is that this Holy-Spirit component relates much more directly to the human ekklesia component than to the human arky-structure component. Whether this be true or not, our one crucial consideration here is to realize that the extraordinary, transcendent quality lent to the church by virtue of its divine component is in no way the same phenomenon as the human extraordinary, self-transcending appearance lent by forming the constituency into ideological power blocs to be manipulated to good effect by "corporate heads." The discussion to follow ignores the divine side of the church, not to deny it, but simply to keep us concentrated on the human phenomena.

As long as the church is defined as *ekklesia,* i.e., the assembling of the (individual) saints, there is no problem. Here there is not only room for, but even the need for, whatever one cares to posit in the way of fellowship, koinonia, gemeinschaft, bodyhood, community. The only thing these ideas add to "individualistic reality" is "togetherness." And "togetherness" is not a new category, nothing that is transcendent or standing superior to individual existence. It is, instead, a natural form, a *function* of individual existence. There is no such thing as "community" except when individuals (as individuals) are *doing* it. As ekklesia (and nothing more than ekklesia), "church" is still a totally anarchic concept; no hint of arkydom is involved.

Where the line is crossed into arkydom is the point at which it is assumed that a grouping of individuals can be given the quantitative value of their sum and then treated as a collective solidarity represented by a corporate head.

From our Western culture we have inherited one of the profound nuggets of human wisdom, namely, that "you can't add apples and oranges" (although I don't know what either apples or oranges

ever did to get stuck with the particular onus of being unaddable).
Actually, of course, apples can be added (on the one pile) and oranges can be added (on the other); the two can even be added
together (as long as what one counts is "fruit"). No, it is only with
God's hair-numbered humans that we run into true unaddability.
But the one mathematical count God will not "countenance" is to
add up, say, fifty-three human ones ("1"s) and get a sum, a new
number of, say, "53 and upwards," which is itself larger and more
powerful than any of the constituent "1"s or all of them put together.
The fact is that God has created human beings to be unaddable:
"you can't add individuals and individuals." Any "1" in there (even
the tiniest) is itself infinitely larger than the "53" that purports to be
their sum. To glom people into a collective (and "glom" is a perfectly
good word contributed by Walt Kelly's *Pogo* and based upon the
very widespread Indo-European root meaning "to mash together
into a *ball*," as in "conglomeration") but to glom people into a
collective never works, as the arkys suppose, to human *magnification*—always to human *degradation*.

Yet the invariable method of arky power is to glom such human collectives into being and then to anoint special individuals
who presume to *represent* that body, *speak for* it, act in *behalf of* it,
and even stand *in place of* it. Of course, God himself can work
something like this—as he did in Jesus Christ. Yet this is to slip over
into the entirely different sphere of "the third component." The
question is whether he has given permission for us to do anything
of this sort for ourselves. I wouldn't even deny that humanity has
worked itself into a place where it can't operate in any other way.
Yet the question remains as to whether God himself ever wills or
blesses the maneuver.

Thus, within the Judaic tradition of the Bible, we find the two
concepts of "church" standing side by side. The temple signifies the
arky, "churchly" one and the synagogue the anarchic, "ekklesial"
one. The temple cult, of course, was based entirely upon the arky
premise that there are special, anointed agents (priests) who are
capable of representing all Israel before God—and that in total disregard of the actual faith-status of any given Israelite and complete
ignorance even of what percentage of individual Israelites might at
the moment be believing or unbelieving. Such a priest was more
than an individual in that he could "represent" the "summated
being" of the corporation before God. And he could perform, in
behalf of other (lay) individuals, actions of cultic effectiveness before

God—actions that no lay individual was capable of performing for himself.

Israel, in such case, obviously is not being considered as an ekklesia, a community of individual existences, but as some sort of arky entity which can be represented to God as a collective solidarity and responded to by God en masse. There is now no reason God even *needs* an individual hair-count. For his convenience, we have gotten ourselves organized so that his salvation can proceed through arky transaction rather than on any person-by-person basis. My question is whether God had any part in that scheme, whether he ever recognizes any reality other than that of individuals—be they sparrows or otherwise.

With the *synagogue,* these arky presuppositions are not so. A synagogue is nothing more nor less than the place of the ekklesia, the gathering of the faithful. It is the place where—although they do it *together* (and I would never minimize the significance of that)—it is still each individual doing his own studying and hearing of the word, his own praying, his own worshiping, his own relating to God, his own performing as a member of the body. The rabbi is a teacher and in no sense a priest. He is only one member of the congregation and can no more represent or speak for it than any other one member can. No "official," arky privilege before God is claimed or wanted.

Clearly, the course of God's way with Israel—beginning with the prophets—was *away* from temple arky and *toward* the anarchic reality of the synagogue. In its turn, Christianity started out as a completely anarchic ekklesia and then drifted into churchly arkydom.

The treatment above might suggest that the issue is one of "sacramentalism" and the sacerdotal powers of a priesthood. Surely, those are involved, but the question is much broader and more profound. It can be put as simply as this: Who is entitled to speak for whom—and by what authority?

I guess *pater familias* is as much of arky status as I have any claim to. Well, then, does being *pater familias* mean that I can "speak for" the family? Don't you believe it! The very idea is an impossible one. It implies that, somehow, above and beyond and independent of the various minds of the individual members, the family has a common mind to which I, as *pater familias,* have access and thus am empowered to speak "for the family." No way. I can speak "for the family" only to the extent that every member gives me both permission to speak for him and the voluntary assent that what I say is indeed an expression of his individual mind as well. If so much as one family member as lowly as Cricket the Cat thinks differently (and when he thinks at all, you can know it will be differently), even though I am *pater familias,* I am still hung up in speaking "for the family" without impermissibly overriding his sacred individuality.

The family has no common mind, no higher mind, no singular mind transcending the plural and various minds of its individual members. If there is no single mind, there certainly is no arky figure who can claim to represent the family as a whole in speaking it. No arky entity ever takes precedence over individual existence; no one can speak for another except at the other's permission and instruction.

I haven't any doubt that God recognizes "families" as "individuals in configured relationship with each other." I deny that he grants reality to any idea of "family" which, without reference to the independent mind of each and every constituent member, posits the sort of collective solidarity that would even make it possible for one special individual to "represent" or "speak for" the whole. Thus, it is precisely "the great realities of our day" (according to arky faith) which turn out to have no real existence in the eyes of our anarchist Father who art in heaven.

We will turn now to specific examples documenting how completely churchly arkydom operates in terms of these abstractions from reality. The easiest and most obvious example would be Roman Catholicism, with its hierarchical polity culminating in one extra-special individual who is presumed to have the power, before God, to represent (stand in place of) and speak for hundreds of millions of actual individuals—and with its sacramental system in which a quite special person, before God, can gain access to grace for a multitude in a way no other member of the group can. The trouble, of course, is that such an example would let Protestants off the hook with a blithe, "But our church isn't that way." So I am choosing, rather, to take our examples from the World Council of Churches and its recent assembly at Vancouver, British Columbia.

We shall give attention to one of the "biggies" from that event. The German theologian, Dorothee Sölle, addressed a plenary session. That much is the truth of what took place, but the significance, the power which the churchly arky (with the aid of the media arky) immediately pumped in was to make it read, "WOMAN Addresses World Council of CHURCHES."

My opinion is that the anarchist God—who recognizes no human reality beyond that of individuals—is fully aware that one

human individual named Dorothee Sölle addressed a gathering of
so many other human individuals named Variously. He could even
give you an as-of-that-moment hair-count for each. But I also am
of the opinion that as soon as the situation was projected into terms
of abstract entities, God would say we had traded human reality for
arky unreality.

Sölle can't *represent* "woman," "women," or "women in general," because there isn't any such entity. There are in the world only
scads of female individuals—with as many minds as there are females. Certainly, there is no one idea upon which the total group
would agree—not even (or perhaps least of all) that women are
systematically misused by men. There is absolutely no collective solidarity that even would make it possible for Sölle (or any other
woman, or any group of women) ever to "represent" or "speak for"
an entity that doesn't exist. Sölle (or anyone else) can represent only
as many individuals as have asked her to represent them and have
given their personal approval to what she shall say.

Yes, I know I am talking about what is called "a symbolic
event." What I am questioning is whether there exists any reality
corresponding to the symbol—and recall what Tillich insisted, that
a symbol must "participate in" as well as "signify" the reality for
which it stands. So, for a symbol to work, there has to be some
reality around somewhere in the mix.

Can God be anything but unhappy, then, after he created people for human individuality, to have their individuality overridden
in the interests of glomming them into collective solidarities for
purposes of arky power? So, just as "woman" was not present at
Vancouver in the person of Dorothee Sölle, neither were any
"churches" present in the persona of dignitaries, officers, or delegates. To suggest that, in God's eyes, something significant regarding
"women in the church" took place at Vancouver is to take arky
abstraction for human reality.

God, of course, knows which actual women, of which actual
hair-count, are playing which actual roles in which actual churches.
He also knows in which cases the woman's presence is contributive
to the life of the church and in which destructive. And it is only in
relation to this reality that talk, opinion, and evaluation of "women
in the church" has any truth value at all. On the level of abstract
ideality and symbolic representation, where one can identify the
reality of neither "women" nor "church," how can it even be said
whether the idea of "women in the church" is good, bad, or indif-

ferent? And yet arkydom regularly prefers to operate with what it takes to be the magnified powers of abstract collectives and their representative persona.

God, of course, also knows which actual women are actually being misused by which actual men. He also knows in which cases the actual woman is by no means an innocent party but is doing her full share of misusing others. It is only on this real level that real behavioral changes can effect progress toward real justice. Consequently, it is difficult to imagine what is gained by approaching the problem at the level of arky abstraction, with such propositions as "Women are systematically oppressed by men." What truth value can the statement have if such collective solidarities as "women" and "men" don't even exist? What relevance do such slogans have for, or what help do they afford to, the actual situation in which male individuals and female individuals must relate to each other? Clearly, such a slogan is even of negative value if it be read backwards as a description of reality—thus, for example, inviting an actual woman to decide she is being misused, simply on the basis that she is a member of that female collective which systematically is misused by the male collective. Just that detached from reality can arky abstraction become. The power of such slogans lie, not in their truth value, but solely in the fact that they *sound* big, sweeping, profound, and important.

With Sölle at Vancouver, then, my guess is that God was listening and interested at an entirely different point from what the churchly audience and media magnifiers were. I doubt whether he even caught the symbolic significance of "women in the church" (since, in any case, he already knows what is the actual status of each actual woman in church). No, given his overweening concern about what is going on with individuals, it seems likely that his main interest would have been: "What is the state of Sölle's personal relationship to me? Is the specific content of her profession of faith consonant with the membership standard of the WCC she is addressing?"

That standard reads: "[We] confess the Lord Jesus Christ as God and Savior according to the Scriptures and therefore seek to fulfill together [our] common calling to the glory of the one God, Father, Son, and Holy Spirit." And the question regarding Sölle's own theology is a legitimate one, because her writings would indicate that, for her, "God" is that mythic ideal which the race, through its religious creativity, continually is developing in the interests of its own moral and cultural advancement—surely, something quite different from what the WCC statement has in mind. If, then, we are to read Sölle at Vancouver on the arky level of symbolic event, what are we to make of it? If Sölle is representative of women in the church, is her theology also representative of the theology of women in the church?

Be clear; I am not at all suggesting that the WCC should have made Sölle's faith an arky concern, with committee investigations, heresy trials, excommunications, and what all. I mean only to suggest that God on the one hand and churchly arkydom on the other apparently operate on completely different wavelengths regarding what is truly real and central to Christianity. The assembly likes generalized, all-inclusive, large-symboled, arky-powerful, headline-grabbing pronouncements about WOMEN in the CHURCH. But God, anarchically disinterested in all that, goes for the loving concern as to what is the state of faith of this daughter of his, this one particular "woman in the church" who is infinitely more real and important to him than all the symbolic abstractions churchly arkydom has ever invented. So as it turns out, what the WCC regards as a "biggie" God doesn't even recognize as being for real. And what God finds most important the WCC scarcely notices.

Let us now turn our attention to the "churches" that supposedly were present at Vancouver to hear Sölle. Although they acted with somewhat more pontifical dignity, there nevertheless was that about them suggestive of a presidential nominating convention. At least the polity of procedure was the same. You've seen it: Some slap-happy pipsqueak in a crazy hat gets hold of the microphone, and then we hear, "Mr. Chairman! Mr. Chairman! THE GREAT STATE OF N'YAWK goes for the next President of the United States, Senator Ted Kennedy!" The guy's own conviction convinces all the rest of us that this is for real, that *he* actually is wielding the representational arky power of THE GREAT STATE OF N'YAWK to determine the course of the nation and, through it, the world. Very many people undoubtedly give more credence to his weighty words than to those of the Revelator: "The kingdoms of this world are become the kingdoms of our Lord and of his Christ." The politician at least spoke with the votes in his pocket, while John had nary a one.

Once more, let's look at the situation through the eyes of God rather than those of oh-ye-of-arky-faith. God knows, of course, that he has a goodly batch of individuals living in the area; he may even know that there are boundaries setting it off as a state named New York. But that there are a handful of politicians who, by means of "representation," can speak for and wield the awesome power of some world-shaping, individual-transcending arky-conglomerate known as THE GREAT STATE OF N'YWAK—well, I doubt whether that has come to his attention. In any case, he surely would have to "come down" in order to see it, as the account tells us he had to do to see the Tower of Babel. We know that his eye is on the sparrow; but whether he can keep it there and at the same time see THE GREAT STATE OF N'YAWK (which obviously has no head the hairs of which it would even be possible to number and perhaps not even any real existence at all), that is another question.

If that is how it is with THE GREAT STATE OF N'YAWK, how is it, say, with THE LUTHERAN CHURCH? No different. It is indubitable, of course, that God keeps track of each and every member of the body of Christ (as he does even of its nonmembers). He may even be aware that some millions of these are called "Lutherans"—no matter what they call each other. But that these millions of Lutherans can then be glommed together into a corporate solidarity called "Lutheranism," from which is squeezed out the power-essence to anoint a representative who can go to Vancouver and *be* THE LUTHERAN CHURCH—that I somewhat doubt. "My strength is as the strength of tens of millions, because my heart is pure Lutheranism!"

Therefore, though it was called a council of CHURCHES and very much hyped as such, I am skeptical that God saw any of them at Vancouver. What he did see was an ekklesia of individual Christians. And in the anarchist eyes of God that, in any case, is a far greater reality than a council of nonexistent churches.

Note, if you will, that mine has been quite a different critique of the WCC than any seen heretofore. Rather than taking one side or the other, mine would apply to all the voluble critics of WCC just as much as to the WCC itself. My example of the WCC was a quite arbitrary selection, the critique itself being just as relevant to any of the constituent (or even nonconstituent) churches and to both religious and secular organizations generally. My anarchist quarrel is pointed no more toward the WCC than toward any other arky. Nonetheless, there would seem no denying that the WCC assembly was an outstanding demonstration of the pomp and circumstance of self-advertised churchly arkydom and its collectivist, power-bloc mentality. I don't even know that the WCC *could* be any different. My only point is that it represents a way of "seeing" which is totally other than keeping one's eye upon the sparrow.

So, if Christian Anarchy identifies a skepticism regarding everything "arky faith" represents, we here are getting at an essential principle. We are back with Blumhardt: "I am proud to stand before you as a man; and if politics cannot tolerate a human being, then let politics be damned." Human individuals, by all means; political conglomerates, never!

Anarchists—whether divine or human—hold that individuals in ekklesia (i.e., in that setting which best serves and preserves their individuality) represent the highest human reality there is. Thus, whenever any arkydom treats them, rather, as "clods" to be glommed together into "mountains" (which God knows to be "molehills"), this represents a degradation of humanity and not a magnification of it.

Anarchist Kierkegaard saw this principle even earlier and more clearly than Blumhardt did. Now, among us, Kierkegaard (with Ellul) regularly gets accused of promoting an "individualism" that is detrimental to any social concept of "church." However, that accusation is accurate depending entirely upon what one means by "church." "Church" as an ekklesia of individuals, they are all for. "Church" as holy arky, they anarchistically despise.

Kierkegaard could state the matter formally and philosophically:

> It is not the individual's relationship to the congregation which determines his relationship to God, but his relationship to God which determines his relationship to the congregation. Ultimately, in addition, there is a supreme relationship in which "the individual" is absolutely higher than the "congregation." . . . When a person first of all and qualitatively is an "individual," the concept "Christian congregation" [we would say "ekklesia"] is secured as qualitatively different from the "public," "many," [or what we would call "arky collectivity"].

Or again:

> In community, the individual is; the individual is dialectically decisive as *prius* in order to form community; and in community the qualitative individual is essential and can at any instant become higher than "the community," namely, as soon as "the others" fall away from the idea [namely, the constituting commitment of the ekklesia].

Kierkegaard could make it brief and biting: "Nothing, nothing, nothing, no error, no crime is so absolutely repugnant to God as everything which is *official* [call it "arky"]; and why? because the official is impersonal and therefore the deepest insult which can be offered to a personality."

He could describe "hierarchy" (pronounced "higher arky") in terms of a pyramid:

> Man is "a social animal," and what he believes in is the power of union. So man's thought is, "Let us all unite"—if it were possible, all the kingdoms and countries of the earth, with this pyramid-shaped union always rising higher and higher, supporting at its summit a super-king whom one may suppose to be nearest to God, in fact so near to God that God cares about him and takes notice of him. In Christian terms the true state of affairs is exactly the reverse of this. Such a super-king would be the farthest from God, just as the whole pyramid enterprise is utterly repugnant to God. What is despised and rejected by men, one poor rejected fellow, an outcast, this is what in Christian terms is chosen by God, is nearest to him. He hates the whole business of pyramids.

Or he could capsulize and conclude our treatment by affirming its thesis that arkydom is unreal:

> *The more the phenomenon, the appearance, expresses that God cannot possibly be there, the nearer he is.* So in Christ. . . . When the appearance expressed that men even denied that he was a man ("See, what a man!"), at that moment God's reality was the nearest it has ever been. . . . *The law for God's farness* (and this is the history of Christianity) is therefore that everything that strengthens the appearance makes God distant. At the time when there were no churches, but the handful of Christians gathered as refugees and persecuted people in catacombs, God was nearer to reality. Then came churches, so many churches, such large and splendid churches—and to the same degree God is made distant.

(The above quotations are taken from my book, *Kierkegaard and Radical Discipleship* [Princeton University Press, 1968], pp. 345, 346, 300, 291, and 332 respectively.)

Originally, this chapter ended here, but several months after its writing a new idea demanded to be put in at this spot. Then, a couple of months after that, the Roman Catholic *exemplum* appeared which will form our capstone. The new idea occurred to me while I was teaching out of Howard Clark Kee's study of the Gospel of Mark, *Community of the New Age* (Macon: Mercer University Press, 1983).

Kee's premise (which seems a sound one) is that Mark composed his Gospel specifically as instruction for the particular church community (possibly a collection of house-groups) for which he had responsibility (Kee thinks in rural Syria). Mark's intention, then, was that his readers understand what he portrays as Jesus' leading and counsel of *his* disciple community (A.D. 30) as being also Jesus' counsel to *their* Christian community (A.D. 65-70).

Accordingly, one characteristic about which Mark is emphatic is that the Jesus community *was*—and thus every Christian community *ought to be*—completely inclusive as to membership. Kee finds Mark's Gospel stressing particularly that women, children, and Gentiles belong in. He then proceeds to observe that Mark's description of "the twelve" defies every effort to make that community reflective of any one socio-economic class. Some of the twelve, of course, were fishermen; but Mark informs us that the father of fishermen James and John had hired servants—which would seem to disqualify them from the peasant class. Another disciple, Levi, was at least a minor official in the tax office.

My own thought ran on to consider that all we know of the Pauline communities and of early Christianity in general would confirm Mark's picture. The Christian church cannot be interpreted as a phenomenon of a particular social class, it being as "inclusive" on this count as it was regarding women, children, and Gentiles. From this I concluded that early Christianity—just as truly as contemporary Christian social thought—was dedicated to the ideal of "the classless society." Nevertheless, it immediately struck me that those two have completely divergent ideas as to how classlessness is to be achieved.

First, as we proceed to think about "class" and "classlessness," we need to keep aware of what a great range of distinctions may be involved. In our day, people are grouped and defined not simply by socio-economics, but also by gender, generation, racial and ethnic identity, level of education, language, voting habits, shopping habits, and religious preference, to name a few. We have enough class distinctions to cut a society every which way you choose.

I don't know enough to speak with authority but my impression is that Marxism was the first popular philosophy to base its whole understanding of social history upon the premises of class distinction, class consciousness, and class struggle—all, of course, dedicated to the goal of a classless society. To this extent, as much as all of modern social thought, Christian and secular, is Marxist:

"class distinction" (and the conflict that involves) is not only the basic fact about society but also its one hope, its means of salvation, the essential instrument for directing society to its classless goal.

(In the following, this is as much as I mean by "Marxism." It is shorthand for "any philosophy that defines social progress in terms of a class struggle toward classlessness." My use of the word intends no other overtones, is entirely descriptive and in no way pejorative.)

Yet all such "Marxisms"—even while being sincerely dedicated to classlessness—see no other possibility of getting there except by taking off 180 degrees in the other direction. Classlessness can be achieved only by first locating the class distinction that is at the root of the difficulty. The "oppressed class" and the "oppressing class" must be spotted and publicly identified. Once identified, the consciousness of the oppressed class must be raised—which, of course, inevitably leads to the raising of the class consciousness of the opposite number as well. A deliberate polarizing is taking place in order that the oppressed class might consolidate its power ("solidarity" is the very word, "ideological solidarity")—this in preparation for the struggle, the warfare, which is intended to eventuate in classlessness.

Obviously, the action serves to exacerbate the very class distinction it is out to eliminate—but there is no other way. The "oppressed but righteous class" *must* gain power over the "wicked and oppressing class" in order then to replace it, destroy it, dominate it, absorb it, or convert it and so leave itself as the one, total, and thus "classless" class. The ideological solidifying and polarizing of the class distinction, with the accompanying intensification of the class struggle, is the only way to classlessness.

Granted, this Marxist theory presents some problems: Are we to "continue in sin that grace may abound"?—play up class antagonism in the interests of classlessness? But I don't know who has come up with any better solution (actually, I do; but I am holding that for a bit). In common practice, of course, the business proceeds according to program through the spotting of the class distinction, the raising of consciousness, the building of ideological solidarity, and the hue and cry of the class struggle—only to hang up on the final step of creating classlessness. For some reason, at that point everything that can go wrong invariably does.

Thus, with the Soviet Union of proto-Marxism, the comrades of the oppressed working classes achieved their solidarity, won their revolution, and even established the bureaucracy which was to be the instrument for creating their classless society. Yet instead of the workers' classless society becoming the total order of the day, lo and behold, the bureaucracy itself introduced a new class distinction— doing this by itself becoming totalitarian over everyone else. So it went; and so it goes.

Yet ever and always we have to give Marxism another try— because what else is there? If class distinctions are the "given," the only entities we have with which to work; and if the inherent conflict between them is that which must be overcome—then what else besides class warfare can there ever be? All the liberation movements of our day show the pattern. I now use one to illustrate them all.

The clear and laudable goal of the feminist movement is to create a society in which the social distinctions between male and female are reduced to adiaphora, matters of no consequence. Not only any hint of inequality but even the distinguishing marks of the two are to be minimized. A true classlessness is to transpire. Yet that classlessness cannot happen by the direct approach of playing down the distinctions; the power of the oppressing class must first be broken. No, the immediate steps must point directly away from the ultimate goal they would serve.

Thus: "Yes, the two genders should be treated without distinction." So, from time immemorial we have had us an English language that enables us to speak by the hour without dropping so much as a hint that two different genders of human beings are involved, that there even exists a distinction known as "gender." Yet, that way hardly serves the raising of feminine class consciousness. Therefore, the rule now is to speak (with doubled pronouns and the like) so that the gender distinction is always prominent, to use gendered terminology in preference to the ungendered, to take care in specifying women at least as often as men. The feminist grammar is designed to serve gender awareness, not the classlessness of gender ignorance.

Thus: "Yes, the goal is that gender distinction disappear." However, on the way to that goal, feminine class distinction is necessary—to the point that one theology cannot be taken as serving human beings indiscriminately. There must now be a feminist theology in which women can have their special concept of God, their definition of salvation, their preferred reading of the gospel. Yes, just that far must the commonality of women and men be denied— for the sake of ultimate classlessness!

Thus: "Yes, we look for the day when the distinction between women and men will be seen as insignificant if not nonexistent." Nevertheless, for the sake of the ideological solidarity necessary to get us there, we find it right to posit an absolute moral distinction between the sexes—namely, that it is *men* who cause wars and that, if given a chance, *women* would create peace.

Please hear me when I say that I am not lifting up these ambiguities and contradictions as being foolish or senseless. No, *under the presupposition that class warfare is the only route to classlessness,* these moves are obvious, proper, and necessary.

In undoubted sincerity, the feminists claim that their interest is not simply in liberating themselves but in liberating men as well. Yet what must be recognized is that this has been the standard revolutionary line of every class war ever mounted. However, the question is whether true classlessness ever can be achieved through one class's gaining the power to dictate the terms of that classlessness. Even more, can it be called "liberation" for other people to take it upon themselves to liberate *you* according to *their* idea of what your liberation should be? It strikes me that "liberation" is one term the person will have to define for himself.

But if "class distinction" and "class struggle" be our chosen means, is it possible that the contradiction ever can be overcome?— that "classlessness" can ever mean anything other than "we are now all of one class, because ours is it"; or "liberation" mean anything other than "you are now liberated, because we are in position to tell you that you are"?

We have not used the term here, yet it must be clear that what we have been calling "Marxism" is but one particular form of "arky faith." It is the faith that the struggle between those arkys called "classes" can be humanly engineered to eventuate in the social salvation called "the classless society."

We now undertake a tracing of biblical history intent to show (1) that the Marxism of "classlessness achieved through class warfare" has proved about as futile an operation as humanity has been foolish enough to try; and (2) that a transition has been made into a Christian Anarchy that can do (and has done) what Marxism never can.

From beginning (almost) to end (almost), the Bible presents a classic portrayal (perhaps *the* classic portrayal) of class struggle toward classlessness. In our context, remember, "classlessness" is a synonym for "justice." The two classes of which we will speak were, at one and the same time, distinguished religiously, ethnically, culturally, and socio-economically—as well as upon the basis of "the oppressed" and "the oppressors." Throughout, the oppressed are "the Jews" and the oppressors "the Gentiles" (of different varieties). Throughout, also, the patterns of Marxism are obvious.

ROUND ONE is the Exodus from Egypt, with the Hebrew slaves as the oppressed class and the Egyptian overlords the Gentile oppressors. There is here no question at all but that the Hebrew slaves' struggle for liberation was an entirely just cause—as is also the case at every point to follow. Our concern has nothing to do with whether revolution is ever justified but solely with whether Marxist strategies ever deliver the goods. Because the Hebrew slaves apparently started with virtually no sense of common identity, a major hurdle in this instance seems to have been the primal need for class consciousness.

Acts 7:25 is quite specific that Moses intended his original killing of an Egyptian taskmaster as a signal of revolt and that the matter fell through because the Hebrews didn't have enough sense of class solidarity to understand what was going on and see their role in it. Before Moses' next try could succeed there was needed the consciousness raising of "*we* are the oppressed slave bloc, God's people; and *they* are the enemy, the oppressing party; and what we are supposed to do is hang together and fight them." The pattern is that of any and all class-warfare before and since.

Again, right on program, the actual struggle is interpreted as "holy war," God siding entirely with the oppressed class against the oppressing one—God not only approving the revolt but actually aiding in the effort and giving the victory.

The Hebrews best the Egyptians all right, and that Gentile threat is eliminated. The trouble is that the victory fails to translate into anything that could be called liberation, justice, or classlessness. What we get, rather, is not simply the hardships of the desert but, more importantly, the spiritual chaos of these freedmen wanting nothing so much as to be back in the slavery of Egypt and, in time, the Old Testament dark ages described in Joshua and Judges. All in the world the Exodus accomplished was to set the stage for the next class struggle.

ROUND TWO pits oppressed Israel against the Gentile Canaanites (and an assortment of other pagan tribes). Apparently it is in the course of this long-drawn struggle that the class consciousness of "us Jews versus them Gentiles" gets burned into the psyche of Israel as its fundamental sense of identity. Now "holy war" becomes an explicit theological concept and reality. With God's help through Kings Saul, David, and climaxing in the reign of Solomon, Israel's holy war is won and the Gentile oppressors driven off the scene. God's people now being in full control, there is not one thing to prevent their setting up the just and classless society for which they had been fighting. So what happens?

Well, I suppose simply to keep people from feeling lost in not having any oppression to complain about, King Solomon volunteered to step into the breach, tax them to death, and even subject fellow Jews to slavery. This, of course, led to the warfare of civil strife and the breakup of the kingdom. And whereas Father David had kicked the Canaanites out the front door, Son Solomon sneaked Canaanite religion in again through the back door with his pagan wives and their followings. One King Ahab, you recall, even married a Jezebel and assisted her in establishing Baalism as the religion of the realm. What, according to Marxist theory, by all rights should have been Israel's accomplishment of her just and classless society turned out, instead, to be the period in which the prophets were barely able to stave off the complete paganizing of Israel's faith.

ROUND THREE is the domination and oppression of the Israelite kingdoms by the Gentile Assyrian invaders. God's people were not in the best position for fighting this one. Israel, the northern kingdom, was lost for good. The southern kingdom, Judah, was saved through a miracle of God. Yet "saved" is used here, of course, in a very limited sense. Judah did not put her "salvation" to any good use; she simply became a puppet state, Assyrianized to the core.

ROUND FOUR of "God's poor" against Gentile oppression is the Babylonian destruction of Jerusalem. At first glance, this would appear to be the one in which the oppressed class lost it all. However, at God's intervention, the period of exile led to a "return to the land" which Deutero-Isaiah proclaimed as the Jews' best-ever opportunity to be the very people of God, a showpiece that "all flesh should see together," bringing even the Gentiles into God's one truly classless and truly just society.

Unfortunately, even while being handed the victory in their class struggle, the liberated ones again blew the payoff. Deutero-Isaiah's wonderful vision did not come to pass (at least at that time and in the way he foresaw). Rather than any bringing of the Gentiles into classlessness, in the return to the land under Ezra and Nehemiah, the class consciousness of "pious Jew versus damned Gentile" was raised to the nasty pitch of bigotry, exclusion, and jingoistic nationalism. Both the book of Ruth and that of Jonah probably were written in direct protest against this mean spirit—a spirit perhaps best exemplified in the edict that Jewish men must cast off and cast out their Gentile wives. Here was a classless society, in the sense that the oppressed class had taken over completely and excluded the very presence of any other classes. But it is not too pretty a picture of "classlessness."

ROUND FIVE (to be treated in more detail in our next chapter) is the revolt of the Maccabean Jews against the Hellenistic Gentiles, the Seleucids. It is again a case of the revolt succeeding but the results being nothing but the newly freed "oppressed" becoming the next generation of "oppressors."

ROUND SIX (to be treated in even greater detail in our next chapter) pits the Zealots, the loyalist freedom fighters of Judaism, against the Gentile Roman Empire. This revolt of the oppressed was undoubtedly the most conspicuous failure of all.

THE FINAL ROUND is the attack upon the Jew/Gentile class problem led by one Jesus of Nazareth. Here—and here only— can it be said that anything remotely akin to true classlessness was the result. Regarding this case—and only this case—an apostle could declare: "There *is* neither Jew nor Gentile, . . . for you are all one in Christ Jesus."

"Oh, so the Marxist strategy has worked and will work . . . if one takes Jesus as its sponsor?"—which is just what many liberationist theologians seem to be saying.

No, no, no, no! Jesus' success came through anything but the *political* method of Marxist theory. His was the *theological* way of Christian Anarchy.

We have seen that the liberationist methodology (here called "Marxism") is essentially a manipulation of those arkys we know as "ideologically constituted classes," aimed at insuring that the innocent classes of the oppressed prevail over the wicked classes of the oppressors. However, rather than through anything resembling "arky theory," *Christianity* comes at the class problem through a radically anarchistic approach. It will simply deny that these "arkys of class" (women against men, poor against rich, slaves against owners, Jews against Gentiles) have any actual power, significance, or reality. It will achieve its classless community—not by trying forcibly to *overcome* the class distinctions—but by ignoring them and living above them, by the grace of God simply proceeding to live classlessly. This Christianity manages to do by the expedient of insisting that human beings are always *individuals* and never ever constituent units of *en bloc* collectives called "classes." It follows, of course, that these human beings are to be *treated* as individuals rather than being glommed into "solidarities" and manipulated in the interest of any class struggle.

The Marxist concept of "class solidarity" is an invention, a fiction, a sham and delusion. It is as "unsolid" a phantasm as ever was fantasized. No one's essential identity is, for example, "woman"— this automatically putting her into ideological solidarity with, making her one of a kind with, even making her a "sister" within whatever power bloc has chosen to label itself WOMAN. No, she is who she is, an individual who—not at all "determined" by her gender— will be "woman" as *she* chooses to define the term; will give herself to whatever "solidarity" *she* picks, rather than being pushed into one by any sort of class distinction; will make of her gender what *she* decides to make of it; will be "sister" to the male chauvinist pigs if that is what suits her (men have "sisters," too, you know). She can ignore her classification and live outside any class, if that is what she wants to do.

A person may be under involuntary servitude—but that does not make him, involuntarily, a member of the "slave class"—does not dictate that he must share the slave mentality, be in ideological solidarity with all other slaves, see his master as an oppressing enemy, or let himself be used as a pawn in any class struggle. Even if 99 percent of all slaves display a particular character, that does not dictate that he *must*. His *individuality* always takes precedence over his so-called *class status*.

If he wants to, a man has the right to be poverty stricken without getting roped in with Charles Wesley's "the humble poor [who] believe." And being wealthy does not inevitably put one into solidarity with "the proud rich who disbelieve," either. Because there are only individuals of all sorts who have come below a particular income level in various ways and are meeting that situation in various ways. . . . And because there are only individuals (quite possibly some of the same people who, ideologically unchanged, had at one time been part of the other class) who have come *above* a particular income level in various ways and are meeting the situation in various ways. . . . Therefore, there are no such entities as a bloc of the "proud rich" oppressing the bloc of the "humble poor." The creation

of a socio-economically classless society hardly will be served by
fostering class warfare between imaginary solidarities.

The apostle Paul, on the other hand, tells about the one society
that has succeeded in true classlessness. Speaking from out the midst
of it, he says: "From now on we regard no one from a human point
of view" (2 Cor. 5:16).

We might think of him going on to say: "No, here we try to
see you as God sees you. In the eye that is on the sparrow, you are
you—and nothing else. If we see that you are a you who needs food,
we'll try to get that for you. If we see that you are a you who has
more money than you need, we'll try to get it out of you. But here
we do not buy the 'human point of view' that insists on identifying
people by class. We refuse to see people as 'humble poor' or 'proud
rich' and try to set them against each other. That's not the way God
sees anybody."

The real Paul, again: "There is neither Jew nor Greek, there
is neither slave nor free, there is neither male nor female; for you
are all one in Christ Jesus" (Gal. 3:28).

And as he might continue: "Of course, I am not denying that,
in our classless society, if we chose to, we could find out whether
you are of Jewish extraction or Greek; whether your legal status is
that of slave or freeman; whether you are of the oppressed sex or
the oppressing. The point is that we don't care. You are a member
of the body of Christ; that's all we want or need to know. Pretending
that these other classifications have significance will only confuse the
truth of who you really are. So please quit telling us you're a 'woman.'
We don't care."

Still again, the real Paul: "Every one should remain in the state
in which he was called. Were you a slave when called? Never mind.
But if you can gain your freedom, avail yourself of the opportunity.
For he who was called in the Lord as a slave is a freedman of the
Lord. Likewise, he who was free when called is a slave of Christ.
You were bought with a price; do not become slaves of men. So
brethren, in whatever state each was called, there let him remain
with God" (1 Cor. 7:21-24).

And as he might continue: "You were bought with a price
precisely that you might be given the one 'classification' that makes
any difference, 'member of the classless body of Christ.' Your one
goal in life should be to remain there with God. Yet the surest way
of losing that classification is to let the world sucker you into thinking its classifications are important. It, of course, insists on catego-
rizing people, defining some categories as 'privileged' and others as

'underprivileged,' then turning people loose to fight themselves into a higher class or else get an entire class privileged above the opposition.

"So you're as much as a slave, a poor Nicaraguan who would love to be as rich as an American. Of course, if you have a chance of bettering yourself, avail yourself of the opportunity. But do you have any idea how *unhappy* rich Americans can be? I advise you to pass up the class-warfare game—which so seldom works anyhow. You already are far more free and much better off among us unclassified members of the body of Christ. Indeed, it may well have been an actual *slave* who first sang: 'I sing because I'm happy;/I sing because I'm free;/For his eye is on the sparrow,/And I know he watches me.' "

One more time, the real Paul: "For freedom Christ has set us free; stand fast therefore, and do not submit again to a yoke of slavery" (Gal. 5:1).

And as he might continue: " 'Freedom' and escaping 'the yoke of slavery'? No, I am not reverting to the lingo of class struggle. I am not speaking of those who, through the exercise of class struggle, have already freed themselves from the domination of the oppressor class and must now maintain a vigilant class consciousness lest the oppressor repossess them. The very opposite: I'm saying that, in Christ's classless society, we have been freed from all this deindividualizing, dehumanizing business of class distinction, class solidarity, and class warfare. Herein lies freedom—definitely not in one class's gaining the ascendancy to where it can impose *its* 'liberation,' *its* 'classlessness,' on the others. And yes, we Christians do need to keep vigilant (toward ourselves) that we do not let the world entice us back into the slavery of what it calls its 'struggle for freedom.' "

Finally, in Ephesians 2:4-22, the real Paul properly theologizes the matter: "But God, rich in mercy, for the great love he bore us, brought us to life with Christ even when we were dead in our sins. . . . It is not your own doing. It is God's gift, not a reward for work done. . . . Gentiles and Jews, he has made the two one, and in his own body of flesh and blood has broken down the enmity which stood like a dividing wall between them . . . so as to create out of the two a single new humanity in himself, thereby making peace." That's what I call classlessness!

Of course I realize that if society had to give up thinking in generalities, give up treating people statistically according to class distinctions and social categories, it would come to a complete halt.

Scientific analyses (and particularly those of the social sciences) would be rendered impossible. It undoubtedly is correct that even Christians and the church must be able to deal in these terms. Laboring under the human limitations we do, we, frankly, don't possess an "eye of God" capable of watching and comprehending each and every person (let alone sparrow) as an individual.

However, what, by the grace of God, we *can* do is know that classification is a necessary evil and not the key to the truth about human society. We can know that classification *always* represents an injustice toward the real individuality of the persons involved. We can *resist* rather than *welcome* class thinking—knowing for a fact that we are being the more godly (and thus closer to true classlessness, liberation, community, and justice) whenever we can manage to think and deal in terms of individuality.

Collectivist class thinking is clearly of the arkys—is *the* means and method of arky power. Just as clearly, the insistence that human beings be considered and treated individualistically represents an anarchical refusal to accept or legitimate anything of arky philosophy or procedure.

Perhaps I also should say once more that the individualism of Christian Anarchy is not in any sense a threat (or even a countermove) to true community. No, the threat to community lies rather in the ideological solidarities of arkydom's class consciousness. What arkydom calls "solidarity" is actually pseudocommunity, the very opposite of true community—and this precisely because it denies and overrides the God-given "freedom of individuality" upon which true community is premised and in which it consists.

An *exemplum* will establish the relevance and contemporaneity of the above discussion. As of the time of this writing, Roman Catholicism is approaching a showdown between the church (i.e., the Vatican) and certain of its priests associated with "the theology of liberation." (As to how many and which thinkers are liberation theologians who fall under the church's indictment, I certainly am not in position to judge. The term "liberation theology" is itself an umbrella large enough to cover a great variety of thought. In the Catholic case, it will be for the Vatican to decide. In our case here, it will be for readers to judge for themselves.)

A couple of news stories name the Brazilian Franciscan monk Leonardo Boff as "one of the leading exponents of the theology of liberation." He is quoted from a magazine article as saying, "The theologians of liberation want to know why poverty exists, not just poverty as a social fact. In this sense, for a liberation theologian, Marx aids in seeing social sin, and in this sense, I think that Marx is useful to the higher cause of theology."

The same accounts then cite the Vatican theologian Cardinal Joseph Ratzinger as attacking "the progressive line that adopts the Marxist notion of 'class war' as historical 'fact' on which to base the church's 'mission of salvation.' " Boff's fellow Brazilian, a second Vatican theologian Cardinal Angelo Rossi, adds, "We can't accept class war as a concept because it leads to violence, and that is against the gospel." (Rossi's observation is true enough, though we have suggested that the essential error comes not just at the point of violence but at the very first step of taking class distinction as the essential truth of social reality.)

The Pope himself gets into the news story with quotations from a message he had recently sent to an African bishop's conference: "The solidarity [he might have chosen a better word] of the church with the poor, with the victims of unjust laws or unjust social and economic structures goes without saying." (Certainly the record of John Paul's own administration supports his statement. The point at issue with the liberationists has nothing to do with whether the church should not be concerned with justice and help for the poor. It has to do solely with whether class warfare is the gospel way—or even an effective way—of social progress.)

The Pope continues: "[But] the forms in which this solidarity is realized cannot be dictated by an analysis based on class distinctions and class struggle. The church's task is to call all men and women to conversion and reconciliation, without opposing groups, without being 'against' anyone." (Sound familiar?)

Finally, Cardinal Ratzinger raises a matter that points to a succeeding chapter of ours: His basic criticism is that liberation theology injects Marxist social theory into "the fundamental postulates of the gospel." "[It] elevates to theology that which in reality should be a social ethic or social theory. [It] mixes two levels, that which is Christianity and that which is social ethics." Ratzinger calls this an abuse of theology.

I must admit I would never have thought of looking to the Roman Catholic hierarchy for support of my idea of Christian Anarchy. But when they offer it, I certainly am not about to turn it down.

Chapter Four

ON SELECTIVE SIN AND RIGHTEOUSNESS

Regarding this chapter, I owe the Holy Spirit (or whoever inspired it) an apology. I got it in the wrong book.

This chapter (in somewhat different form) appeared in my previous book, *Towering Babble*, from Brethren Press (from which kind permissions have been obtained). Granted, it almost didn't make it there. The idea came late, after the rest of the manuscript was already in process at the publisher. It was my mistake to think it was given me for the book already marked *finis* when actually it is all about Christian Anarchy. However, the Spirit didn't have the grace to tell me it was about anarchy (all right, I wasn't really listening). But at that time I didn't even know there was such stuff— let alone that I was into it and had been elected to write a book about it. How was I to know the crazy chapter was meant as the nucleus of a new book rather than an untimely born appendix to the old? I apologize—but I still don't think it was entirely my fault.

The thesis now is that an almost invariable characteristic of "arky faith" (whether that of the establishment legitimizers of the Right or the new-order revolutionists of the Left) is what shall here be called "zealotism." The insight came to me by way of the studies of a professor of New Testament from the University of Tübingen (Germany), Martin Hengel—though he's had no more idea that he's actually been talking about Christian Anarchy than I've had. That's how it is with us accidental anarchists—so I better tell the whole story.

Hengel has specialized on the first-century Jewish revolution against the Roman military establishment, the proponents of which came to be identified as the Zealots. The spirit these revolutionaries represent ("zealotism," we shall call it) marks, I would say, a great deal of modern Christian thought. So in the following, a capital-Z

"Zealotism" designates the first-century phenomenon and lower-case-z "zealotism" the perennial manifestation of it.

Hengel has two slim (almost booklet) volumes, *Was Jesus a Revolutionist?* and *Victory over Violence* (both from Fortress Press and both, unfortunately, out of print). As one of our top experts on the socio-political background of the Bible from intertestamental times through the earliest Christian centuries, he is eminently qualified to tell us the stories of two Jewish revolutions. The first—a century and more before Jesus—was the Maccabean revolt against Hellenistic oppressors (the Seleucids). The second—getting underway during the time of Jesus and running almost fifty years beyond him—was the Zealot revolt against Roman oppression.

The ultimate purpose behind Hengel's study—his being an unknowing anarchist—is to critique the revolutionist, liberationist, radical-social-change, political-activist theologies of our own day. "Revolution"—as we have been using the term all along—might be defined as "an all-out, holy-arky effort to unseat an evil regime (the Establishment) and replace it with a just one (the Revolution)." The word "violent" does not appear in our definition; but the question is whether such revolution has any chance of succeeding without resort to at least some forms of violence. Thus, to avoid confusion, Hengel is careful not to follow popular thought in using the terms "revolution" or "revolutionary" in reference to Jesus. Surely, the way of Jesus was something quite different from that of human-heroic arky power.

Hengel uses the two Jewish revolutions as models of revolutionism in general—models of revolutionary idealism and ideology as well as models of revolutionary procedure and outcome.

There is no question but that both the Maccabean and Zealot uprisings met every possible qualification for "good," justifiable revolution: (1) In every aspect of life, the populace had been pushed to the extremes of oppression; their grievances were real; they were in despair and without hopeful alternative. (2) The revolution arose out of the lower, oppressed classes and was the spontaneous expression of their need. Their leadership came out of their own ranks. They were not being manipulated for the political advantage of any ideological clique. (3) Their goals were entirely right and good. They sought no more than simple justice; their demands were in no way exorbitant or self-serving. (4) Their religious motivation was strong and pure. They wanted truly to obey God, to be free to worship him and establish his justice. They were not prostituting the faith in the service of their revolution. (5) Each of these revolts turned to violence only as a last resort; any observer would have had to agree that no other political possibility was open to them.

The main difference between the two was that the Maccabean revolt succeeded and the Zealot revolt failed. The sad sameness was that both came to an identical end—"success" or "failure," no appreciable difference.

The Maccabees were quickly successful in achieving their revolutionary goals: they won back the temple and reconsecrated it; they fought themselves free of the Seleucids—their taxation, their enslaving of people, their cultural hegemony. Yet, in the process, the revolutionists had become power hungry and couldn't bring themselves to stop fighting. In their turn, they became imperialist toward the Gentiles. The revolutionary leadership became corrupt and extortive, fell to fighting among themselves, actually became collaborationist with the Hellenists they had set out to oppose. Perhaps saddest of all, the revolution which originated as resistance to Jews being forced to give up their religion and become Hellenist wound up with the Jewish establishment forcing Gentiles to be circumcised. At the very time Jewish revolutionaries were defeating the Hellenist oppressors, Hellenist morality was subverting Judaism. And it is easy to show that this is not the only revolution in history to have "succeeded" in just this way.

With the Zealots against Rome, there was also some initial success—a gaining control of at least one section of Jerusalem. But again, the revolutionary leaders fell to fighting among themselves, and in this case the Roman military responded with a vengeance. The population was killed or went refugee. Jerusalem was leveled to the ground and burned. God's holy temple was gone for good, and, at Masada, the Zealot survivors committed suicide in one of history's most gruesome and ghastly episodes. It is no thanks to the heroic freedom fighters that Judaism itself survived either of these revolutions. Their efforts would have lost it; the survival is owing solely to the grace of God. I do not believe the case can be made that either of these revolutions went bad because of poor decisions that a wiser leadership (say, modern Christians like ourselves) would have avoided. No, disaster somehow seems to be built into the very economy of arky revolution.

However, Hengel uses his exercise to show that the style of Jesus is as opposed to the arky faith of revolution as it is to that of the establishment—and this in an entirely fundamental way, not simply on the matter of physical violence. Of course, some proponents of liberation theology argue that the only reason Jesus doesn't show up as much of a political revolutionary is that the situation of his day didn't really provide for such a role. They imply that, if Jesus were around today, he would undoubtedly be out there with the best of them.

Hengel's answer is that first-century Palestine showed just as true a revolutionary ferment as any hot spot of the world today; that, had he had the inclination, Jesus easily could have joined (or led) about any sort of revolution he chose to; and that, rather than accidentally missing the revolution, he deliberately disavowed it root and branch.

I have some doubt that Hengel was aware how big an idea he was onto or how close he was to identifying Christian Anarchy; but in his treatment of "Jesus and the Tribute Money" (Mark 12) he gets to the very heart of the matter. We will let Hengel explain things his way (*Was Jesus a Revolutionist?*, pp. 32-34) and then I get to say what I think it all means. What follows is a paraphrase of Hengel— my English may communicate better than his translated German:

There is no evidence that Jesus ever had anything good to say about the Zealot revolutionaries—although he was probably even more strongly opposed to the establishment Jews who were cozying up to the Roman occupation. Nevertheless, Jesus' stating that the tax coin should be given to Caesar in no way can be understood as his legitimizing and siding with the establishment. Consider that the question about tax payment had been put to him as the hypocritical trick of some establishment-types. They knew—and were depending upon the fact—that he would never align himself with them, would never favor collaboration with the Romans. So, if they could work him into a corner where he would have to say that taxes should be withheld, he would be as much as an admitted Zealot. They could then report him to the authorities as an enemy of the state.

Yet the Zealots, it must be understood, were much more than simple tax withholders such as we know today—and much more radically consistent. Because the tax coin, the Roman silver denarius, bore the likeness and inscription of Caesar, the Zealots considered it both traitorous and idolatrous even to look upon one, let alone possess it. To so much as hold the things and profit by them would itself have been a collaboration with the foreign oppressor. No one could accuse these resisters of *taking* Caesar's money with one hand while refusing to give him his percentage with the other; their dissociation from the evil system was as complete as they could make it. Accordingly, in showing their allegiance to God, they were as willing to knife a Jewish collaborator as a Roman overlord.

That Jesus had to *ask* for a denarius surely is meant to indicate that he didn't own one and, to that extent, might qualify as a Zealot. Conversely, that the questioners immediately produced one clearly identifies them as collaborators. The setup poses Jesus an inescapable choice—he must recommend either supporting the establishment by *paying* taxes or supporting the revolution by *withholding* them.

The first meaning of Jesus' answer is to the effect that those conscientiously able to take money *off* Caesar (his image on the coin is proof enough as to where they got it) had better also find themselves conscientiously able to pay back the share he demands—that's part of the bargain; they're already committed. Notice, however, that this has nothing to do with the either/or choice. Collaborators (and that they *have* Caesar's coin is proof enough that they owe) should pay their taxes; yet that says nothing as to whether one should or should not possess coins and be a collaborator.

The zinger comes, then, with Jesus' second meaning (which, by the way, is not an answer to the question that was put). This, the text tells us, left them "amazed." "How did he come up with that one? We thought we had him with no way out." Hengel suggests that the Greek of the connective should be translated "but" in place of the usual "and": "Render to Caesar the things that are Caesar's—*but* to God the things that are God's."

With that, Hengel observes, the whole debate about what does or does not belong to Caesar becomes irrelevant in view of the nearness of God. Choosing God is really all that matters—not the choosing between the Establishment and the Revolution. All choices other than the choosing of God become what Hengel calls "adiaphora," i.e., things of no real consequence. It is senseless to take them too seriously, either positively or negatively. Neither the Establishment nor the Revolution, neither paying taxes nor withholding them has anything to do with the coming of the kingdom of God. And recall what Ellul observed regarding this text: that Jesus elsewhere identifies mammon as being a product of evil's realm and nothing God is particularly interested in claiming as his own.

According to Hengel,

World power [whether establishment or revolutionary] is neither justified nor condemned. It is deprived of its significance,
however, through that little word "but," which pushes everything to God's side. True freedom from the powers [whether
establishment arkys or revolutionist ones] *begins* with an *inner
freedom;* and inner freedom, in the New Testament sense, only
he achieves who has grasped in faith the nearness of the love
of God which leads him away from himself to his fellow man.

Choosing God with this sort of intensity must entail the denial
that the outcome of history is being decided in the contest of the
human arkys we have chosen to designate as "good" and "evil."
Consequently, Christians refuse to become embroiled in the contest,
whether investing themselves in the arkys of the one side or the
other. And this stance is what we have been calling "Christian
Anarchy."

After picking up this interpretation from Hengel, I found other
prominent New Testament scholars not only in agreement but con-
tributing further insights of their own. In his book cited earlier,
Howard Clark Kee analyzes Mark's Gospel, not simply as a historical
report of what Jesus had said and done thirty-five to forty years
earlier, but as Mark's on-the-spot instruction to and statement of
the position of his own Palestinian church community—which was
living right up against the Jewish-Roman War of A.D. 66-70.

Kee suggests that "four main options were open to Jews of
Palestine in the period prior to the first revolt":

1. "The first was to collaborate fully with the Roman overlords
and their puppets, the Herodian tetrarchs and petty kings" (p. 97).
As is regularly the case, this position was that of the aristocratic
elite, the "profiteers" who could do themselves a bit of good by
playing along with the oppressors.

2. "Or the Jews could assume the more passive form of acquiescence to Roman rule and to Rome's economic standards. It
was this attitude that was adopted by the Pharisees, who concerned
themselves largely with the maintenance of personal and group piety
within their own community" (p. 97).

3. "The third position, of which we hear nothing directly in
the gospel tradition but which has significant kinship with primitive
Christianity, is that of the Essenes. . . . The Essenes [unlike the
Christians] withdrew from society [and] clustered in their desert
settlements" (p. 98).

4. "The remaining position was that of the insurrectionists" (pp. 98-99). Kee uses Josephus in describing how widespread and pervasive revolutionist activity was in the Palestine of Mark's day.

5. However, "the community of Mark adopted a position that was not consonant with any of the options. . . . Their rejection of the use of political power or physical force, as shown by Jesus' denunciation of the power play by the sons of Zebedee [to which he responded with the words: 'You know that those who are supposed to rule over the Gentiles lord it over them, and their great men exercise authority over them, but it shall not be so among you . . .'—10:35-44] and their concurrent acquiescence in the payment of tribute to Caesar (12:13-17) would have enraged the revolutionaries" (pp. 99-100).

At another point in his book, Kee sums up his reading of the Markan community:

> Since messianic language is political language, since the chief image for the new age in Mark is "the kingdom of God," and since Jesus had, according to Mark 14–15, been executed as a pretender to the Jewish throne, it was difficult for the Markan community to avoid sympathies, if not connivance, with those who were working to free Palestine from Roman control. But Mark records Jesus as refusing to make a move in that direction. . . . Between persons [such as those of the Markan community] who shared this strange view of the coming of the kingdom solely by divine grace and those who seized initiative in taking it by storm there could be no common ground. (P. 93)

After this chapter and the book itself were long completed, I remembered that Günther Bornkamm and his turning-the-corner-on-Bultmann study, *Jesus of Nazareth* (Harper & Row, Eng. 1960) [Ger. 1956]) belong very much within the present company. Bornkamm has an exegesis of Mark 12 (pp. 120-24) which harmonizes completely with what we have had from our other New Testament scholars—but in which he comes closer to actually saying the words "Christian Anarchy" than any of them do. More importantly, although again without using our terminology, he finds a profound Christian Anarchy within Jesus' Sermon on the Mount—where I don't know that anyone else has perceived it.

First, on Mark 12, he opens by spotting the major theme of the pericope: "Seen against this background (the Roman oppression of Palestine), it is most astonishing and remarkable that political problems should take second place in Jesus' preaching. The reason for this is without any doubt the expectation of the approaching reign of God" (p. 121). As we will be observing time and again, it is another case of the Arky of God crowding any and all human arkys out of their places of primacy, as it were.

Then, after arguing that "Render unto God the things that are God's" is the heart of the passage, he concludes: "But the very fact that here the entire problem of the state is thus put in the margin, and that its fundamental problems are not allowed to come to the surface, is obviously a very important word on the whole matter. . . . Herewith Jesus' word opposes all attempts, be they Jewish or Christian, reactionary [Bornkamm must here have intended 'radical' or 'revolutionist,' if the pattern of his sentence is to hang together at all] or conservative-loyal, to improve the world with ideologies" (pp. 123-24). Read: "Christian Anarchy."

Second, his anarchical interpretation of the Sermon on the Mount is revealed in a section entitled "The New Righteousness" (pp. 100-109). He is examining Jesus' attitude toward the Old Testament "law," the *torah*. To appreciate the full weight of Bornkamm's argument we must know that Israel's torah represented the compendium of the divinely bestowed, culturally inherited definition of and instruction about what is good and right and wise regarding personal, moral, religious, social, economic, and civic aspects of life. Perhaps no other people has ever had all its tradition so neatly collected and codified; yet it must be correct to say that every society has its own *torah*, in however scattered and disorganized a state it may be.

Whether, then, one has in mind first-century Judaism or any other culture, Bornkamm suggests that people take one of two different "fronts" regarding their *torah:* "The first is the front of the fanatics who wish to claim Jesus for their own as the great revolutionary, as the prophet of a new world order, as the bringer of a new era, to which must be sacrificed all that has gone before. . . . For them, the will of God which has ever summoned and bound us is a burdensome chain which must be discarded. This picture of the future of the world is now made the only valid law. . . . This movement rushes towards a dreamed-of-future, right past the law of God and heedless of it" (p. 101). This, of course, is what we have been calling the revolutionist, or liberationist, view of those whose arky faith lies in the new world order to be introduced by Christian creativity and virtue.

Jesus dissociates himself from this leftist front, Bornkamm suggests, with the words, "Think not that I have come to abolish the law and the prophets: I have not come to abolish them but to fulfill them" (Matt. 5:17). Jesus will neither join nor approve those who reject the torah by damning it as "the dead past" from which they are moving *away* as they proceed toward "the new, dreamed-of-future."

Conversely, the second "front" regarding one's torah is that of those who see it as the means of society's salvation. Certainly not by moving away from the torah but by moving *toward* it in ever closer attention, respect, and obedience—it is in this way that both individuals and society will find their beatitude in the will of God. This, of course, is the alternative we have been identifying as "the establishment," or "legitimization."

Bornkamm suggests that Jesus just as explicitly dissociates himself from this front (only three verses later, in Matt. 5:20) with the words, "For I tell you, unless your righteousness exceeds that of the scribes and Pharisees, you will never enter the kingdom of heaven." With the scribes and Pharisees, to move *toward* the torah as one's goal is just as wrong as moving away from it.

Bornkamm then proposes that the literary pattern of the remainder of Matthew 5 both underscores Jesus' rejection of the rightist arky faith of salvation by obedience to the torah and points to his own distinctive stance (which we will show to be Christian Anarchy). "You have heard that it was said to men of old . . . but I say to you." (a) It was said not to kill; I say don't even be angry. (b) It was said not to commit adultery; I say don't even look lustfully. (c) It was said to divorce properly; I say not to divorce at all. (d) It was said to swear properly; I say not to swear at all. (e) It was said an eye for an eye; I say don't even resist. (f) It was said to love friends but hate enemies; I say to love even enemies. It is plain that Jesus' authoritative innovation is to push the torah to be more strict and demanding than even the scribes and Pharisees had it.

At first blush, Jesus' move appears to be an effort to get even closer to the torah than the legalistic legitimizers have managed— in consequence making obedience even more impossible than it has proved for them. Yet, Bornkamm suggests, this is not at all what Jesus has in mind. Jesus is not making the torah itself his end and goal—as the conservatives do. No, his move is to punch *through* the torah to get to the Giver who stands behind it. Once that is accomplished, it becomes apparent that obedience to the torah was simply another human arky-faith proposal for getting ourselves saved. Yet after we get past that arky to stand directly before God, then, as something of a fringe benefit, we find the grace, transformation, and power which enables us to obey even "the intensified torah" in a way we could never have done simply on our own. Although claiming no righteousness in having done so regarding their obedience to the torah, Christians who are living out of the grace of a direct relationship to God actually exceed the obedience of the scribes and Pharisees who are seeking righteousness as an end in itself.

So, if the torah is not "the dead past" from which we must liberate ourselves in order to enter "the new future," and if it is not "the way to life" that could be ours by following it—then what is it? You don't suppose it was from Jesus that Paul learned to see the torah neither as jailer nor savior but as the household servant whose job is simply to get the children to school, delivering them directly and safely into the care of the one true Schoolmarm (Gal. 3:24)?

Again, this is a case of renouncing any form of arky faith in order to go all-out with the Arky of God. If you will, it is a case of rendering to the torah as much as actually belongs to the torah but, of infinitely greater importance, rendering to God what belongs to God. For Jesus carefully to pick his way, avoiding either establishment "salvation *by* torah" or revolutionary "salvation *from* torah"— well, that strikes me as one rather fundamental variety of Christian Anarchy.

Our scholars have brought us this far; from here on out we're on our own.

What Jesus accomplished in that Mark-12 confrontation, I suggest, is this: he makes the distinction between the one, ultimate, absolute choice and all lesser, relative choices. So draw on your mental blackboard, if you will, a horizontal line. As poles of an "either/or" choice, label one end THE ARKYS OF ESTABLISHMENT and the other THE ARKYS OF REVOLUTION. You need not go to the mental effort of writing them in; but consider that subhead labels could be "Collaborate with the Romans" at the one end and "Resist the Romans" at the other; "Conscientiously Pay Taxes" at the one end and "Conscientiously Withhold Taxes" at the other. A little additional thought would show that, in addition to "The Establishment vs. the Revolution," any number of other morally contested arky alignments (such as "pro-torah" vs. "anti-torah") would fit the diagram as well. Any and all such horizontal polarities, such human alternatives, we will call "relative choices."

In Mark 12, Jesus says that none of these represents the real issue of human existence and social destiny. These, one and all, are "adiaphora" in comparison to the one choice that really counts. So, at the other end of your blackboard (you haven't already erased that first diagram, have you?) draw a vertical line—except, don't make it a solid, continuous line (dots, dashes, or other forms of tenuousness will do nicely). At the top of this line, then, write GOD. At the bottom of the line, however, we want to put the entire "Establishment vs. Revolution" alignment, plus every other possible horizontality—and summarize the whole bit with the word WORLD.

Now this vertical alignment—in which a person either chooses "God" or chooses something else which, however good or evil it might seem, is obviously "not-God"—this constitutes the only AB-SOLUTE choice there is or can be. It is what Jesus was talking about when he said: "The eye is the lamp of the body. So, if your eye [this choice] is sound, your whole body will be full of light; but if your eye is not sound, your whole body will be full of darkness. If then the light in you is darkness, how great is the darkness! No one can serve two masters; for either he will hate the one and love the other, or he will be devoted to the one and despise the other. You cannot serve God and mammon" (Matt. 6:22-24). The book of Revelation is after the same idea in insisting that, at any given moment, every person bears either, on his forehead, the seal with the name of the Lamb and his Father or else, on his hand, the mark that names the Beast.

Thus, this choice is absolute in that everyone must make it; to fail to choose God is already to have chosen the world. Of no relative choice is this the case. The whole point of Jesus' response to the tax question is that refusal to join the Revolution is *not* the equivalent of joining the Establishment (or vice versa). In Scripture, it is only God in Christ who can say, "He who is not with me is against me." The assumption that one must either absolutize the state-arky as a god (as does the establishment) or else absolutize it as a satan (as does the revolution) is utterly false. Jesus asks us to absolutize God alone and let the state and all other arkys be the human relativities they are, at once relatively good and relatively evil—even as you and I are.

The choosing of God—and only this choice—is absolute in

that everything else hangs on it. Only here does "your whole body" become full of either light or darkness.

This choice is absolute in that it is the only true "life and death choice," the only "black and white choice," the only choice between "light and darkness" (to use Jesus' own terminology). Between "God" and "the world" there is no natural connection, no possibility of gradual transition, no shadings of gray, no middle ground, nothing shared in common between the two ends of the choice (which is why, on your diagram, you were asked to make that vertical a non-line). Here and only here are we invited—or even permitted—to "hate the one and love the other, be devoted to the one and despise the other."

This choice—and only this choice—is absolute in that there is no room for dialogue or discussion between the poles, no room for seeking what is true and good in each, for effecting any sort of reconciliation or compromise. Here there can be no conversation (as there could be none when Jesus chose not to debate Pilate), for when God is that which is to be chosen, "To whom then will you compare me?"—as it is put in Isaiah 40:25. No, all one can do is *choose* and choose *absolutely*—"let goods and kindred go; this mortal life also."

Once one has absolutely chosen *God*—it needs to be said—*then* it is perfectly proper to turn to the *world* and find all sorts of relative values there. Thus the issue is not the customary one of being either world-rejecting or world-affirming; it is rather the question of primacy—who's master, God or the world? But once that has been settled, there is no end to the amount of *discriminating* world affirmation that can take place.

Now the root sin of arky-faith's zealotism is the penchant for absolutizing what are actually relative choices, for treating as vertical those alignments that are actually horizontal. The contest between two different "not-God" positions is treated as though it involves a choosing of "God," as though one of the positions were the position of "God" and only the other a "not-God" position.

However, the truth of the matter is that relative choices represent an entirely different alignment from the absolute choice and must be approached in an entirely different manner. God, of course, has the right to demand that every person choose him or, in failing to do so, choose the world. *We* have no right to demand that anyone choose between our *humanly* defined alternatives. Being humanly defined, the alternatives we set up are never black and white; at best, they are only differing shades of gray. It is hardly our place, then, to suggest that people must choose what we define as "the Revolution" or else be damned as part of what we define as "the Establishment," choose what we define as "liberalism" or else be damned as what we call "a conservative," choose what we define as "peacemaking" or else be damned according to our definition of "a warmaker."

Just the opposite of the way it is with the absolute choice, relative choices—in their comparative grayness—must recognize the essential commonality of the two poles; they are two varieties of the same thing. Both the Revolution and the Establishment are nothing more than arky ideologies regarding the use of political power. Either may be capable of making some real contribution to human welfare, and each is capable of really messing up things. Neither can guarantee anything, whether good results or bad ones. Establishment types are sinners and revolutionaries are sinners—you can take that as axiomatic. Consequently, what horizontal alignments present as "opposite poles" are actually different points on a continuous spectrum of relative good and evil (which is why you drew your horizontal as a solid, connecting line between the two "poles.")

Thus, just where the vertical, absolutist alignment emphasizes polarization and prohibits conversation, horizontal relativism calls for the opposite. What it presents as polar distinctions are not such and dare not be treated as such. Instead, what is called for from both ends is humility, honesty, openness—a spotting what is wrong and a looking for what is right in both the one position and the other; a give-and-take that is mutually affirmative as well as mutually critical; two-way recognition and correction; a search for reconciliation through the discovery of new locations on the spectrum where the values of each can be preserved as the "poles" move closer together. Precisely because the alignment is relative, each position must be taken as only relatively right or wrong, relatively fixed, relatively important.

Kierkegaard, perhaps, has put it best: "Whatever difference there may be between two persons, even if humanly speaking it were most extreme, God has it in his power to say, 'When I am present, certainly no one will presume to be conscious of this difference, because that would be standing and talking to each other in my presence as if I were not present'" (*Works of Love,* p. 315).

Nevertheless, just because—in comparison to the absolute choice, in comparison to God and his kingdom—all relative, human choices are seen as adiaphora is not to say that they are of no importance at all, that they merit no concern or attention from us. To say that each pole represents a shade of gray is not to say that, in every case, it is the same shade. It is not to say that one arky might not have a relative advantage over another, a moral advantage well worth striving for. I don't know that Jesus ever condemns our involvement with and struggle over the relative arky choices that confront us. In fact, he gives instruction and counsel regarding many of them. However, what he does condemn is our bypassing the absolute choice in the interests of absolutizing some relative choice which we choose to make all-important. Consequently, we dare not, *in principle,* declare the Revolution always to be preferable to the Establishment (or vice versa). Each case is *relative* to its own merits.

We now can define "zealotism" as that moral zeal which gets so carried away in its holy cause that it takes its own relative righteousness for the absolute righteousness of God himself. The anti-Roman Zealots of the first century are a good example of the disease; yet we need to realize that, even there, "zealotism" was by no means confined to the Zealots. The collaborationist Jewish establishment, for its part, was just as zealously certain that its arky represented the "God-pole" of the alignment. And each could adduce good arguments. The establishment held the temple, the priesthood, the Scriptures, and religious learning—and stood for law and order. The revolution represented the eschatological hopes of the people—and stood for righteousness, justice, and the liberation of the poor. The fact that *each* had a convincing God-claim would seem a rather good indicator of the relativity of both. In his anarchical response, Jesus displayed the very wisdom of God when, rather than choosing between them, he renounced the zealotism of both.

Yes, zealotism can and does show itself across our spectrums—political, religious, socio-cultural. It is nothing peculiar to the radical Left. In our day, for instance, the Moral Majority shows as much absolutizing zeal as anyone. However, because most readers of this book are likely to be left-leaners, I will continue to take my examples from and make my applications to the revolutionist end of the spectrum.

If the above analysis is correct, the Zealot movement did not *become* sinful only when it became violent. In its absolutizing of the relative (insisting that one's readiness to resist Rome is *the* test of true faith), it was sinful from the beginning and would have been so even if it had somehow managed to avoid physical violence. In fact, my guess is that it is the very action of absolutizing that makes violence as much as inevitable. Once a party is convinced it represents "God" over against "Satan," it is in position to justify whatever action proves necessary in taking out that satan.

The sin of absolutizing the relative could, I suppose, be called idolatry; but I'm not sure that quite says it. It is not so much a case of setting up a god besides Yahweh as it is our presuming to locate God, to say where he stands (namely, at the position of our arky's good cause and against the other arky's bad cause). We do this rather than allowing God to locate us (namely, as sinful, lost, and helpless). But whatever such sin should be called, it is bad—a form of Eden's "titanism" in which man presumes to set the rules by which God must play, assigns him his position on the field, and even tries to coach him. Zealotism signifies something much more serious than simply an enthusiasm for God that accidentally overdoes a good thing.

Starting out bad, zealotism inevitably gets worse. We defined it as "moral zeal for a holy cause"—but that was to put the matter as charitably as possible. With some regularity zealotism comes across more strongly as "moral zeal *against* unholy causes." Although the first-century Zealots *claimed* (undoubtedly honestly enough) that their motivation was the liberation of the poor, what they became best at was sticking it into the ribs of the rich (to the extent that they even came to be known as "the knifemen"). True to form, contemporary zealots prove much more proficient at denouncing whomever they choose to call warmakers than they are at positive peacemaking.

Now it may be thought that these two—loving the good and hating the evil—come to the same thing, that they are simply two sides of the same coin, but that just isn't so. Jesus showed us that they are not—at the same time showing that he was not a Zealot. He loved the poor—but did it without hating the rich. He loved the poor, indeed, while showing love toward different rich people at the same time. In fact, in his book *Money and Power* (pp. 137-73), Ellul argues well that Jesus didn't even draw the good-poor/bad-rich distinction in the same simplistic terms we do. None of this, of course, is to deny that Jesus did recognize an important although relative distinction between the poor and the rich. How did he manage it? He managed it by anarchically keeping relative alignments relative, refusing to absolutize them. It is only those absolutely certain of their own rightness who can afford to take out after those they know to be absolutely wrong.

Indeed, there is reason to believe that, at least in some cases, behind the zealous castigation of a particular sin or sinner lies the castigator's need to buttress his own holiness. He centers in on a selected sin (which is not his) in the interests of promoting his own selective righteousness. Such clearly was the case with the scribes and Pharisees whose zealous hatred of immorality had them ready to kill the woman taken in adultery. Plainly, their actual concern was not so much her sin as the promotion of their own righteousness. They were out to use her—absolutizing her relative moral defect as a way of simultaneously absolutizing their own (defective) moral righteousness. Zealotism's outlook of "us good guys versus them bad guys"—white-hatted heroes versus black-hatted villains—lends itself to just such grotesquery: the black, black, blacker I can paint my selected enemy, the white, white, more heroic white it leaves me. "I thank God that I am not like other men—notably Ronald Reagan" (Luke 18:11).

In this regard, there is at least one conspicuous difference between all forms of "biblical theology" on the one hand and the contemporary "liberationist theologies" on the other—whether those target Third World poverty (liberation theology), racism (black theology), sexism (feminist theology), or war (peace theology). Even if biblical thought has now to be stigmatized as "Western-white-male-military theology," it must still be admitted that that theology is dedicated to bringing Western white male warmakers (along with everyone else) into confrontation with their own sinfulness. Yet with modern liberationist theologies, things are otherwise. The regular pattern is to find out and denounce the sin of the enemy and leave one's own constituency smelling like a rose. These theologies are so deeply invested into society's arky struggles that they can't afford to give the enemy an inch by admitting even the possibility of wrongness in themselves. Zealotism simply does not make for good biblical theology.

As we proceed to analyze the character of Christian zealotism on the current scene, perhaps the one best example lies in the "peace movement," that arky opposing nuclear armament. We will stick with it as our example, our case study—although with the understanding that it is only an example. Zealotism itself is a widespread disease which readers, on their own, will have no trouble spotting and diagnosing throughout our bodies politic and ecclesiastic.

Current church literature and teaching often give the impression that we Christians consider it more important for a person to join us in opposing the nukes than in worshiping Jesus Christ as Lord and Savior. We use a person's stand on nuclear arms as a truer test of a person's Christianity than his stand on the biblical proclamation as to who Christ is. This is a zealotism, the prioritizing of a human arky above the true God.

Likewise, the movement shows the zealot tendency of becoming highly sensitized to the selected "sin of the day" (which is regularly someone else's rather than our own) and as much as totally insensitive to sins that come closer home. As Jesus put it, we get quite agitated about the speck in the other person's eye while completely ignoring the log in our own. So, for purposes of log/speck comparison, let's put the sin of nuclear armament up against, say, the sin of adultery—first being reminded that the same set of ten commandments which says, "You shall not kill," also says, "You shall not commit adultery." I find nothing in the text of those commandments inviting us to categorize its prohibited sins into those which are really, really bad and those which aren't really bad at all.

That paragraph *sets* my argument about adultery but hardly *constitutes* it. Much more needs to be said about the basic character of sin and how the sinfulness of given behavior is to be evaluated. The criterion cannot be simply the statistical-sociological one of how many individuals are adversely affected in what way. Much more important is the discovery of the spiritual economy involved, what the sin has to say regarding the sinner's relationship to God. "Sin" always is defined in relation to God before it is in relation to neighbor (although I do not mean to suggest that the two aspects are ever separable). Yet the modern tendency is to be completely blind to the Godward side of sin.

Regarding nuclear armament, then, its principal and essential sinfulness is certainly the effrontery of the nations in wresting from God's hands the power and authority to direct the course of history and dictate the future (or non-future) of the planet. It is the Tower of Babel all over again. By the way, this has been the sinfulness of militarism since the beginning. Nuclear capability marks a technological advance but hardly a qualitative leap in the spiritual economy of the sin itself. No, the sinful determination to power history into going our way undoubtedly has been a constant throughout the life of the race.

Regarding, then, in its turn, the sin of adultery, the Bible's paradigmatic treatment will best tell us what we need to know. Although, as far as we are told, King David's was a one-time affair that was quickly repented, yet we must be impressed by how seriously God took the matter—sending a prophet especially to get things straightened out and having the story written up in Scripture as a critical juncture in the history of his people. Plainly, more was involved than a bit of sexual misbehavior that incurred God's legalistic displeasure in having one of his commandments broken.

No, with David—as probably with most of his celebrity colleagues in this sin—it seems not to have been his intention to challenge the rightness of the Seventh Commandment. In fact, he was probably all for it . . . as a rule for common, run-of-the-mill sinners. They need such constraint; it helps keep them on the straight and narrow. Yet the case is entirely different with His Royal Majesty, King o' the Realm David. It is given to kings to *make* the laws—definitely not to *obey* them along with the hoi polloi. David's clearly was an "elitist adultery," a matter not so much of "executive-" as of "titanic-privilege," the privilege of being "big man."

Thus, the sin of David was not so much "adultery" as the pretension of claiming to be "like God." God himself well understood what was involved and so had the affair commemorated as marking both David's personal decline and the progressive breakup of his kingdom. If the spiritual economy of nuclear armament is that of Babel, the spiritual economy of this sort of adultery is that of Eden. And who would presume to say which is a log and which a speck?

Yet the evidence is that the sin of "elitist adultery" is still very much with us and that God's spiritual diagnosis of it is correct. A recent biography of Lyndon Johnson makes it plain that he was of the company—and quotes him something to the effect that "power" is a wonderful aphrodisiac (an observation that gets to the very heart of the matter).

In a syndicated newspaper piece, columnist Joan Beck raises concerns similar to ours—this in connection with the abysmal personal morality of different members of the Kennedy family, as that has been exposed in a number of recent books about them. Regarding President Kennedy, she writes:

And didn't voters have a right to know that he cheated routinely on his wife—or that he used the Secret Service to sneak women in and out of the White House and that one of his longer dalliances was with the mistress of Mafia leader Sam Giancana? Or that when there were no Hollywood stars or starlets around, he used two blonds from the secretarial pool whom he and his friends called "Fiddle and Faddle" (while Jackie, who knew about them, dubbed them "the White House dogs")?

Please hear me when I say that my point in speaking of these two presidents has nothing to do with any desire to attack or derogate them. My one interest is the extreme selectivity and inconsistency with which Christian zealotism applies moral standards. By what logic do we see it right to scream bloody murder about the sinfulness of nuclear armament and show virtually no concern about the sort of adultery that goes on among bigwigs in the worlds of religion, business, and entertainment—as well as politics?

It will not do to try the usual dodge of suggesting that nuclear armament is a matter having widespread *public* repercussions while adultery is a purely *personal* matter. It strikes me that Beck's picture identifies President Kennedy as extremely *sexist*—a matter interpreted as anything but "one's private business" in our day. So why is it writers who fail to conform to feminist decrees regarding good English who regularly get accused of sexism, while the most prominent feminist of the country names President Kennedy as one of her favorite men? Could this be selective moralism?

Further, John F. Kennedy's taking of Roman Catholic wedding vows (with a nuptial mass) "before God and these witnesses" was a deliberately *public* act of solemn covenant-making. Deliberately public, also, was his carefully nurtured, politically essential image as husband, father, and family man. So, if President Kennedy was this quick to put the satisfaction of his carnal appetites ahead of honesty and the integrity of his solemn oath-taking, what assurance have we that he would not treat his solemn oath of office the same way?

I submit that this sort of power-privileged deceit and infidelity (to God and these witnesses just as much as to his wife and family) is every bit as much a threat to the *moral* existence of society as nuclear armament is to its *physical* existence—which, I think, is why in the first place God wanted the commandment against adultery in there right along with the one against killing, and why he gave special attention to David's case. Consequently, I was greatly disturbed when, in reviewing one of these Kennedy books, *The Christian Century* opined that, although the Christian public once would have been disturbed by such presidential behavior, it now can take it in stride. Does this not reflect a most highly selective moral standard?

What is going on when, regarding President *Nixon,* we are determined to take every step to ferret out his "sin," damn it in no uncertain terms, broadcast it to the ends of the earth, and dog him with it to his grave? So what is going on when, at the same time, regarding President *Kennedy,* we treat his "sin" as something we'd just as soon not hear about and, having heard, would prefer to forget and not have broadcast any further. Nixon's sin we play up to be as heinous as we can make it. Kennedy's we play down as a peccadillo Christians ought lovingly overlook. So what is the principle of selection behind so obvious a practice of selective sin and righteousness? Let me make a try at that one.

In the first place, this selectivity must be an indication that our "moral standards" come from somewhere other than an absolute commitment to the absolute God. The hallmark of his justice is its impartiality, its refusal to show bias or play favorites. "You shall not be partial in judgment; you shall hear the small and the great alike; you shall not be afraid of the face of man, for the judgment is God's"—as was understood as early as the writing of Deuteronomy 1:17. Our moral selectivity has to have come from somewhere other than God.

My understanding is that this selectivity indicates a zealotism born of the worldly arky contest. Could it be that what actually triggered our moral indignation against Nixon was the fact that he was a Republican "conservative" with a less than winning personality? Could it be that what calls up our moral leniency toward Kennedy is the fact that he was a Democratic "liberal" of very winsome personality? Could it be that, in our zealotism, we adapt our "moral standards" to serve as weapons of arky warfare? Could it be that we have our moral sensitivity honed to a fine point when there is opportunity for using its righteous indignation to shaft the enemy with whom we disagree and whom we just plain don't like? Could it be that we have that moral sensitivity just as conveniently blunted as soon as there arises the possibility that its judgment might fall upon ourselves or the friends we do agree with and very much like?

Could it be that *selective* sin and righteousness is a far cry from the real thing, namely *God's* understanding of both sin and righteousness?

Apart from "biased morality," zealotism leads to other difficulties. Apparently, along with the absolutist sense of being *right* comes also the license to say about the opposition anything that pops into your head—as long as it is bad. The assumption seems to be that it is manifestly impossible to malign the devil—whether that devil be the U.S. Government or the National Council of Churches (Left and Right, tit for tat). But regularly, one of the first casualties of zealotism (and a most serious loss) is the biblical command to "speak the truth in love" (Eph. 4:15).

That command has two aspects, both of which are essential. "To speak the truth" surely intends a scrupulous regard for fact—both in taking pains to get the facts (all the facts) before presuming to speak and in sticking to the facts when one does speak. Plainly, this obligation is the more weighty when we set out to accuse an enemy than when we are out to compliment a friend. We need to be aware of and ready to correct for our personal bias and proclivity.

To speak that truth "in love," then, adds a further obligation. Kierkegaard once pointed out that, although our natural propensity is to be very strict toward other people's sins and very lenient toward our own, Scripture would have it the other way around: we should be most suspicious of our own perceived righteousness and most ready to forgive and make allowance for what we perceive as the sin of others.

However, it is in his treatment of "Love Hides the Multiplicity of Sins (1 Peter 4:8)" (in *Works of Love,* pp. 261ff.) that Kierkegaard becomes most pointed. One of his theme statements reads: "Love hides the multiplicity of sins, for what it cannot avoid seeing or hearing, it hides in silence, in a mitigating explanation, in forgiveness." And it is his middle term—"a mitigating explanation"—that is particularly germane to our topic of speaking the truth *in love.*

In almost every case, even after the facts are in hand and have been given their true value, there is still a great deal of leeway, still room for a number of different interpretations, differing explanations of what those facts actually *mean.* Zealotism, out of its abso-lutizing need to make the black-and-white contrast as stark as possible, regularly gives the most negative interpretation to the behavior of "the enemy" and the most positive ("taking in stride") to that of "the friend." Love, Kierkegaard insists, always opts for the most positive, even (or especially) in the case of enemies. Of course he is not asking that we ignore or twist the facts in the interests of love. Rather, in telling the truth, we should make it as loving as the facts will allow.

As we come to specific examples, we are still sticking with the peace movement. Our point can better be made with one case study than by banging away, hit or miss, all over the place. However, let me reiterate that I am not singling out the peace movement for special criticism. The "loose speaking" of zealotism could be documented on one issue or another, with party after party, left, right, and probably middle—all across the political (and theological) spectrum.

Let me say at the outset that I believe very few if any peace zealots, of whatever persuasion, to be deliberately unloving speakers of untruth. Recall that our initial definition of zealotism included the words "carried away"; this must be the very truth regarding these obviously well-intentioned people—whether of the Left or the Right (including even the first-century Zealots and their Establishment enemies). Nevertheless, zealotism often fails to speak the truth (whether in love or not) and that by several different means.

Half-truth: We seek out and speak loudly the worst things about the enemy, while neglecting to as much as mention the good things that would round out and balance up his picture.

Half-truth: We single out our selected villain and really roast him, carefully ignoring the fact that, if he were compared to those around him, he might even show up as the best of the bunch.

Half-truth: As per the suggestion Kierkegaard already has made, we give the worst possible interpretation to what may even be accurate facts about our enemy.

Half-truth: We keep the probing spotlight fixed on him and are careful not to let it fall upon ourselves.

Regarding the peace issue, the enemy surely should be identified as that nationalistic pride and pretension which proposes to take over and run things its own way—in defiance of God, the public welfare, and humane concern. But at the same time, it should be recognized that this disease is and has been endemic to every state or government (rightist or leftist) that has ever been. "Impositional power" is the very name of the arky game. More, this sort of pretension is a disease that can and does infect cause-groups and individuals as well as nations. It has not even been demonstrated that zealots themselves are immune to it.

But zealots can't be content with a targeting that might possibly splash even onto them. The villain has to be more narrowly selected. Nationalistic warmaking now is seen to be the particular sin of the technological West.

With that, absolutism is taking over, and the truth we are committed to speak is slipping away. Both historically and presently the Third World has warred and killed with all its limited technological skill—just as the West has with its almost unlimited technological skill. But that the wars of the Third World have been notably smaller than those of the West is no credit to those people's moral restraint—any more than the grand scale of Western war is a sign of those people's greater depravity. Both are intent on doing the best sinning possible with what they've got. And the more I learn about Pol Pot's purge in Cambodia, the more I wonder whether any Western state will ever be able to play in that Third World league. To damn Western war and leave the Third World looking like lovers of peace simply is not speaking the truth.

But with zealotism, things get worse rather than better. It turns out that the black heart of the black West is the United States of America. "More than any other event in history the worldwide human experience of those August days in 1945 (Hiroshima and Nagasaki) was a recapitulation of the primeval Fall." In the totality of human history there has been but one sin to compare with Adam's, and our own United States of America has the honor of having committed it. We win out over the Babylonian destruction of Jerusalem, Judas' betrayal of Jesus, the crucifixion of Jesus, the Roman destruction of Jerusalem, the Turkish genocide of Armenia, the Nazi Holocaust, Stalin's purges, you name it. Compared to us, everything else is innocence.

Why would it not be nearer to speaking the truth in love to say some things such as these: "In World War II, every combatant that possessed atomic capability used it. That some did not possess it is of no moral credit to them. The evidence is that all would have liked to have it and would have used it if they had had it—as would the Romans (or the Zealots) if it could have been theirs in the first century. So where is this quantum jump in moral evil?

"Whereas Hiroshima was destroyed with a single bomb, other cities in other nations and other wars have suffered similar devastation from conventional (if not primitive) weapons—it just took a bit longer to do it. So where is the quantum jump in moral evil?

"Although we are not obligated to agree, we are obligated

seriously to consider and thoughtfully to respond to President Truman's rationale for using the bomb. His explanation cannot simply be waved aside as disingenuous."

One characteristic of zealotism is to pooh-pooh and airily dismiss—rather than face and confute—arguments from the other side. But Truman's stated purpose was to end the war quickly and thus save great numbers of both Japanese and American lives which very surely would have been lost if we had had to fight our way into Japan and Tokyo. For that matter, if the Zealots must share the moral responsibility for what the Romans did to Jerusalem, why should not the Japanese High Command share moral responsibility for the fact that they refused to surrender even after we had given them every possible signal that this was their only alternative? *They* did have it in their power easily to end the war with the saving of countless lives. *We* could end it only through one of two alternatives (the bomb or the invasion)—each very costly. Construe the facts any way you honestly can, there hardly seem grounds for accusing President Truman of a quantum jump in moral evil. But to continue:

"That the Hiroshima bomb was not 'history's most evil event' as the zealots make it out to be is shown clearly by its context. The bomb was not used as a first strike but as one blow in a raging war in which every combatant already was throwing everything he had. And this war the U.S. had not started but had entered only under the provocation of what was indeed a dastardly first strike. The U.S. purpose in using the bomb clearly was to achieve a surrender and a cessation of hostilities, and was in no way a genocide of the Japanese people. In defeating the Japanese, the U.S. did not practice the sort of torture and atrocity the Japanese had practiced very freely in their turn. The subsequent occupation of Japan shows for a fact that the U.S. had no imperialistic designs and no interest in the sort of domination and exploitation that was the case, say, in the Roman occupation of first-century Palestine."

Now I am opposed to war—all war, including the U.S. involvement in World War II. But in my anti-war manual of the Bible I find not one little bit of this business of playing fast and loose with the facts in order to single out one nation's "war demon" as the special recipient of true Christianity's righteous rage. I find it suggesting, rather, that from Cain on, all war has been very much the same, a manifestation of the same spirit of sin, no matter who's doing it how—even if it should be the "peace people's" war against the U.S. Government.

I find nothing in my Bible of the white-hatted "us" being paired off against the black-hatted "them"; picking out one party as the particular villain while letting off others as comparatively innocent; interpreting technological advance as the measure of moral regression. And for the life of me, I can't figure out how this polarizing approach is supposed to improve our chances of finding peace. I'll take speaking the truth in love every time. In fact, it strikes me that the only statement in the vein of the opening quotation that Scripture would allow is: "I can't speak for others, but in my heart I know that I myself have recapitulated the primeval Fall."

It was most interesting for me to discover that what is to my mind the one best answer to and refutation of this sort of anti-Western, anti-American zealotism was written by a scholar who is himself the sharpest in spotting social, political, and spiritual sin— a man frequently quoted so by the peace zealots themselves. This is, of course, no less than our first-to-be-named anarchist Jacques Ellul— in an essay, "The Defense of the West," from his book *The Betrayal of the West* (New York: Seabury, 1978). I recommend it.

Another example of the zealotism good anarchists deplore is this from a Bible scholar arguing the case for tax resistance and having some trouble with Paul's Romans 13 words about paying taxes, honoring the emperor, and all: "It should be clear [he says] that it does not do simply to quote Paul as if the nuclear situation and the modern state were no different than the Roman occupation forces."

I contend the man now has bigger trouble than he had before he spoke. He does not see the implication, but as a conservative biblicist he has lost his authoritative Bible. There is no reason why the logic of his statement couldn't as well be worded to read, "It should be clear that it does not do simply to quote the New Testament about the resurrection of Jesus when modern man knows that resurrections cannot and do not occur." His way, the Bible comes totally under our control; we can make it say whatever we prefer: "Of course, if Paul were writing *today,* he would say the opposite of what he said then."

But more, what under the sun could this writer come up with if he were called upon, speaking the truth in love, *to document* such categorical moral superiority of the pagan Roman military over the modern U.S. Government that, inspired by God, the apostle Paul would be impelled to contradict himself, commanding his first readers to obey the Romans but commanding *us* to disobey the U.S.?

Why, the very way the U.S. Government handles *this very writer's* own tax resistance, compared to the way Rome handled tax resistance in its day, shows that he has his moral comparison completely wrong end to. Ellul's sharp question would seem to apply: "Is anyone really unable to see the difference between the United States and Hitler or Stalin?" Our Bible scholar is, without doubt, a learned and honest man; I think he simply got "carried away."

More than just moral bias is involved in this peace zealotism, however. I earlier said something to the effect that the stated issue is "war or peace" *as the zealots themselves choose to define those terms*. What I had in mind is this: A great many honest Christians see themselves as devoted wholly to peace—even while believing that nuclear deterrence is the only possible way of preserving it. Yet, in our moral zeal, we are not about to let that sort be considered "peace people" along with ourselves. We aren't about to credit either their honesty or sincerity; they are black-hatted warmakers as much as any.

Of course, the truth of the matter is that they are as sincere in their desire for peace as is any of the zealots, and they are not fools. Whether one winds up agreeing with them or not, their argument deserves a hearing and response. After all, it is true that deterrence already has succeeded in preventing nuclear holocaust for much longer than early predictions said it could. And it is a fact that the longest interval of European peace on record is the one in which we are now living, inaugurated by the nuclear age. Now I happen to find the deterrent argument a mix of truth and error (as I find the unilateral disarmament argument)—and I would like to talk with the deterrentists about that. But what is certain is that this crucial dialogue can't take place as long as, in our zealotism, we find it right to reject these honest peacemakers out of hand, as being nothing other than evil warmakers.

What may be an even worse violation of speaking the truth in love is our righteous zeal in refusing to make any moral distinction between *having* nuclear weapons and *using* the same. As one writer has it: "Even if Cain, because of some fear, had held back the lethal blow and had contented himself with murder fantasies and pantomimes when Abel's back was turned, the ghastliness of his intent would have remained. With megakill, too, an unspeakable ghastliness of intent for a hundred-million-fold murder is there."

The analogy has an evil brother intent on doing in an innocent brother with his back turned. The writer doesn't say how those roles are to be allotted among the superpowers—except that the U.S. Government is regularly his villain. However, the more serious question is "Whom is he accusing of entertaining murder fantasies, of being *eager* to nuclearize vast populations and ready to do so in an instant if it were not for the restraining fear of retaliation?" Is he suggesting that every U.S. president in the nuclear age has had this ghastly intent?—or only the Republican ones? Or, since his charge is entirely general and open-ended, are we to understand that anyone (his fellow Christians included) who does not buy his program of immediate and total disarmament can be taken as *wanting* to use the nukes? Read it as you will, it strikes me as a totally unsubstantiated calumny against one's brothers and sisters. I think the writer got "carried away."

What simply cannot be right is our joining the first-century Zealots in their identifying their own small party as the locus of godly righteousness and consigning everyone else to the outer darkness of demonism. As they wound up knifing even those fellow Jews they decided were "collaborators," so we wind up damning as murderers many fellow Christians who are as concerned for peace as we are but who happen not to share quite our view of how to get there.

Finally, even as I find zealotism unbiblical and un-Christian, I can't figure out how it is supposed to work, how it shows any possibility of accomplishing its declared purpose. If the peace movement be understood as a battle against the forces of evil, I guess zealot methods of battling at least fit the picture. However, if the purpose of the peace movement is to help pacify the conflicts and tensions of a storm-vexed world, I can't figure how zealotism stands a chance of making any contribution at all. For instance, a tax-resister publishes an article arguing his position and winds up telling the reader: "I fully expect that you will be able to put me down with theological arguments, or discredit me with a self-righteous application of Scripture taken out of context to justify and rationalize your position." What possible purpose is that line meant to serve?

I suppose there must be some satisfaction in being so sure of your position that you can brand all dissenters as frauds without even hearing what they have to say. I can see a certain cathartic effect for an author, coming on as the White Knight to take his whacks at the foulest monster of human history since the serpent in Eden. I would guess that zealot literature goes great in zealot circles. Of course, it does nothing to encourage one's fellow zealots in examining themselves, looking for their own sin, but it certainly must serve to confirm them in the righteousness of their cause and the wrongness of everyone else's. Yet I would think the cause of peace (perhaps above all others) should be focused upon reaching out—upon dialoguing with others, becoming reconciled with others, attracting others, convincing others, winning others for the peaceable kingdom.

Yet why should anyone want to consider tax-resistance after being told that, if he raises any questions, it can only be that he is putting down the author and self-righteously distorting Scripture? This is meant as an invitation to dialogue? Why should any believer in peace through deterrence be willing to consider Christian pacifism after being told that he is a murderer awaiting only the opportunity to push the button? Why should anyone consider a peace action when that means accepting the premise that the U.S. is so much more depraved than the Roman military in Palestine that the Bible is to be read the opposite of what it says? Why would any sensible patriot consider aligning himself with the peace movement if that means agreeing that the United States of America committed history's one greatest recapitulation of the Fall of Man?

There is no way wild accusation can amount to a positive contribution to the cause of peace. Personally, I doubt whether the irresponsible denouncing of bad people (and I have been denounced by some of the most righteous people around) is ever much help at all—at least it has never been of any help to me. For sure, this was never the mark of Jesus' approach to sinners, even though his righteousness would beat that of all the world's zealots put together.

So let us have done with the business of polarizing what ought to be reconciled, denying kinship where we should be finding commonality, shouting down what ought to be heard, putting down those who should be helped up, blackening reputations where we should be cleansing them, making enemies of those who might be made friends, displaying our righteousness at the cost of the other guy's, absolutizing issues that should be left relative, doing violence (yes, violence) to both truth and love.

What is the cure? Where is the way out? Whether either Jesus or Hengel-Kee-Bornkamm knew they were speaking Christian Anarchy, Jesus said it and they caught what he said: "But give to God what belongs to God." Make him the absolute that shows up all other choices as relative. That way, and only that way, lies freedom—freedom from the false absolutizing of the arkys (whether absolutizing the state as a god or, what is just as bad, absolutizing it as a satan); freedom to treat relative choices as the human relativities they truly are; freedom in which "world power is neither justified nor condemned but is deprived of its significance"—by giving to God the absolute loyalty and obedience that belongs to God.

NOTE: Allow me to emphasize some of the qualifications I have already stated. That I chose to center upon "peace zealotism" is not because I think it the only zealotism around. It may be that any important cause—and many an unimportant one—develops its own zealotisms; such is the propensity of arky advocacy and cause-making. Yet if I had tried to be "inclusive" regarding zealotism, this chapter would have taken over the book. Consequently, I chose to be "intensive"—in expectation that readers would have no trouble spotting the pattern and making the application to other zealotisms far and near.

Likewise, I chose a left-wing zealotism, not because I think zealotism is in any way confined to the Left, but only because, for the readers of this book, left-wing zealotism will be closer home. Yet the chapter intends no discrimination regarding the zealotisms of any part of the spectrum; each variety is equally bad.

None of the zealots I have known are dishonest, malicious, spiteful people. They are regularly good, sincere, devoted Christians who get "carried away." I can say that from my experience with zealots of the Left. I think we ought to be just as quick to say it regarding zealots of the Right.

Chapter Five

KARL BARTH
A Theology of Christian Anarchy

In an earlier chapter, you may recall, in which I listed those thinkers who, to my mind, constitute the modern tradition of Christian Anarchy, I centered upon Blumhardt and named Barth and Bonhoeffer as more-or-less followers who consequently were themselves more or less anarchical. Being only more or less sure of myself, I was that tentative so as not to invite anyone to call me out and challenge me to *prove* that Barth was a Christian anarchist.

Recall, then, that the very idea of "Christian Anarchy" had been triggered by Bernie Ramm's saying that he had read something on the subject that named Blumhardt. Well, when Ramm finally got around to disclosing his sources, it turned out that what he had been reading was nothing particularly about Blumhardt but a book which (incorrectly as we shall see) identified *Karl Barth* as an anarchist—a *political* anarchist, that is. Inevitably, this as much as forced me to investigate Barth—and whoever it was wanted to call him an anarchist. In the course of that investigation, I was brought to the conclusion of this chapter title: that Barth's is actually "a theology of Christian Anarchy."

The book Ramm had been reading was George Hunsinger's *Karl Barth and Radical Politics* (hereafter: *Hunsinger*) (Westminster, 1976). That book—of which Hunsinger is simply editor and contributor of one essay—is a debate (all right, "wild brawl") involving both Continental and American scholars. It concerns, first, how Barth's political stance is to be described and identified and, second, to what degree that stance was determinative for his theology. The different writers argue so many different conclusions that the book's total impress is simply confusion.

However, because *Hunsinger* was the best source I had or knew of, I originally wrote this chapter over it—simply by gleaning Barth quotations from various of the *Hunsinger* contributors. Then, long after my manuscript was at the publisher, I came across a much superior source which, in effect, obliged me to junk that first effort and re-do the whole thing. (At one point Barth complained that he had to write everything twice—once to get the ideas down and then a second edition to get them "right." And at least to that extent, I'm a Barthian.)

My new source was a truly amazing book, Eberhard Busch's *Karl Barth: His Life from Letters and Autobiographical Texts* (hereafter: *Busch*) (Fortress, 1976—now distributed by Eerdmans). During the last years of Barth's life, Busch was his secretary and assistant. And, having total access to Barth's works and papers, what Busch produced would need to be called "a constructed autobiography." The words are predominantly Barth's own (or Busch's careful paraphrasing)—with no attempt at interpretation or critical analysis. Most importantly, they are all properly placed in the *biographical* context of Barth's personal history and development (and my citations of Busch will preserve that feature by bracketing in the date of Barth's various statements). Quite apart from the purposes of this chapter, I recommend *Busch* as the best one-volume means both of meeting the man Karl Barth and getting a perspective on his total theology and work.

Where *Busch* has it all over *Hunsinger* is in showing that it was never Barth himself who was confused about his political stance, his Christian Anarchy, or anything else. That confusion has been the contribution of the scholars who were trying to make sense out of him. However, we will now come at Barth's Christian Anarchy by letting him tell it *his* way. Let us be clear as to what we are attempting: It is *not* that we will do a *selective* reading, picking out those statements of Barth having to do with his political stance—then to propose that one particular (and minor) strand of his overall theology might be identified as Christian Anarchy. Not at all; we will let Barth (through Busch, of course) identify his own major themes—and then show that, all together, those add up to what with complete accuracy can be called "a *theology* of Christian Anarchy."

I. The Birth of Barth's Dialectical Theology
From World War I to Romans II *(1914-21)*

The story of this seven-year period is abundantly clear. Barth is the Reformed pastor in the Swiss village of Safenwil. With him at every stage of development is his close friend and neighboring pastor, Eduard Thurneysen.

1. The "Givens" of Barth's Upbringing and Education

There are two dominant realities standing as the unquestioned (and unquestionable) assumptions of Barth's religious worldview; they had been bred into him. The first is the general theological stance which will be referred to under many different names but which we will here try to pin down as "Neo-Protestant Liberalism." It is this theology he will come to repudiate as "the counter-Barth," the heresy, the enemy, the threat to Christian truth.

Only in the course of time following our initial period will Barth pinpoint the specific loci of this theological abomination, but what it comes to is this: The historical fountainhead was Friedrich Schleiermacher. The one of Barth's own teachers and mentors best exemplifying it was Adolf von Harnack. The three of his contemporaries and colleagues giving him the most trouble over it were Friedrich Gogarten, Emil Brunner, and Rudolf Bultmann (with Paul Tillich so far out of it as to go virtually unnoticed). Brunner caught Barth's most pointed attack—though this may have happened precisely because Barth knew that Brunner was more biblically oriented than any of the others and so held out more hope of bringing him to repentance. Gogarten was simply scratched off as a bad deal. And Bultmann was the most troublesome. Barth had known him from student days. Bultmann had a popular following—some of his students even attended Barth's classes. The two men made repeated efforts to get together—only to have to face the finality of their theological opposition.

A final manifestation of this theology—which won't quite fit the term "Neo-Protestantism" but belongs here in any case—is the Roman Catholic doctrine of *analogia entis*.

The second "given" of Barth's religious milieu was a profound and serious *social concern*—which, in these days, focused primarily upon "world peace" and "the plight of the working man." The channel of action for this concern was a widespread religio-political party, Religious Socialism. As Safenwil pastor, Barth not only preached and lectured on these social themes but also was very much politically involved with them.

However, come the turnaround, Barth will be far from totally repudiating his social concern—as he did his Neo-Protestant theology. His social concern will remain as strong as ever; what he will repudiate is the theological rationale of Religious Socialism. The *expression* of his social concern will have to take a quite different form.

2. The Collapse of Barth's Religious World

The collapse can be dated to the day—August 1, 1914, the outbreak of World War I. Karl Barth, in retrospect, says:

> On that very day "ninety-three German intellectuals issued a terrible manifesto, identifying themselves before all the world with the war policy.... And to my dismay, among the signatories I discovered the names of almost all my German teachers.... To me they seemed to have been hopelessly compromised by what I regarded as their failure in the face of the ideology of war...." Thus "a whole world of exegesis, ethics, dogmatics, and preaching, which I had hitherto held to be essentially trustworthy, was shaken to the foundations, and with it, all the other writings of the German theologians." (Busch, p. 81)

> For Barth the outbreak of the World War was "a double madness," involving not only his theological teachers but also European socialism.... "All along the national war fronts we saw it swinging into line, ... the failure of German Social Democracy [that day's 'peace movement'] in the face of the ideology of war" (Busch, p. 82).

Note well *what* it is specifically with which Barth is so completely disillusioned: "arky faith," namely, the confidence that the organized human piety of a nation's leading Christians (the progressives, even) could bring society to moral health—or at least preserve it from moral death. And *this* faith of his (thank God) Barth was never able to recover.

Another aspect of this disillusionment must be mentioned. Recall that both Barth and Thurneysen are *pastors*. Once the poverty of neo-Protestantism had been exposed, they were desperate to find a gospel that could be *preached* as help and good news to their people. Throughout his career, Barth's one interest in theology had nothing to do with his own intellectual satisfaction; he simply wanted to find the message that could truly be *preached* as gospel.

3. Turning to Blumhardt

Christoph Blumhardt, a friend of the Thurneysen family, had occasionally visited in that home. A sister of Barth's mother—his beloved Aunt Bethi—was a Blumhardt follower who regularly resorted in Bad Boll. Both Thurneysen and Barth had visited Bad Boll from time to time during their school days. But when, in April 1915, Barth spent five days there—that was different: it was a deliberate seeking of help.

Above all, it has become increasingly clear to me that what we need is something beyond all morality and politics and ethics [i.e., beyond arky faith]. These are constantly forced into compromises with "reality" and therefore have no saving power in themselves. This is true even of the so-called Christian morality and so-called socialist politics. . . . In the midst of this hopeless confusion, it was the message of the two Blumhardts with its orientation on Christian hope which above all began to make sense to me. ([1915] Busch, p. 84)

The unique feature, indeed the prophetic feature (and I use the word deliberately), in Blumhardt's message and mission was in the way in which the hurrying and the waiting, the worldly and the divine, the present and the future, met, were united, kept supplementing one another, seeking and finding one another. (Busch, pp. 84-85)

Call this way of thinking "dialectical." Although Barth's will be called "dialectical theology" as early as 1922, we will discover that it took him some time to get his theology as well dialecticized as Blumhardt's already was. But then consider that the very thinkers we have been identifying as Christian anarchists are also the ones best known for their dialectic method. Christian Anarchy is dialectical by nature.

"Soon after his return [Barth] began to read Zündel's book on the older Blumhardt. He found that he was extremely moved by what he encountered in Bad Boll" (Busch, p. 85). "A longing began to stir in Barth 'to show himself and others the essentials' " (Busch, p. 86).

"[Blumhardt] simply passes over dogmatic and liberal theologians, those interested in religious morality and us socialists. He is friendly, but quite uninvolved. He does not contradict anyone, and no one needs to feel rejected, but at the same time he does not agree with anyone's view. . . . I think that he would also have all sorts of things to say about the conflicts and problems which now affect us. But he does not want to say it; it is not important enough, because other things are more important to him" ([1916] Busch, p. 85). Wherever has Christian Anarchy been better characterized?

4. The Spin-Off

Here we will spot the themes and emphases Barth develops between the time of his Blumhardt visit (1915) and the 1918 publication of his first book, *The Epistle to the Romans* (hereafter: *Romans I*). He ascribes none of these ideas directly to Blumhardt, but it is obvious that all of them were prominent there.

The Poverty of Human Arky. "[Is it not that] the whole of human independence and self-assurance are weighed in the balance and finally found wanting? . . . [This] is *the* question which then came down on me like a ton of bricks round about 1915" (Busch, p. 91). "We must begin all over again with a new *inner* orientation to the primitive basic truths of life; only this can deliver us from the chaos arising from the failure of conservative or revolutionary proposals and counter-proposals" ([1916] Busch, p. 89). "The problem of 'war or peace?'—about which there was so much talk and writing—had to give way to the radical and deadly serious problem of faith: 'With God or—as so far—without him?' " ([1916] Busch, p. 84). (How long has it been since anyone else ever gave the question of God priority over that of war or peace?) "Above all, it will be a matter of our recognizing God once more as God. . . . This is a task alongside which all cultural, social, and patriotic duties are child's play" ([1916] Busch, p. 89). (And how long has it been since a theologian has seen "theology" as his first order of business?)

The Wholly-Otherness of God. "It was Thurneysen who whispered the key phrase to me, half aloud, while we were alone together: 'What we need for preaching, instruction, and pastoral care is a "wholly other" theological foundation' " ([1915] Busch, p. 97). This theme will become both crucial and controversial—so keep an eye on it. Notice (surprisingly enough) that it begins as a *pastoral* concern. Then consider that it is simply the other side of the coin to "the poverty of human arky"—on the way to minting the double-sided piece of Christian Anarchy. "Wholly other than what?" Than human arky, of course. A Good wholly other than our human idea of "good." A Justice wholly other than our human idea of "justice." A Power wholly other than the "power" of our human exercise. A Glory wholly other than our human vision of "glory." An Arky of God wholly other than even the best and most Christian of human arkys.

"[With us] everything—above all everything that has to do with the state—is taken a hundred times more seriously than God ([1915] Busch, p. 87). (Ain't it the truth?) "The kingdom of God is the kingdom of *God*. We cannot conceive radically enough [the magnitude] of the transition from the analogies of divine reality to human reality. The pattern of [the moral] development [of the race] is a failure. . . . The new Jerusalem has not the least to do with the new Switzerland and the revolutionary state of the future; it comes to earth in God's great freedom, when the time has arrived" ([1919] Busch, p. 109). (I just happened to read the review of a book by a prominent Christian social ethicist of our day, in which the reviewer reports: "[The author] is convinced that the kingdom of God can not come until institutional structures are changed in North and Latin America." So much for God and *his* kingdom!)

A New Look at the Bible. This one is as critical an aspect of Christian Anarchy as any—the Bible being its one source and authority. "We tried to learn our theological ABC all over again, beginning by reading and interpreting the writing of the Old and New Testaments more thoughtfully than before. . . . I sat under an apple tree and began to apply myself to Romans with all the resources that were available to me at the time" (Busch, p. 97). And under that apple tree began the move toward the Romans books that would climax the whole development.

In 1917, Barth delivered a lecture which was the first public account of his new biblical studies. He called it *The Strange New World within the Bible:* "In the Bible we find something quite unexpected: not history, not morality, not religion, [not human arky,] but virtually a 'new world': 'not the right human thoughts about God but the right divine thoughts about men' " (Busch, p. 101). This is more than just a new look at the Bible; it is looking at the Bible as the word of God in a new (a more honest and open) way.

The Eschatological Orientation of the Gospel. "I began to be increasingly preoccupied with idea of the kingdom of God in the biblical, real, this-worldly sense of the term" (Busch, pp. 92, 97). "For Barth, the question of according God a place of central importance was becoming more and more fundamental. And since he had met Blumhardt, it was very closely connected with the eschatological question of the Christian hope" (Busch, p. 87). "Nothing new, Barth argued, was to be expected from 'secular circles,' among which Barth also included human attempts at reform and even the church: 'The world is the world. But God is God'—the *'but'* is there because new things are to be expected from God" ([1915] Busch, p. 87).

Religious Socialism: Barth, Kutter, Ragaz. This matter was a most sticky one for Barth and is most crucial regarding Christian Anarchy—partly because it involves political praxis rather than just theological theory. We have now a triangular relationship between three dedicated religious socialists—all three of whom appeal to

Christoph Blumhardt as mentor. (Recall that, much earlier, Blumhardt himself had been very much into religious socialism—joining the party, running for office, and representing it in the Württemberg legislature. Yet somewhat later he had decided to withdraw completely.) In addition, Barth, Kutter, and Ragaz were all three Swiss—sharing a common sphere of influence—and all three had begun their careers as pastors in the Reformed Church.

Hermann Kutter represented the "waiting" pole of the Blumhardtian dialectic and Leonhard Ragaz the "hurrying" pole—without either managing to dialecticize the relationship. "Accordingly, the two sought to exploit the upheaval caused by the First World War in very different directions: Kutter with a summons to tranquil reappraisal, Ragaz with appeals for pacifist action" (Busch, p. 86). Yet no more than Jesus did regarding the tribute money was Barth about to let himself get trapped into that "either/or." He chose to go dialectical with Blumhardt: "Isn't it better to strive for the point where Kutter's 'no' and Ragaz's 'yes'—Kutter's radical tranquility and Ragaz's energetic tackling of problems . . . come together?" (Busch, p. 86). "Barth realized even more clearly that he was 'always forced to follow Kutter in matters of emphasis' but that he 'could not rule out Ragaz's position on any important issue' " (Busch, p. 86).

In 1916, "under the title 'Wait for the Kingdom of *God*,' Barth had sent Ragaz a review of Blumhardt's *House Prayers* for [the magazine] *Neue Weg*. In it he wrote some words which were unmistakably directed against the Religious Socialists: 'Our dialectic has reached a dead end, and if we want to be healthy and strong we must begin all over again, not with our own actions, but quietly "waiting" for God's action.' Ragaz refused to publish the review because he rejected its argument as being quietistic" (Busch, p. 92). "Ragaz and I roared past one another like two express trains: he went out of the church [which he felt to be a 'drag' on his social activism], I went in [feeling the church was the 'place' for a new theology]" (Busch, p. 92). And years later, Kutter wrote a letter to the effect that he could only regard Barth as a 'general rejection' of his own theology (Busch, p. 162). Barth's anarchy lost him his friends at both ends of the dialectic.

In 1918, then, "Barth now even dissociated himself clearly from Ragaz and Religious Socialism—for all his acknowledgement of it and dependence on it. 'Pacifism and social democracy do not represent the kingdom of God, but the old kingdom of man in new forms [almost Blumhardt's exact words when he was in the similar situation]' " (Busch, p. 101). As a powerful example of Christian Anarchy, Barth shows the inherent dialecticism that refuses to commit itself to either the quietist or the activist alternative—either the conservative or the revolutionist—in the struggle to give to God what belongs to God.

Religious Socialism: The Tambach Conference. For Barth, his disillusionment with Religious Socialism did not imply his dropping of membership, participation, or interest. Rather than an "annihilation," his was a "desacralizing" or "profaning" of that arky. Simply and honestly as sheer human arky (and nothing more than that), he would have been quick to grant that it was one of the best around. No, it was only when it went on to claim for itself kingdom-significance as an object of Christian faith and hope—as a subunit, or authorized deputy, of the Arky of God—it was only then it became for him an abomination of desolation.

"I regard the 'political pastor' in any form as a mistake. But as a man and a citizen . . . I take the side of the Social Democrats" ([1915] Busch, p. 88). He spoke of his "very limited interest in socialism. For the most part it was only *practical* [italics mine—VE]. But I was only marginally interested in socialist principles and ideology" ([1917] Busch, p. 104). (Spoken like a good Christian anarchist.) "Thou shalt not have your heart in your politics. Your souls are and remain alien to the ideals of the State" ([1919] Hunsinger, p. 208). "[Let there be] strike, general strike, and street fighting if there must be, but no religious justification or glorification of them; . . . military service as soldier or officer, if it must be, but on *no* condition as military chaplain; . . . social democratic but not religious socialist" ([1919] Hunsinger, p. 208).

Those statements introduce a crucial idea, to be explored in depth in Chapter Seven. One must be entirely clear as to which actions are those of "a man and a citizen," done within the *political* horizon of cause-and-effect results calculated as sheerly human probabilities and possibilities—and which actions are those of "a Christian," done within the *theological* horizon of obedience to God and in the faith that *he* can use them as he will to produce the incalculable results of his grace and power. But just as soon as human, political arky of the one sphere tries to justify itself with religious, Christian pretensions from the other, it has usurped the place of God to become idolatrous.

Barth's relationship to Religious Socialism came to a head when, in 1919, at Tambach, Germany, he addressed a conference of about a hundred religious-socialist leaders from Germany and

Switzerland. The formal response to Barth's paper was made by one
Eberhard Arnold, who observed that the lecture was "a rather complicated kind of machine that runs backwards and forwards and
shoots in all directions with no lack of both visible and hidden
joints" (Busch, p. 110).

(Arnold could have been prophetic if he had only gone on to
say: "—which is just how an engine of Christian Anarchy should
operate." Eberhard Arnold was himself within a year or so of found-
ing that Christian community which has survived to the present day
as the "Bruderhof" movement. In examining Arnold's own thought
in the recently published anthology of his works—*God's Revolution*
[Paulist Press, 1984]—it becomes apparent that he is Blumhardtian
enough that any Christian Anarchy ascribed to Blumhardt would
have to apply to Arnold as well. Yet it is Arnold who may take the
prize as the very first person to use the term "anarchism" according
to the exact definition and with the exact application we intend now.
In the Introduction and Survey to his 1926 sourcebook—*The Early
Christians* [Baker, 1979]—he wrote: "At the same time, it was within
the Church that monasticism once again achieved that radical 'anarchism' of faith responsible to God alone which had been alive in
the beginning" [pp. 52-53].)

In his Tambach address, then, Barth made

> a clear and fundamental distinction between Christ or the king-
> dom of God on the one hand and human actions, whether
> conservative or revolutionary, on the other. "The kingdom of
> God does not first begin with our movements of protest. It is
> the revolution which is *before* all revolutions, as it is *before* the
> whole prevailing order of things." In contrast to both conser-
> vatives and revolutionaries it is radically new, in such a way
> that says "no" to both of them—though in this "no" the one
> is qualified by a relative affirmation of the other. Thus on the
> one hand protest against the prevailing order of things is cer-
> tainly part of the kingdom of God. But on the other hand
> Barth also reckoned with "parables of the kingdom of God,"
> "analogies of the divine," on the earthly scene. And in any case
> he found himself compelled to dissociate himself from the
> danger which he now recognized as such, "of secularizing
> Christ" for the umpteenth time, e.g., today for the sake of
> democracy, or pacifism, or the youth movement, or something
> of the sort—as yesterday it would have been for the sake of
> liberal culture or our countries, Switzerland or Germany.
> (Busch, pp. 110-11)

Take note, this early in Barth's development, of the positive references to "parables of the kingdom of God" and "analogies of the divine" on the earthly scene. We will give them specific attention later—but they do not signify any change in his evaluation of human arky.

Barth's first book—"Romans I." We just step backwards a year from the Stambach Conference to look at the publication of his first book in 1918. That study of Paul's Epistle to the Romans does not belong in the direct line of Barth's relationship to Religious Socialism; but it is a very clear statement of Christian Anarchy (with some insights we have not encountered earlier):

> All the Christian groups, trends, and "movements" of his time could not carry on as they were doing. [With them,] "everything had always already been settled without God . . . [which means that,] whatever ensues, it cannot be new action or aid on God's part. In the last resort it will prove to be a reform, or the old situation in a new guise. From God's standpoint that is more of a hindrance than a help, since it continues to delude people about the need for the coming of *his* kingdom. Our 'movements' then stand directly in the way of God's movement; our 'causes' hinder his cause; the richness of our 'life' hinders the tranquil growth of the divine life in the world. . . . The collapse of *our* cause must demonstrate once that *God's* cause is exclusively his own. That is where we stand today." (Busch, pp. 99-100)

> Men can never make "God's standpoint their own partisan standpoint" and therefore no individual or group simply stands on God's side over against others. . . . All human distinctions—between the religious and the irreligious, the moral and the immoral—become relative. . . . The kingdom of God is not "a rebellion within the old aeon but the dawn of a new one"; it is not "a development within previous possibilities but the new possibility of life." Thus there is a clear distinction between this kingdom and all human attempts at reform. . . . But there is also a clear distinction between this kingdom and man's religious and moral possibilities: "they do not create anything new." (Busch, p. 100)

Barth's Discovery of Anarchist Kierkegaard. This input came at just the right time to give Barth a powerful confirmation of his own theological development. "[Kierkegaard] only entered my thinking seriously and more extensively, in 1919, at the critical turning-point between the first and second edition of my *Romans*. . . . What we

[Barth and Thurneysen] found particularly attractive, delightful, and instructive was his inexorable criticism, which went on snipping and snipping. We saw him using it to attack all speculation which wiped out the *infinite qualitative difference* [my italics—VE] between God and man" (Busch, p. 116).

The two contributions for which Kierkegaard is credited are, of course, again the two sides of the one anarchical coin. The inexorable, critical "cutting down to size" of the arkys (all arkys) is simply the necessary move in enabling the infinite qualitative distinction to stand tall and clear. Later, Barth will claim theologically to have moved away from Kierkegaard—though it can be debated endlessly as to whether that represented a real move or only a misunderstanding of Kierkegaard. In either case, it is plain that the two thinkers never were in disagreement on the points stated here.

II. Romans 13 according to Barth's *Romans II*

1. The Character of Romans II

It was in 1920 Barth decided that he needed to entirely rewrite *Romans* for its second edition of 1921. "Only now did my opposition to Schleiermacher become quite clear and open" (Busch, p. 114). In *Romans II* he wrote: "For this [Schleiermacherian] theology, to think of God meant to think in a scarcely veiled fashion about man— more exactly about the religious, the Christian religious man. To speak of God meant to speak in an exalted tone, but once and again and more than ever about this man—his revelations and wonders, his faith and his works [i.e., the potential of his arky power]. There is no question about it: here *man* was made great at the cost of *God*" (Busch, p. 119). (And consider now, more than sixty years later, just how completely modern theology is done in this Schleiermacherian mode.)

So Busch characterizes *Romans II* by its "abundance of *negative* definitions (this is where the second edition of *Romans* differed from the first); [Barth] stressed that God could not be conceived of, that he was beyond this world, the wholly other" (Busch, p. 119). (It might lead one to suspect that Kierkegaard had a hand in Barth's decision to rewrite.)

2. Barth's Treatment of Romans 13

This book already has made it plain that, regarding a thinker's Christian Anarchy, his handling of Romans 13 (along with Mark 12) is the litmus test. And in being so tested, Barth gives us what must now be considered "a classic statement of Christian Anarchy."

Clearly, what Barth sees as being his first order of business is the dissolving of all we customarily have accepted as being the natural continuity, affinity, or relatedness between the following "unpairs." There is no possibility of "bridging" between one element and its counterpart:

THE ARKY OF GOD / ALL HUMAN ARKY
CHRISTIAN ANARCHY / POLITICAL ANARCHISM
GOD'S SOCIALISM / POLITICAL SOCIALISM
GOD'S REVOLUTION / HUMAN REVOLUTIONS

Some of these represent my terminology and some Barth's, yet the anarchical presupposition is the same in any case.

Rather than "the Establishment vs. the Revolution" (our terminology of the previous chapter), Barth speaks of "the principle of Legitimism vs. the principle of Revolution." Same difference. Barth, along with all Christian anarchists since Paul himself, is clear that the apostle has not the slightest desire to legitimate any human arky as being "of God" (perhaps the Roman arky least of all). Yet there was certainly no reason for Paul to hammer *that* point. After all, his readers were Christians living in Rome within recent memory of the Emperor Claudius's having strong-armed and man-handled them a bit. Who there would feel any temptation to hallow Rome, of all arkys?

No, Barth agrees with what we said earlier, that Paul (as also was the case with Jesus and the tribute money) immediately is concerned to apply the anarchistic warning much more against Leftist revolution than against Rightist collaboration. Paul certainly has no interest in legitimizing Rome; but his particular concern is that his Christian readers not legitimate revolution against Rome, either.

However, when it comes to the question as to *why* God wants a Roman Empire in place, why he wants it left there rather than being knocked out and replaced by a truly godly arky of the Christian revolutionaries, Barth offers a new interpretation. Our earlier suggestion was simply that God was "putting up with" the Roman Empire out of his respect for human freedom—the freedom of allowing the world to be as sinful as it chooses to be. If God grants the Roman Empire the freedom to be whatever it has in mind for itself, who are we to try to deny it that freedom?

But Barth comes at the question from an entirely different

(and most intriguing) direction. He proposes that, in God's eyes, the Roman Empire of Paul's day—and thus *any* state, or in our parlance, any human arky—stands as a "sign" of God's own Arky (the kingdom of God).

"Hey, wait a minute! That's the *liberal* line—in fact, a gross extension of the liberal line. Liberals would say that only their holy leftist arkys are signs of God's Arky—not that rightist Roman arkys are, for goodness' sake. Barth's idea doesn't make any sense at all. He is actually 'pairing' the things he supposedly set out to 'unpair.' "

That's what you heard, because you didn't let me finish what I was saying. Barth's understanding is that every human arky is intended by God as a NEGATIVE sign of his own Arky. He wants all those arkys in place to keep his people reminded that anything we have now is not yet the kingdom, that even the best of human arkys is no acceptable substitute for God's Arky. And come to think of it, the Roman Empire did serve God's purpose very well in that regard. The book of Revelation makes it clear that the early Christians owed it solely to the Roman Empire that they kept praying, "Come, Lord Jesus." The very presence of the empire added a certain fervency to that prayer. Thanks to the empire, among them, the kingdom of God became what might be called "a felt need."

It was no accident that the church's taking that arky to its bosom as being the HOLY Roman Empire coincided in point of time with its ceasing to pray for the coming of the Lord Jesus. Once we get in with an arky that treats *us* all right and serves our own personal interests, we tend to lose all hunger for the Arky of God. We think a Holy Empire which befriends rather than persecutes the church is "good enough," "as much as can be hoped for"—no matter what it may be doing on other counts. Yet this experience is no indication that God's idea of "negative pairing" was a bad one but, rather, that we exercise our penchant for misusing every good thing (such as a bad arky) the Lord provides us.

In this, the logic of Barth's thought might say that the *worst* arky (from our standpoint) is the *best* (for God's purposes). Yet this cannot be taken to mean that Christians ought to be out encouraging bad arkys for the sake of their spiritual benefit. The natural supply of bad arkys certainly is sufficient for our every need. And if we had our eyes open, we would see that even our *best* arkys are *bad* enough to leave the Arky of God a consummation devoutly to be wished. For Barth's "negative pairing" to drive us to God does not call us to *do* anything regarding the arkys, but only to clarify our own perceptions of them. Yet, by *negatively* pairing human arky and divine arky, Barth has gone beyond even the mere "unpairing" of them. Let's call his "anarchy-squared."

(In their turn—not being as intellectually or theologically sophisticated as either Barth or Ellul—the sixteenth-century Anabaptists generally derived their Romans-13 anarchism by an argument different from either of these other two. Why does God want the arkys in place and forbid his people to try to overthrow or revamp them? The Anabaptists tended to latch onto Paul's observation about the arkys' being a threat only to bad conduct and an instrument of God's punishment of evildoers. The argument then went that God's own people, the Christian believers, are not evildoers, that the arky license therefore does not extend to them, and thus they are anarchistically free from any arky power or authority. It did not necessarily nor even regularly do so, but this interpretation *could* lead to a certain disregard over whatever hurt the arkys might be inflicting on non-Christian "evildoers." Nonetheless, my perception is that, whether the exegesis be that of Ellul, Barth, or the Anabaptists, it all comes out at the same Christian Anarchy. Paul's text will support any of the three; each can be accepted as true; there is no need to choose between them.)

Now, whether or not it proceeds from a common negative principle, Barth's proposal that *God* "negatively" correlates his Arky and human arky is paralleled by another. His new proposal is that Paul actually is counseling that *our* relationship to the arkys should take the form of what we "not do" concerning them rather than what we "do" do. This idea of "doing" God's will by a deliberate "not-doing" that of the arkys can be very helpful in our reading of Romans 13. However, it will not work as a general principle that can be used independently of very careful attention to what the apostle actually says. The difficulty is that any command of either "doing" or "not-doing" can be *worded* the other way around and still *mean* the same thing.

For instance, revolutionary civil disobedience and tax withholding *could be* thought of (and perhaps most often are) as belonging to the "not-doing" alternative, i.e., as being a defiant refusal to do what the civil-arky demands. By the same logic, Paul's "being subject to the authorities" would be seen as the "doing" alternative, the doing of whatever the state asks of you. Yet, in effect, Barth argues that Paul means things to be worded the other way around.

Revolutionary civil disobedience and tax withholding are now the active and aggressive "doing" of entering the worldly contest with an offensive play (i.e., the political power of a good arky) intent to bring pressure against those arkys perceived to be evil. Conversely, for Paul, "being subject" is the Christian "not-doing." It is the *not* doing of any arky-style response, the *not* doing of rebellion and self-assertion. It is Paul's own "*not* being conformed to the world" and "*not* paying evil for evil." It is Jesus' "*not* resisting one who is evil."

Paul, of course, is one who knew best that "being subject to the authorities" in no way threatens the prior principle that we must obey God rather than man. He had been in trouble with the law no telling how many times for not stopping preaching when the authorities had ordered him to. Yet, even when such obeying of God necessitates the disobeying of an arky, this is no abrogation of the principle of "being subject." It does not amount to a "doing" of revolt and contest. It probably shouldn't even be called "civil disobedience"—that term customarily denoting a disobedience for the sake of disobedience, as a political means of attacking the bad arky, challenging, protesting, provoking, and exposing its evil. No, in cases like Paul's refusal to stop preaching, the action is still a "not-doing" of revolution. The intent is entirely that of obeying God— it being entirely incidental that, unavoidably, the arky had to be disobeyed in the process. Indeed, the disobeyer can even remain entirely subject to the authorities by expressing regret that his obedience to God left him no recourse but to disobey the arky.

Barth's distinction between "doing" and "not-doing" is admittedly a fine one—although not for that reason less true or less helpful in getting us to the heart of Romans 13. At which job we are now ready to let Barth speak for himself.

We will follow Barth's exegesis but be free to supplement *Romans* quotations with quotations from elsewhere in Barth. We will find him confirming many of the anarchical observations made in previous chapters. (I know it can be questioned as to who is confirming whom. Granted, he had *written* long before the present book was even a gleam in its father's eye [or better *I* was even a gleam in my father's eye]; but I had not *read* until after my previous chapters were already in black and white.)

Set not your mind on high things (Rom. 12:16)—and a "not-doing" counsel, notice. Regarding which, Barth says:

> Christianity does not set its mind on *high things*. It is uneasy when it hears men speaking loudly and with confidence about

"creative evolution"; when it marks their plans for perfecting the development of pure and applied science, of art, of morals and of religion, of physical and spiritual health, of welfare and well-being. Christianity is unhappy when men boast of the glories of marriage and family life, of Church and State, and of Society. Christianity does not busy itself to support and underpin those many "ideals" by which men are deeply moved—individualism, collectivism, nationalism, internationalism, humanitarianism, ecclesiasticism. . . . In all these growing towers Christianity beholds at least a parable of death. . . . It finds itself unable to place serious confidence in the permanence of any of these "important" things, or in the value of any of these "values." Christianity perceives men moving, it is true, but moving to deprivation. (Romans, pp. 462-63)

"Why, the man indiscriminately mixes good arkys and bad arkys as though they were all the same!" Yup, that's anarchy—although it is not that the arkys are all the same but that our hallowing of, our "serious confidence in" them is. For instance, Barth, as we will discover, knows very well that Christianity sides with the poor and lowly. Yet, long before "liberation theology" was invented, he saw that even so worthy a concern easily could become "arkyized": "It may therefore be that those whom we think to be *lowly* have long ago become in fact exalted. It may be that their humility has been turned long ago to horrid pride. It may be that their ambiguity has been formed into an idol, and their 'brokenness' into some new popular theology" (Romans, p. 464).

The root difficulty here is what we earlier identified as "zealotism," the unquestioned confidence that, in our perception of right and wrong, we are as much as infallible:

[Man] is only a dilettante, a blunderer, in his attempt to distinguish between good and evil, right and wrong, acting as though he really has the capacity to do it. . . . Neither in his own cause nor in that of others can he be a wise and righteous judge. (Hunsinger, p. 165)

In Genesis 3, the desire of man for a knowledge of good and evil is represented as an evil desire, indeed the one evil desire which is so characteristic and fatal for the whole race. (Hunsinger, p. 166)

I am already choosing wrong when I think that I know and ought to decide what is right, and I am doing wrong when I try to accomplish that which I have chosen as right. I am already putting myself in the wrong with others, and doing

them wrong, when—it makes no odds how gently or vigor-
ously I do it—I confront them as the one who is right, wanting
to break over them as the great crisis. (Hunsinger, p. 166)

"Break over them as the great crisis"—which is to say, "force them
to choose between what *I* present as the great options of Good and
Evil."

That to which Barth is objecting is that which is most characteristic of arky faith. Has he not here spotted the most fundamental (and most impositional) power of arkydom, namely, the
power of knowing oneself to be an elect representative of "the
right," asserting my strength as that of ten, because I know my heart
is pure? And what virtue is so utterly lacking in the arkys as "humility"? Barth is even thoughtful enough to put the matter into the
"absolutist/relativist" language of our previous chapter:

> Let us not deceive ourselves. Our conceits are haphazard. To
> this rule there are no exceptions. . . . [The] relativity of the
> ethics of grace is the axe laid at the root of *our own haphazard
> conceits* (Rom. 11:25). The root from which our conceits spring,
> the secret which lies behind all human exultation, is disclosed
> in the persistent regularity with which men crown themselves
> with the security of some absolute answer. By putting an end
> to all absolute ethics, Christianity finally puts an end to all the
> triumph and sorrow that accompanies the occupation of any
> human eminence. (Romans, p. 466)

Inevitably, then, our *sense* of absolute rightness moves us to
promote and enforce that righteousness:

> Am I also to take into my own hands the preservation of that
> right? . . . Our determination to introduce the higher righ-
> teousness is precisely that which renders it altogether lost: *For
> the wrath of God is revealed against all ungodliness and unrigh-
> teousness of men* (Rom. 1:18). The wrath of God is revealed
> against human ungodliness in doing evil and in doing good;
> it is revealed against the enemy and against me, if I purpose
> to be the enemy of my enemy. This is the criticism of milita-
> rism, but it is, in passing, a criticism of pacifism also. But who
> among us does in fact leave room, not for the wrath of men,
> but for the wrath of God? Who among us does seriously
> reckon with the fact that human action will, not only here but
> everywhere, be driven off the field by the pre-eminent action
> of God? (Romans, p. 473)

Then, in a rather cryptic statement out of a quite cryptic passage, I *think* Barth picks up our idea about arkys using the unreality of collective solidarities to override the real individuality of sparrows and human beings. He is talking about "encountering the great positions of Church and State, of Law and Society" in which they claim to have all the answers. Then he says, "In all of them the plurality of individuals has been limited by the Whole" (Romans, p. 477).

As Barth moves into his central argument—that which says, in effect, that Christian Anarchy equally rejects both legitimism of the arkys *and* revolution against them, he claims to be following Paul in very *unequally* giving his attention to revolution. That takes some explaining which gets him to the very heart of his anarchical concern. We begin with some crucial statements from outside his *Romans* book:

"The little revolutions and attacks by which [the powers of history] seem to be more shaken than they really are can never succeed even in limiting, let alone destroying, their power. It is the kingdom, the revolution of God, which breaks, which has already broken them. Jesus *is* their conqueror." (Hunsinger, pp. 90-91)

"At this point there can be no reversal. The victory of Jesus Christ, and thus what can be called the victory of light over darkness, can never be inferred from any victories of humanity—never at any rate with real certainty." (Hunsinger, p. 94)

Here and in the following is the idea we had in mind when presenting "God's Revolution/Human Revolutions" as one of the couples Barth was intent to "unpair." And in the above Barth is doing little more than quote Blumhardt. Back, then, to the *Romans* book:

> Why is it that we [with Paul and Jesus] have to watch so carefully the forces of revolution? Why are we not equally anxious about the manifest dangers of conservatism? . . . We are anxious about the forces of revolution and not about the forces of conservatism, because it is most improbable that anyone will be won over to the cause of reaction—as a result of reading the Epistle to the Romans! . . .

[Barth was addressing the liberal intelligentsia of the Continent and knew that none of them were candidates for conservative legitimism. Whether he considered that Romans 13—with its "Let every person be subject to the governing authorities"—could and often would be used as counsel of legitimism, we do not know.

Even so, he is still correct: a fair reading of the entirety of Paul's "Epistle to the Romans" could never be made to serve "the cause of reaction." Barth continues:]

"The revolutionary Titan is far more godless, far more dangerous, than his reactionary counterpart—because he is so much nearer the truth. To us, at least, the reactionary presents little danger; with his Red brother it is far otherwise" (Romans, p. 468).

The phrase "Red brother" alerts us to when it was Barth wrote these words and introduces us to an intriguing aspect of his personal anarchism. Writing in 1920, Barth was in the atmosphere of the Bolshevik "socialist" revolution getting its regime into place—about the same time Walter Rauschenbusch was calling it the world's best hope for peace and brotherhood and Malcolm Muggeridge's friends were visiting Russia and being entranced. In calling the Red brother "so much nearer the truth" than the political conservatives, Barth is saying simply that the rhetorical line of the revolutionary Left always is superior to that of the Right. With its talk about freedom, justice, equality—about helping the poor and oppressed—it even *sounds* very much like Jesus. It is precisely in that similarity that the danger lies—the danger of our taking it *for* Jesus.

In 1919, Barth "spoke about the Russian revolution, which he saw as an attempt which had to be made but was not to be imitated. He was also well aware of the problems in this attempt: violent revolution (which meant the establishment of the new society 'on the old foundations'), the exclusiveness of the working class (in contrast to the abolition of classes) [see Chapter Three], and minority rule ('the acknowledged shortcomings of democracy are not improved by its abolition')" (Busch, p. 106).

It will become entirely plain that, throughout his life, Barth's own socio-political preference was that of "socialism." Yet already we have seen him repudiate Religious *Socialism;* now that of the Union of Soviet *Socialist* Republics; and yet to come the National *Socialist* German Workers Party (Nazism). Of course, he is aware of the moral distinctions between these different forms of socialism, but his repudiation of each is not based upon that assessment of relative morality. Fundamentally, each is equally out of order for being a human arky claiming messianic status for itself. So Barth's rejection of Soviet socialism is in no sense that of an ideologue who brands that arky as demonic in the effort to get his own preferred holy arky (say, capitalism) into its place. No, Barth is the Christian anarchist who is not about to legitimize Soviet socialism but who is not about to legitimize any other arky's fighting against it or trying to replace it, either. "Give to God what belongs to God."

Years later, the liberal theologian Reinhold Niebuhr—whose own arky faith always wanted him on board the arky "nearest the truth"—became highly incensed with what he saw as Barth's political flip-flopping. Yet right here in Romans II, we see the consistent (though anarchical) principle that makes sense of Barth: always warn against that arky nearest the truth, the one Christians will most be in danger of taking for the Arky of God.

> [The travesty of it all is] that men should, as a matter of course, claim to possess a higher right over their fellow men, that they should, as a matter of course, dare to regulate and predetermine almost all their conduct, that those who put forward such a manifestly fraudulent claim should be crowned with a halo of real power and should be capable of requiring obedience and sacrifice as though they had been invested with the authority of God, that the Many should conspire to speak as though they were the One, that a minority or a majority (even the supreme democratic majority of all against one) should assume that they are the community. . . . This whole pseudo-transcendence [claimed by] an altogether immanent order is the wound that is inflicted by every existing government— even by the best—upon those who are most delicately conscious of what is good and right. [Even so,] the more successfully the good and the right assume concrete form, the more they become evil and wrong—*summa jus, summa injuria.* . . . If, for example, the Church of Calvin [for Barth, the nearest-to-the-truth church] were to be reformed and broadened out to be the Church of the League of Nations, this doing of the supreme right would become the supreme wrongdoing. (Romans, p. 479)

Now that's anarchy (though I claim it would still be just as good anarchy even if Barth had put it into shorter and clearer sentences).

> From this perception of the evil that lies in the very existence of existing government, Revolution is born. The revolutionary seeks to be rid of the evil by bestirring himself to battle with it and to overthrow it. He determines to remove the existing ordinances, in order that he may erect in their place the new right. . . . The revolutionary must, however, own that in adopting his plan he allows himself to be *overcome of evil* (Rom. 12:21 [which is, by the way, another "not-doing" command]). He forgets that he is not the One, that he is not the subject

[the creator] of the freedom which he so earnestly desires, that, for all the strange brightness of his eyes, he is not the Christ. . . . What man has the right to propound and represent the "New," whether it be a new age, or a new world, or a new . . . spirit? . . . Far more than the conservative, the revolutionary is *overcome of evil,* because with his "No" he stands so strangely near to God. This is the tragedy of revolution. Evil is not the true answer to evil. (Romans, p. 480)

Overcome evil with good (Rom. 12:21). What can this mean but the end of the triumph of men, whether their triumph is celebrated in the existing order or by revolution? And how can this be represented, if it be not by some strange "not-doing" precisely where men feel themselves most powerfully called to action? . . . What more radical action can [one] perform than the action of turning back to the original root of "not-doing"— and NOT be angry, NOT engage in assault, NOT demolish? This turning back is the ethical factor in the command, *Overcome evil with good.* There is here no word of approval of the existing order; but there is endless disapproval of every enemy of it. It is God who wishes to be recognized as He that *overcometh* the unrighteousness of the existing order. (Romans, p. 481)

When an arky takes it upon itself to impose upon society what *it* chooses to call "God's good," it is being just as defiant of God as is the arky intent to do evil.

Let every man be in subjection to the existing ruling powers (Rom. 13:1). Though "subjection" may assume from time to time many various concrete forms, as an ethical conception it is here purely negative. It means to withdraw and make way; it means to have no resentment, and not to overthrow. Why, then, does not the rebel turn back and become no more a rebel? [I propose that the reading here must have intended: "Is there, then, no reason for the rebel to turn back? Yes, there is; simply because. . . ."] Simply because the conflict in which he is immersed cannot be represented as a conflict between him and the *existing ruling powers;* it is, rather, a conflict of evil with evil. Even the most radical revolution can do no more than set what *exists* [namely, "a human reality"] against what *exists.* Even the most radical revolution—and this is so even when it is called a "spiritual" or "peaceful" revolution—can be no more than a revolt; that is to say, it is in itself simply a justification and confirmation of what already exists [namely, a sinful human arky we have chosen to absolutize as demonic and one we have chosen to absolutize as holy]. (Romans, pp. 481-82)

What, then, is the Christian to *do* about the arkys?

It is evident that there can be no more devastating undermining of the existing order than the recognition of it which is here recommended, a recognition rid of all illusion and devoid of all the joy of triumph [i.e., a recognizing of them for what they are, "full of sound and fury, signifying nothing"]. State, Church, Society, Positive Right, Family, Organized Research, etc., etc., live off the credulity of those who have been nurtured upon vigorous sermons-delivered-on-the-field-of-battle and upon suchlike solemn humbug. Deprive them of their PATHOS, and they will be starved out; but stir up revolution against them, and their PATHOS is provided fresh fodder. (Romans, p. 483)

Consider that this is another counsel of "not-doing": we are *not* to credit the arkys for what they present themselves as being.

"To *be in subjection* is—when it is rightly understood—an action void of purpose, an action, that is to say, which can spring only from obedience to God" (Romans, p. 483). And it follows that, even if an action springing only from obedience to God happens in the process to involve disobedience to the existing arky, it still represents "being subject" and ought not be identified as a revolutionary action of "civil disobedience."

Barth, then, makes his point about God's ordaining the arkys as "negative signs" of the kingdom:

Is not, therefore, the *existing order* a pregnant parable of *the Order that does not [yet] exist? For the creature was subjected to vanity, not of its own will, but by reason of him who subjected it in hope* (Rom. 8:20). . . . But the existing order is justified against revolution precisely at this source; for here the demand is made that the revolutionary should not take the assault and judgment into his own hands, but rather should recognize that the evil of the existing order bears witness to the good, since it stands of necessity as an order *contrasted* [italics mine—VE] with THE Order. (Romans, p. 485)

Vengeance belongeth unto me (Rom. 12:19). Our subjection means, therefore, no more than that vengeance is not our affair. . . . [That revolutionaries lay their hands] upon the sword of judgment cannot be excused on the ground that the *power* has already employed the same sword against them. That is *its* judgment, not their right. The moment when they rise up in protest is the moment when a protest must be directed against them: *Wherein thou judgest the other, thou condemnest thyself; for thou that judgest dost practice the same things* (Rom. 2:1). (Romans, p. 486)

Regarding, then, the Christian who, in obedience to God, is "being subject to the existing ruling powers," Barth says:

> All unsuspecting, rulers rejoice over a citizen so remarkably well-behaved; but they are in fact rejoicing over one whose behavior [signifies nothing other than] the judgment of God [against the rulers themselves]—one who has so much to say that, [there being no point in doing so,] he no longer complains of them. And, in spite of the irony of his position, [the Christian] really does make a "good citizen," [in that] he has turned back to reality and is rid of all romanticism. Having freed himself of all idolatry, he does not need to engage himself in endless protestations against idols. Nor is he continually busying himself with pointing out the manifest inadequacy of each solution of the problem of life as it is propounded, of each form of government as it is erected, of each human road along which men propose to journey. And this is because he knows that the shadow of the judgment of God which spreads itself over them all is the shadow of righteousness. (Romans, pp. 487-88)

The Christian doesn't have to fret and fight regarding every evil of the world, because he knows that all will be made right in God's good time and in God's good way.

> Calm reflection has thus been substituted for the convulsions of revolution—calm, because final assertions and final complaints have been ruled out, because a prudent reckoning with reality has outrun the insolence [about] "warfare between good and evil," and because an honest humanitarianism and a clear knowledge of the world recognize that the strange chess-board upon which men dare to experiment with men and against them—in State, Church, and Society—cannot be the scene of the conflict between the kingdom of God and Anti-Christ. (Romans, p. 489)

> On this board we make no move that is not met by some dangerous counter-move; no step that does not in some way have back at us; no possibility that does not contain its own impossibility. Whether we support or oppose the existing order, we stand on the same level with it, and are subjected to one condemnation. Occupying some position, positive or negative, on the plane of the existing order, we are bound to have to pay for the fact that all [positions] are relative. . . . The encroachment of revolution [God] meets with the *sword* of

government; the encroachments of government with the *sword* of revolution. And in the fate of both we behold our own destiny—in fear and in pity. The wrath of God falls upon all of us. Upon each one in some way or other the *sword* is drawn; and it is not drawn *in vain*. Whether we attempt to build up some positive human thing or to demolish what others have erected, all our endeavors to justify ourselves are in one way or another shattered in pieces. We must now assert that all these endeavors of ours not merely *cannot* be successful, but *ought not* be so. (Romans, p. 490)

Finally, we get Barth's reading of Paul on a detail considered earlier: "*For this cause ye pay tribute also* (Rom. 13:6). Ye *are* paying taxes to the State. It is important, however, for you to know what ye are doing. Your action is, in fact, pregnant with 'not-doing,' with knowledge, with hope" (Romans, p. 491).

That is to say, if you are *paying* those taxes as a "doing," as a positive legitimation of the state and its evil activity, you are wrong. If, the other way around, you are *withholding* those taxes as a "doing," as an act of protest and rebellion against the evil state, you are wrong again. "But what other option is there?" Perhaps the difficulty is that we have been stating the case wrongly. If Jesus is correct that Caesar's image on the coin is proof enough that it "belongs" to him, then, rather than saying that we *do* pay him taxes, wouldn't it be more correct to say that we *do not* try to stop him from collecting what belongs to him (a true case of "not-doing")? As Barth has it, "It is important for you to know what ye are doing [or, in this case, 'not-doing']."

As we move on to the tracing of Barth's career, we jump backwards in his treatment of Romans—to pick up a statement made-to-order as our transition. When speaking of the human world as a strange chessboard which cannot be the scene of the conflict between the Kingdom of God and Anti-Christ, he continued: "A political career, for example, becomes possible only when it is seen to be essentially a game; that is to say, when we are unable to speak of absolute political right, when the note of 'absoluteness' has vanished from both thesis and antithesis [i.e., both our position and that of our opponents], and when room has perhaps been made for that relative moderateness or for that relative radicalism in which human possibilities [regarding absolute right and wrong] have been renounced" (Romans, p. 489).

3. Barth's Own Retrospective View of Romans II

A common explanation has been that, subsequent to 1921, Barth rather quickly moved beyond and away from his position of *Romans II*, into a new and different theology. We would do well to hear what *he* has to say on that point.

In 1954, he described his 1921 "dialectical theology" in these terms:

> This theology has aptly been called a "theology of the Word"; the term "dialectical theology" is less apt, but it does describe its characteristic thought-forms. . . . "In contrast to the historical and psychological account which the 'religious man' tended to give of himself at the beginning of the century," the characteristic feature of this theology was "its question about the superior, new element which limits and determines any human self-understanding. In the Bible this is called God, God's word, God's revelation, God's kingdom, and God's act. The adjective "dialectical" describes a way of thinking arising from man's conversation with the sovereign God who encounters him." (Busch, p. 144)

In 1961, he opened by quoting a line from *Romans II:*

> "Christianity that is not eschatology, utterly and without remainder, has absolutely nothing to do with Christ." Well roared, lion! . . . I still think that I was ten times more right than those against whom my remarks were directed. . . . My remarks at the time were rash . . . but not because of their content. It was because they were not matched by others equally sharp and direct to compensate for their total claim. (Busch, p. 120)

What he needed to do—and proceeded to do—was make his "dialectical theology" truly dialectical.

> He thought that there was not a "new Barth," "as many people have hastily assumed today." "But it is true that I have learnt some things on the way. At least I hope so. . . . While once man apparently had no place in my theology, I think over the years I have learned to speak of God the Creator and his relationship with man as his creature in a way which allows man a greater prominence. . . . I do not think that I have forgotten and denied anything of what I learned and put forward earlier. But I think that in thinking and speaking about the great cause of God and man I have become more peaceful and happier than I could be when I was arguing fiercely against the attitudes current at that time." ([1956] Busch, p. 418)

"A *genuine* revision does not amount to a retreat after second thoughts; it is a new advance and attack in which what was said before has to be said again, but in a better way." Barth certainly did not want to retract . . . the recognition that God is *God*. ([1956] Busch, pp. 423-24)

We need to see *how* Barth manages to better "dialecticize" the God/man relationship and give man more prominence—yet without at all compromising either his "wholly-otherness of God" or his "Christian Anarchy" (indeed, actually enhancing both). Recall that, as early as the Tambach Conference of 1919, he had spoken of "parables of the kingdom of God" and "divine analogies" that appear on the earthly scene. In 1955, he was ready even to say:

In the form in which she exists among them [the church] can and must be to the world of men around her a reminder of the justice of the kingdom of God already established on earth in Jesus Christ, and a *promise* of its future manifestation. *De facto,* whether they realize it or not, she can and should show them that there already exists on earth an order based on that great transformation of the human situation and directed toward its manifestation. To those outside she can and should not only say, but demonstrate by deed, . . . that *things can be different,* not merely in heaven but on earth, not just some day but even now. (Hunsinger, pp. 89-90)

This easily *could* be read as Barth's backing off from his earlier "wholly otherness" of God. Yet we heard him insist that the forming of a *dialectic*—let's call this one a dialectic tension between "the glory of God's wholly-otherness" and what Kierkegaard calls "the glory of our common humanity"—that the forming of the dialectic in no way marks a repudiation (or even deemphasizing) of either truth. Consequently, the "glory" of our humanity cannot be a glory of the same quality as the "glory" of God, thus putting our glory into *competition* with his, making us "like God" (which, recall, was the *serpent's* line in Genesis 3). Indeed, it is just here that the principalities and powers of human arkydom are disallowed—for claiming a glory competitive with that of God.

No, it is *Kierkegaard* who dialecticizes the matter best—doing it throughout that major part of his writings he calls "discourses" (better: "biblical meditations") and especially in the two entitled "The Glory of Our Common Humanity" and "Man's Need of God Constitutes His Highest Perfection." The glory of the human, he tells us, lies, not in our being "like God," but in our "imaging" of him, being in his image—a relationship of *correspondence* rather than *competition*.

As Kierkegaard once put it: with a ship in the water, its *reflection* appears to extend precisely as far below the surface as the ship itself stands above it. The "glory" of our humanity is a "reflected glory" that can *worship* God in a way truly corresponding to *his* "glory." Rather than a glory that challenges or threatens God's "wholly otherness," humanity's is the glory of confessing, praising, and reflecting that very otherness. Or let me try an illustration of my own: A clever cyclist invents and builds for himself a wonderfully new sort of bicycle. Yet certainly, the "glory" of that machine is not meant to be apparent simply in looking at and examining the bicycle itself. No, its true glory is manifest only with the rider aboard, showing what it can do (actually, what *he* can do on it). Man's is, indeed, a true glory—yet always very much of a reflected one. (And by the way, had not the necessity for polemics lain so heavily upon Barth at the time, either his mentor Blumhardt or Kierkegaard could have taught him this dialectic from the outset.)

Yet regarding Barth's passage about the church being a sign of the kingdom, the question must be put as to what "church" he had in mind. All the way through, he lumps in "Church"—along with "State," "Society," and other such arkys—often enough to make it plain that the church he here "pairs" with the kingdom *cannot* be the arky church, that church which sees itself primarily as a sociopolitical entity and considers its greatest contribution to be its holy power-bloc influence in the world of arkydom. No, what Barth has in mind must be the anarchical church, what we have called the ekklesia—the community of gathered saints who strive in themselves to live out the arky of God but who have no interest in trying to impose that or any other order on the world about them.

Indeed, it is as much as incredible to find this noted cleric of the established Church of Calvin opposing that very church's arkydom on so many fronts: denying the validity of "episcopal or synodical authority"; of infant baptism; of anything the church calls "sacrament"; of formal liturgy; of houses of worship which incorporate "pictorial and symbolic representations" or pipe organs (cf. Busch, pp. 320, 329, 343, 399, 428, 444, 474). If any church is "a sign of the kingdom," it clearly is not through any features of this sort. Just as much as if he were an Anabaptist, Barth's Christian Anarchy applies to the church as to any other arky.

There is, then, one other specification I think Barth would

have wanted to make: As he says, even now churches (better: ek-klesia-communities) *can* perform as signs, witnesses, and presentiments of God's coming kingdom. Yet that depends entirely upon God's gracious choice and empowerment of the community rather than the community's desire to qualify itself for the role. So, as soon as any group presumes to claim and to name itself as a sign of the kingdom—this, then, as an excuse to pull rank and start foisting its ideas of holiness upon the world—at that point we are on the way to Holy Roman Empires, the Crusades, and all manner of clearly *negative* signs. No, the last thing a true kingdom-sign community will do is to recognize itself, nominate itself, or promote itself under that identity. "Then the righteous will answer him, 'Lord, when did we see ourselves as, or program ourselves to be, a sign of thy kingdom?' " "Signs of the kingdom" give the glory to God rather than claiming it for themselves.

In time, then, Barth came to realize that his original "wholly-otherness of God" needed to be balanced up by "the glory of our common humanity." But this did not affect his Christian Anarchy. It is true, of course, that Christian Anarchy involves a putting down of human *pretension*—but not by that token a putting down of the *truly human*. Quite the contrary, Christian Anarchy is dedicated precisely to the *liberation* of the truly human—i.e., *God's* freeing it by putting down the enslaving principalities and powers.

III. Barth as a German
Professorships at Göttingen, Münster, and Bonn (1921-35)

In 1921, with the publication of Romans II, there came also the call for Barth to leave the pastorate and assume a professorship in Germany. A detail it will be important for us to remember is that, on the Continent, university professors are actually civil servants. This connection, in 1926, led to Barth's taking on *German* citizenship—in addition to his native Swiss citizenship. Throughout the period we are now to consider he is essentially a *German*—which period will end with his leaving Germany to spend the rest of his life as a *Swiss* professor.

1. New Development of Old Themes
Under this head, we will simply establish the continuity of Barth's thought by seeing him add insight to what he has said before.

The Pastoral Orientation of Theology. "One can . . . say that to ground theology in the church and especially in the work of the pastor and to make it relevant is a characteristic of the whole theological renewal movement" ([1922] Busch, pp. 136-37).

The New View of the Bible. Barth is insistent in correcting the "liberal" use of Scripture: "Barth contrasted his view of the Bible as evidence of the concrete revelation of God with the view of the Bible as a general religious document" ([1922] Busch, p. 134). "The Bible, an earthly, human book, is a witness to revelation and thus itself the Word of God. So it is not merely a source of Christian knowledge, but its critical norm" ([1923] Busch, p. 161).

Barthian vs. Bultmannian "Eschatology." Rudolf Bultmann's own "eschatology" had him wanting to talk about "last things"— by which he meant the ultimate issues of life the religious individual must face in his own experience and regarding which he must make momentous decisions (i.e., momentous for his own existence as a person). Bultmann asked Barth how he understood "eschatology"; and Barth responded that eschatology had to involve an actual transformation of the whole world order: "He only speaks of *last things* who would speak of the *end* of all things, . . . of a reality so radically superior to all things that the existence of all things would be wholly and utterly *grounded* in it and in it alone; i.e., he would speak of their end which in truth would be none other than their beginning" ([1924] Busch, p. 149). Notice that only a Barthian eschatology will do for Christian Anarchy; the Bultmannian variety has no way of even recognizing the objective, historical existence of principalities and powers—let alone their being overcome by a kingdom of God.

Yet Barth also wants to say how essential eschatology is to the full revelation of God and how relevant it is to the Christian life here and now:

> "Because it speaks of the boundary, of the end, Christian eschatology is fundamentally conscious of saying things which only God can say directly as they are [i.e., human wisdom and invention are of no help here]." Thus, "its object is not *the future [per se]* but *the ONE* [caps mine—VE] *who is to come.* . . . Christian eschatology is not interested in the last things for their own sake. . . . The revelation which constitutes the Word of God is itself eschatological. . . . Christian eschatology is no idle knowledge"; it has "the character of a claim to faith and obedience which directs itself specifically to man." ([1925] Busch, p. 166)

2. The Fight against "Natural Theology"

During the period now under consideration, we find Barth making a change of terminology and something of a change of emphasis— yet actually intensifying the earlier polemic. Rather than speaking so much of the wholly-otherness of God, he now turns his fire on the falseness of the man-centered theology which the wholly-otherness of God was meant to correct. No longer is the term "Neo-Protestant" much used to identify that false theology; "natural theology" takes over as a more general, more inclusive, and more accurate identification. It covers any variety of thought proposing that—outside and independent of God's special revelation to us through Jesus Christ and recorded in Scripture—there are "natural" affinities and connections giving man sufficient access to the divine that he can come to know God on his own. Man, now, does not have to wait for God to reveal himself; he has his own means for initiating encounter.

Picking up from where we left Barth, he is now willing to concede that there are signs of the kingdom on the human scene— but he will not budge an inch toward making these the seed of a natural theology: "[Barth] could say that 'the work of culture . . . *can* be like a parable. . . . It can be a reflection from the light of the eternal Logos who became flesh. . . . [But] the hope of the church rests *on* God *for* man; it does not rest *on* men, not even on religious men—and not even on the belief that men *with God's help* will eventually build and complete that tower (of Babel)' " ([1926] Busch, p. 171). In the same address from which these lines were taken, Barth also said that this address represents "a rather different view" from what he had expressed at Tambach seven years earlier. I suggest that it is not actually as different as it sounds; the basic Christian Anarchy, the complete disallowance of any sort of arky faith, is fully preserved.

Schleiermacher Is Still the Villain. "[Barth] saw the theology of Schleiermacher as an attempt to make 'religion, revelation, and relations between God and man comprehensible as a predicate of *man*. . . . [The secret now is] that theology had long since become anthropology' " ([1926] Busch, p. 169). "[Schleiermacher] was seen [by Barth] as the representative of a theology in which 'man is left master of the field in so far as he alone has become the subject, while Christ is his predicate' " ([1933] Busch, p. 221).

The Arky Faith of Natural Theology Must Collapse. It is still the *preached* message in the life of the congregation that is at issue: "Christian preaching is a proclamation 'of the mighty acts of God' and not 'a proclamation of the acts and works of man' " ([1927] Busch, p. 176). " 'From a man's point of view, in its decisive act, *faith* [italics mine—VE] is the collapse of every effort of his own capacity and will and the recognition of the absolute necessity of that collapse. When a man sees the other aspect, [namely,] that when he is lost he is *justified* [italics mine—VE] . . . he sees himself from God's point of view.' But 'this righteousness does not become a psychological capacity; it remains in God's hand' " ([1927] Busch, p. 172).

Along with "Natural Theology," "Natural Ethics" Must Go. This subpoint calls for special notice in that "Christian ethics" is probably the area of theology done in the greatest disregard of God and his word, done sheerly as human calculations of what is right or wrong, good or evil. But Barth says, " 'Ethics, too, is concerned with reflection on the Word of God'—and 'especially with the reflection on the claim that this Word of God makes on man.' . . . 'What is good?' 'Man acts well in so far as he acts as *one who has heard* the Word of God, and obedience is good' " ([1927] Busch, p. 182).

The Secret Battlefield against Natural Theology. In 1931, Barth published his most off-beat book—a study of the medieval Catholic theologian, St. Anselm—from which he proceeded directly to begin his gargantuan *Church Dogmatics.* Roman Catholic scholars in particular had trouble accepting Barth's book as an accurate understanding of what Anselm was talking about. Barth responded that he didn't really care whether he had Anselm right or not—what he wanted was for people to understand what *he* was talking about.

> My interest in Anselm was never a side-issue for me. On the contrary, whether my historical interpretation of the saint was right or not, I took him very much to heart. . . . Most commentators have completely failed to see that this Anselm book is a vital key, if not *the* key, to understanding the process of thought that has impressed me more and more in my *Church Dogmatics* as the only one proper for theology. (Busch, p. 210)

Just what is that key? This: "[freeing my thought] 'from the last remnants of a philosophical or anthropological . . . justification and explanation of Christian doctrine. . . .' 'The book on Anselm of Canterbury's proof for the existence of God . . . I think I wrote with more loving care than any other of my books and . . . it has been read the least of all my books' " (Busch, p. 206). In effect, the Anselm book and the whole of the *Church Dogmatics* were dedicated to the absolute elimination of arky faith and any vestige of natural theology.

What the "Nein" to Brunner Cost Barth. From the public view, this 1934 pamphlet was Barth's strongest blast against natural theology. It had to be the costliest and most painful to Barth from a personal standpoint. He certainly realized that, of all the "name" theologians of the era, his Swiss compatriot, biblically committed colleague, and fellow Blumhardtian Emil Brunner was the one whose thought stood closest to his own. Yet he publicly humiliated Brunner with "an out-spoken piece of polemic." And why? "[Because] Brunner had put forward the argument that 'the task of our theological generation is to find a way back to a legitimate natural theology' " (Busch, p. 248). Obviously, for Barth, what was at stake was not simply a point of intellectual, theological argument but the very truth of the gospel of Jesus Christ.

Analogia Entis as the Catholic Form of the Heresy. Barth had to fight his war against natural theology on (at least) two fronts at the same time. Yet the Catholic front opened up long after the Protestant—only in the early 'thirties. The Catholic doctrine of *analogia entis* (analogy of "being") proposes that God's divine nature and our human nature each include qualities of "being" analogous (similar) enough to make them mutually attracting. Thus, naturally, our human "being" rises to meet God even as God's divine "being" comes to meet us—plainly a "like God" relationship rather than a "correspondent image" one. "I regard the *analogia entis* as *the* invention of Anti-Christ, and I believe that because of it one cannot become a Catholic" ([1931-32] Busch, p. 215).

Without using the term, Barth hangs the idea upon Augustine:

> Augustine is "the classic representative of the Catholic view . . . that there is a continuity between God and man which is to be thought of as originating from man's side and which constantly threatens to make man his own creator and reconciler." [In Barth's view, however,] Because the connection between God and man—which also exists from man's side—is an "event" in the Holy Spirit and only in him (that is, only as a gift of God), there is no connection apart from this "event"— either before, as an innate property, or afterwards, as the product of some "infusion." ([1929] Busch, p. 188)

> [Barth] thought that there was probably an analogy, a point of correspondence, between God and man, by virtue of which man is "capable" of knowing God. But . . . this "point of

correspondence" is not given to man by nature, by virtue of
his situation, ontologically. It will, however, be given to him
in faith *(analogia fidei)* since the only possibility of knowing
God and his Word is to be found in the Word itself. ([1931-32]
Busch, p. 216)

"Analogy of faith" suggests that it is only God's faithfulness to us
that creates in us a "faith" correspondent to it.

3. Joining the German Social Democratic Party (SPD)
Our attention now turns from the *theological* side of Barth's Christian Anarchy to its *political* side, from theory to praxis. Recall from
his first period that Barth treated his membership with Religious
Socialism in a most anarchical way, as a peripheral matter in which
he was every bit as quick to criticize the party as to support it. At
that time, also, we heard him warn that we dare not put our "hearts"
into our politics; that our political careers must be treated as "a
game"; and that, above all, we dare never use "God" (i.e., religion,
theology, Christianity) as justification or support for what are actually our own political, human-arky ideas. In his political involvements now to be described, Barth will continue to be entirely
consistent with these principles of Christian Anarchy.

It was in 1932, as a full-fledged German citizen, Barth took out
membership in the German Social Democratic Party (SPD). At
about the same time, he made an important statement regarding the
church's involvement in politics: "The proclamation of the church
is by nature political in so far as it has to ask the pagan *polis* to
remedy its state of disorder and make justice a reality. This proclamation is good when it presents the specific commandment of God,
and is not good when it puts forward the abstract truth of a political
ideology" ([1932] Busch, p. 216). The church can (and should) speak
Scripture to the state; but once the church starts identifying itself
with the arkys of particular political philosophies and cause groups,
that is bad.

The true significance of Barth's taking SPD membership becomes apparent only when we are aware of the general political
situation in the Germany of that day. The following is Barth's ret-
rospective description of what he saw as early as 1926:

I also saw and heard the so-called "German nationals" of the
time—in my memory the most undesirable of all God's crea-
tures whom I have ever met. . . . With their inflammatory

speeches they probably made the greatest contributions towards filling to the uttermost a cup of wrath which was then poured out on the German nation over the next two decades. ([1947] Busch, p. 189)

"German Nationalism," of course, is what in time will lead to the horrors of Nazism. Yet that which Barth here finds so offensive cannot be those horrors—which haven't surfaced yet. No, what incenses Barth is the blatant pretension that the Germanic spirit (culture, nationalism, and blood) qualifies as God's holy, messianic arky for the saving of the world. But at the time Barth joins it, the SPD is clearly the "opposition party," the minority party standing as an alternative to the rising National Socialism of the Nazis. Barth's choice is a deliberate act of refusing to legitimize Nazism. Yet as a true Christian anarchist, he isn't going to stoop to the level of trying to fight or subvert the Nazis, either. He will concentrate, rather, on giving to God what belongs to God.

Barth explained in a letter to Paul Tillich:

> Membership in the SPD does not mean for me a confession to the idea and world view of socialism. According to my understanding of the exclusivity of the Christian confession of faith, I can "confess" myself neither to an idea nor to a world view in any serious sense. Hence I also have no necessary intrinsic relation to "Marxism" as such. . . . As an idea and world view, I can bring to it neither fear nor love nor trust. Membership in the SPD means for me simply a practical political decision. . . . I saw [the] requirements for a healthy politics fulfilled in, and only in, the SPD. Therefore, I choose this party. (Hunsinger, p. 116)

Barth does his politics as a "not-doing" of politics; he shows nothing of arky faith, the messianic "gung-ho here we go" zealotism that marks normal politicking. He joins the party, rather, as an anarchist with no illusions about the holiness of the arky; no talk about God's leading him to join; no implication that all good Christians should be there with him; no talk of serving God's kingdom through the party; no dreams of the party's accomplishing "the victory of Good in the world."

By March 1933, the Nazis held enough power that it could mean trouble for government employees (including university faculty members) to be known as SPD members. In that situation, the party itself recommended that, rather than jeopardizing their posts,

SPD faculty members simply resign their party membership and continue their activity in private. Tillich accepted this as a good idea; but Barth would have none of it. For him, this was the very time *not* to back down on one's formal, public commitment. "Anyone who does not want me like this cannot have me at all" (Busch, p. 225).

Without any hint of defiance, Barth straightway communicated his decision to the proper official, the Prussian Minister of Cultural Affairs, asking whether, as a SPD member, he would be allowed to continue his teaching for the summer term. The minister gave permission—on the condition that there would be no "formation of cells." However, in June, before the summer was well underway, the SPD was disbanded and prohibited nationwide. At this point the administrative head of the university asked Barth how he saw his relationship to the SPD. "I said: 'I have arranged things with the Minister himself.' So perhaps I was in fact the last member of the SPD in the Third Reich" (Busch, p. 225).

Notice, Barth was not about to let himself be pushed around; he was adamant against doing anything that could possibly be interpreted as a legitimizing of German Nationalism. Yet, the very figure of courtesy and propriety, he is just as careful not to be guilty of defiance, rage, condemnation, and rebellion against the established arky, either. His stance can be typified as nothing other than "anarchical."

4. The Nazis Bust the Professor

Hitler's take-over of January 30, 1933, caught Barth in bed with the flu; but he knew immediately "where I stood and what I could not do. In the last resort, this was simply because I saw my dear German people beginning to worship a false god" (Busch, p. 223). Barth realized that the quick and easy capitulation of the German people— including many even of his faculty colleagues and former students— was owing to the fact that the church had for so long been buying into whatever cultural or political arky made messianic noises that it saw this as just one more instance of the same. "It transpired that 'over the centuries the Protestant church had in fact been "assimilated" as a result of all kinds of other less ostentatious and aggressive alien pressures to such a degree that it simply could not *repudiate* [italics mine—VE], promptly and confidently, the crude assumption that the church, its message, and its life could be "assimilated" into the National Socialist State'" (Busch, p. 223). Notice, then, that

Barth's own "resistance" to the State is not all an "attack" upon it but simply the refusal to "assimilate" or "legitimize."

But what, then, is Barth (or any Christian) to *do* in the face of such monstrous evil? He speaks as a true Christian anarchist: "His 'first priority' . . . [was] 'to urge the students for whom I was responsible to keep on working as normally as possible in the midst of the general uproar, . . . to maintain the biblical gospel in the face of the new regime and the ideology which had now become predominant' " (Busch, p. 224). The *theological* task of preserving the biblical gospel from ideological take-over is much more important to the course of history than is the *political* effort to destroy Hitler's regime.

Barth's first eyeball-to-eyeball confrontation with that regime came with the directive that all university classes were to open with the Hitler salute. Barth's never did. As he explained to the administration, he had understood it as being a "recommendation" rather than an "order." Besides, it was his custom to open class with a hymn and prayer—and the Hitler salute didn't seem to quite fit. The administration decided not to make an issue of the matter, and Barth carried the day on that one (Busch, p. 242).

On the next go-around, Barth was not so fortunate. The university prescribed an "oath of loyalty to the Führer." And was our professor so defiant as to refuse? Of course not! "Granted, 'I did not refuse to give the official oath, but I stipulated an addition to the effect that I could be loyal to the Führer only within my responsibilities as an Evangelical Christian' " (Busch, p. 255). However, apparently Der Führer didn't find this loyalty quite enough. Immediately suspended from teaching, by 1935 Barth was permanently "busted" from the university and had moved (he would hardly say "fled") back to Switzerland to finish his career there.

With neither the salute nor the loyalty oath can Barth be said to have practiced "civil disobedience" (in the sense of Chapter Eight here following). He did not stage his disobedience as a calculated political power-play. He made no effort to organize his own ideological bloc to contest that of the evil regime. He did not play up to the media as a form of public demonstration, protest, or witness. He exhibited no rage toward nor condemnation of his adversary. He refused to treat the State as "enemy." He was intent only to give to God what belongs to God. And in doing that, he was careful to tread the fine, anarchical line between legitimizing the establishment on the one hand and legitimizing revolution against it on the other.

5. The Barmen Declaration and the Confessing Church

We must back up to 1933 before moving forward again with this line of development. But Karl Barth was the central figure in the inter-denominational church "struggle" that came to be identified as the Confessing Church; he was himself the main author of its consti-tuting Barmen Declaration.

At the outset, Barth established the guideline that the church stick to theology and not politics: "I cannot see anything in German Christianity but the last, fullest, and worst monstrosity of Neo-Prot-estantism" (Busch, p. 230). The problem is essentially a theological one; the answer to it must be essentially theological as well. "Barth began by declaring that at this very moment it was important to do 'theology and only theology'—'as though nothing had happened. This, too, is an attitude to adopt . . . and indirectly it is even a political attitude' " (Busch, p. 226). Just so; it is the politics of "not-doing politics"—which, by the way, the Nazis found most difficult to handle. Regarding "straight politics," they knew just what to do and could counter every move, but "Barthian not-doing politics" had them out of their field. How does one counter *that*? This Chris-tian Anarchy business is a real pain!

"Above all, [Barth] warned against mere church-political tac-tics: 'We must be men who *believe* [my italics—VE], first and last. That—and nothing else' " (Busch, p. 231). And when a visitor asked how the American churches could help, "Barth emphasized that the Anglo-Saxon churches should now support the Confessing Church in one way and only in one way, by showing *theological* solidarity with its struggle against [not the Nazis but] *natural theology* [italics mine—VE]" (Busch, p. 231).

Then, regarding the 1934 Barmen paper:

> An important clause in the declaration stated that the "real problem" of the present was *not* [my italics—VE] "how one could get rid of the German Christian nonsense, if that was God's will—but how it was possible to form a front against the error which had devastated the Evangelical Church for centuries," . . . namely the view that "alongside God's revela-tion . . . man also has a legitimate authority of his own over the message and form of the church." (Busch, p. 236)

Well then, was the Confessing Church a "resistance movement"? Yes indeed, one of the best—as long as Karl Barth was running it and as long as the "resistance" was that of Christian Anarchy rather than "holy arky power play."

IV. From the Demonic Man to the Royal Man
From Hitler to Barth's Treatment of Jesus (1939-55)

The war against Hitler marked a decisive turn in Barth's thought. We now start with that and run our survey up to the writing of his second classic presentation of Christian Anarchy, the Royal Man passage of 1955.

1. Barth's (Momentary) Fall from Anarchy: World War II

I consider Barth's role in the fight against Hitler to mark a serious defection from his own understanding of Christian Anarchy. He started out well enough: "I considered my most immediate and important duty to play my part in seeing that theology should be carried on, thoroughly and 'as if nothing had happened,' in at least one place in an insane Europe—in our Swiss island" (Busch, p. 299). But he was not able to hold that course. It must be said that he did rather quickly recover himself—which has the effect of making the episode all the more instructive for its contrast to both the "before" and the "after" Barth. Our comprehension of Christian Anarchy will be enhanced in here seeing what it is not.

To my mind, Barth's defection came—not so much in his resort to violence—but in his mounting a *Christian* rationale and justification for the same. This, from the man who had been so consistently opposed to allowing any political, human arky to claim Christian, theological standing. I propose that Jacques Ellul (in his book, *Violence*—with the subsequent "rectification" in *Christianity & Crisis,* Oct. 19, 1970, p. 221) offers us the best framework in which to evaluate Barth's actions.

Within the horizon of *political activity*—limited to human actions that can be calculated to produce particular cause-and-effect results according to sheerly human probabilities and possibilities—within this sphere, Ellul suggests, it does seem to be the case that situations arise in which violence shows up as inevitable and *necessary*. The "pacifists" who, still from entirely within this horizon, argue that there can never arise a dilemma which does not include the option of a workable, humanly practical, nonviolent solution—these people are utopians, showing no sense of political realism at all. Of course, no one is saying that *every instance* of human violence has been or is necessary; that leaves all sorts of room for political peacemaking to quell a great deal of our violence. Nevertheless, Ellul would seem to be correct that there are situations in which violence is *necessary;* in which we have no other choice; in which, therefore, violence is *politically* justified. The political distinction between "necessary and unnecessary wars"—"just and unjust wars"—is absolutely essential if we are to make moral judgments in the matter at all.

However, *politically* justified is NOT to say *Christianly* justified. Christians, of course, know that the political horizon is not the final limit of reality. That limit (if as "limit" it should be thought of) certainly opens out to include God and all of God's possibilities— even to the point of resurrection from the dead, the kingdom, and all kingdom possibilities. From out of this larger sphere, for anyone to say that violence is *necessary* is nothing short of blasphemy—a suggestion that God himself is under the same constraints of necessity we are, that violence is something even he has not the wherewithal to avoid. For that matter, Ellul suggests, God has given us Jesus Christ for the very purpose of freeing us from all human *necessity*—the necessities of sin, greed, hard-heartedness, self-centeredness, violence, and what all. What is necessarily necessary *within* the horizon of human politics becomes totally unnecessary once the God-possibilities are taken into account. *Christianly,* then, violence is *never* justified—though Christians can, of course, still recognize the *relative political* justice and injustice of different wars and conflicts.

So, Ellul concludes, whenever Christians support or participate in violence, what this indicates is that—for at least that moment, in that action—they have had a failure of faith; have not truly trusted in God and his possibilities; have forgotten their freedom in Christ, rather to slide back into the realm of necessity, taking the political limit for the actual limit of reality. For such a lapse—as for any other—there is, of course, forgiveness; yet any Christian capitulation to the necessity of violence is a denial of the freeing work of Jesus Christ and consequently a *sin.*

I consider it indisputable that Karl Barth knew all this and could have written the above paragraphs better than I have done. But under the terrible pressures of Hitler, he forgot.

In 1938, Barth wrote a letter in which "he told Czechoslovakia, threatened by Hitler's attack, 'that now every Czech soldier will stand and fall not only for the freedom of Europe, but also for the Christian church'" (Busch, p. 289). Later he explained, "In my letter to Hromádka—for the sake of the faith—I issued a summons to armed resistance against the armed threats and aggression which are now being made. It was not a call to a World War . . . but certainly to resistance" (Busch, p. 289).

Why couldn't Barth have been content to address this political situation *politically*—arguing the political *necessity* of Czech resistance (for which a good case could have been made)? Why did he have to go against all his own theological principles—bringing in "the Christian church" and "the faith"; anointing the Czech army as a holy arky sponsored by and in the service of God? Christian anarchists know better than that!

> "If political order and freedom is threatened, then this threat also indirectly affects the church. And if a just state tries to defend order and freedom, then the church, too, is indirectly involved." Granted, "as a church it can struggle and suffer only in the spirit," but "it would not be taking its own proclamation seriously if it remained indifferent here." ([1938] Busch, pp. 289-90)

We can be grateful for at least the hint that the way of the church might be different from that of the state, although he still has "the church" and "the just state" in closer collaboration than Christian Anarchy will be comfortable with.

"*Unconditional* resistance must be offered against Hitler—both ideological *and* military. . . . [The churches] should not [raise the objection] that the people of the democratic states are fighting against God; they should tell them that *for God's sake* [italics mine—VE] we may be human and must defend ourselves against the onslaught of manifest inhumanity with the power of despair" ([1939] Busch, p. 303). Here Barth not only fails to recognize any God possibilities beyond the immediate political possibilities, he actually asks us to capitulate to political necessity—*for God's sake*. No, earlier (when he was in his right mind) he had it: if we see no other possibility, let's fight—but let us at least have the grace not to say that it is for God's sake we are doing it.

"He said that the Christians were on the way to a final battle which was 'much harder and more momentous' than earthly wars, but which spurred them on to fight 'transitory' human wars boldly and justly with human means" ([1940] Busch, p. 305). Our human wars are now *positive* signs of God's eschatological war for the kingdom? Personally, I much prefer the Barth of *Romans II*, when he had it the other way around (and right): Our human wars—and all other such arkys—are *negative* signs indicating the absence, the not-yet, of the kingdom.

While he did not see Switzerland as a Christian country (rather, it was an "unholy Switzerland"), he nevertheless understood it as a country with a Christian foundation. As "a community of free peoples of free individuals allied by law," the Confederation was in fact, though undeservedly, "like an Alpine twilight, a reflection of the gospel of Jesus Christ proclaimed to us and to all the West." To preserve *this* Switzerland, its people were confronted with the uncompromising alternative "either to surrender or to resist." ([1941] Busch, p. 310)

Now he would have us believe that it is "a Switzerland reflecting the gospel of Jesus Christ" that is the anointed arky and positive sign of the kingdom. But can Swiss nationalism be depended upon to be all that much better than German nationalism turned out to be? Why couldn't Barth have presented "democratic freedom" as being simply a *political* value in its own right—a value which *political necessity* dictates must now be defended by force of arms? As it is, he is losing (momentarily) the very distinction between politics and theology that has been the hallmark of his Christian Anarchy.

Yet, by 1942 Barth is back on the right track. In a message to the American churches he warned against

> any "crusading ideology": the church must not . . . provide "the necessary religious accompaniment" to the "terrible sounds of war." Nor should the war be understood as "an instrument of divine vengeance" instead of as "the last terrible instrument for restoring the public order which has been damaged and destroyed by common guilt." It was only possible to have "a good conscience" if the war against the Germans was "in fact also being carried on *for* [italics mine—VE] them." (Busch, pp. 317-18)

Welcome home, Professor! The war is to be understood as a tragic necessity brought about by the constrictedness of the political horizon of human arky. Although it may have been fully justified *politically*, there shouldn't have been even the thought of trying to justify it *theologically*.

Regarding both Barth here and Bonhoeffer in the chapter to follow, I don't believe there is even a question of their having made a theological about-face, rejecting their earlier thought and heading off in a new direction. I see them, rather, as two human beings who—under terrible pressure—simply found themselves unable to live up to their own ideals. So, to whatever reader has never found in himself the same failure of faith, I herewith extend the invitation to step forward and cast the first stone.

2. WCC: *Amsterdam '48 | Evanston '54*

Barth was invited to address the World Council of Churches Amsterdam Assembly but was reluctant to accept: "Formerly I took no part, or only a small part, in the 'ecumenical movement'; indeed, I had all kinds of criticisms to make of it, since I have always been suspicious of all movements" (Busch, p. 357). That, obviously, is a back-on-the-track anarchist speaking. So when he actually did get to Amsterdam, he took the occasion to lecture the movement about Christian Anarchy:

> There was a serious danger that Christianity might come to grief not only in its human descriptions and assessments of earthly needs, but finally also in its human plans and measures for fighting against these needs and overcoming them. . . . He criticized the preparatory studies above all for the view, which could be found in all of them, that "as Christian men and as church people *we* [italics mine—VE] ought to achieve what [actually] God alone can accomplish and what he *will* [italics mine—VE] accomplish completely by himself. . . . We shall not be the ones who change this wicked world into a good one. God has not abdicated his lordship over us. . . . All that is required of us is that, in the midst of the political and social disorder of the world, we should be his *witnesses*." ([1948] Busch, p. 358)

Barth participated in the preparations but was not able to make the 1952 WCC Assembly at Evanston. He felt that the theme should not be "The Hope of the Church and the World" but, as you might guess, "Jesus Christ, the Crucified Lord, the *Only* [italics undoubtedly his] Hope for the World." And "when [Reinhold] Niebuhr, reflecting on the conference theme, had left eschatology 'on one side,' Barth became angry and, having given up hope [not his "Christian hope," of course], wanted to go home. . . . [He] regretted above all 'that we have to tear our hair so much over Christian hope, of all things, instead of rejoicing at it' " ([1951] Busch, p. 396).

3. *Picking Up on Old Themes*

The Church, State, and Politics. "[The church should exercise] an active and responsible participation in the state. [But] of course, the church's decisive service to the state was, in Barth's view, its preaching: 'By proclaiming the divine justification, it performs the best service to the establishment and maintenance of human justice' " ([1938] Busch, p. 288). But what socially concerned churches today are even preaching the divine justification, let alone considering that their primary political service? Talk about doing politics by a "not-doing" of politics!

In 1946, Barth gave Konrad Adenaur "an urgent warning . . . not to found a Christian Democrat Party. He thought that while the church should indeed have political commitments, these should not take the form of a Christian party" (Busch, p. 333)—which would, of course, imply God's election of a particular human arky. "He thought that the church could neither prescribe a political decision nor leave it open (as though it were merely a 'matter of discretion'); its task was to make the issues quite clear" ([1952] Busch, p. 386). This "clarifying of the issue" I take to mean an open presentation of all interpretations and points of view rather than the pushing of one line the pastor (or somebody) has already decided is the Christian one. Good (anarchical) advice.

If It Isn't Biblical and Pastoral, It Isn't Christian Theology. Regarding scholars and teachers of theology, "he thought that people would notice 'at every turn' if these would-be teachers had never made 'the *kerygma*—to which there was so much appeal—their own responsibility; if they had never presented it in its canonical Old and New Testament form, with humility and patience, with delight and love, in preaching, instruction, and pastoral work, serving a real community, instead of always just thinking *about* it and talking *about* it' " ([1950] Busch, p. 353). "He also believed 'that the question of the right hermeneutics cannot be decided in a discussion of exegetical *method*, but only in exegesis itself' " ([1952] Busch, p. 390).

The Case against Natural Theology Is Refined but Not Changed. We here may have his best word in answer to the *analogia entis*. Years before, he had repudiated it and, in its place, proposed the *analogia fidei*—the analogy of faith in which our "faith" is actually but the reflection, the correspondent image, of God's prior "faithfulness" to us. Finally, now, we get the *analogia relationis*—the analogy of relationship that finds its reflection down from level to level of human experience: "Barth's explanation of the image of God in man . . . consists [first in] the trinitarian 'self-encounter' of God the Father and the Son [which, second,] is 'reflected in God's relationship to man' and [third], in turn, in the human encounter of 'I and Thou,' [to fourth,] 'of man and woman' [by which I take him to mean 'husband and wife']" ([1942] Busch, p. 317). Notice that, consistent with the rest of his thought, this "analogy" is strictly unidirectional. That is, the reality at each level "creates" the reflection below it; at every point it expresses God's defining us rather than our defining him.

> "Christian Humanism" is flawed steel. . . . "The central concern of the gospel is also with *man*. But what *the gospel* [italics mine—VE] says *about* man, *for* man (even *against* man) and *to* man begins where the various humanisms cease. . . . In the light of the gospel one can understand all these humanisms, affirm them to some extent and allow their validity. . . . But in the end one must also counter all humanisms in the light of the gospel. . . ." "I myself spoke of the 'Humanism of *God.*' By that I did not mean any humanity contrived and brought about by man, but the delight in man taken by *God* [italics mine—VE] as the source and norm of all human rights and all human status" [wording re-ordered for clarity—VE]. ([1949] Busch, pp. 366-67)

And in what is it, specifically, that God "delights"? He delights in that which his own grace has brought up in man.

Barth takes on "the natural theology of freedom" in words our modern liberationists need to hear: "Barth argued that freedom was neither a natural right nor a possession which was bestowed by nature. It was God's gracious gift, grounded in God's own freedom. Freedom was not a formal power of control, a freedom of choice, but freedom in encounter, freedom *for*" ([1953] Busch, p. 400).

"The Natural Theology of Ethics" Is Noted, Too. "In Barth's view the law follows the gospel and therefore ethics has the task of declaring 'the law as the form of the gospel. . . .' [What ethics presents] therefore is not an 'ideal,' but a commandment which has already been fulfilled. Ethics is an 'ethics of grace, or it is not a theological ethics at all.' And so the answer to the old question 'What are we to do?' is, 'We should do whatever corresponds to this grace' ([1939] Busch, p. 302).

> He began by decisively rejecting the doctrine of "ordinances of creation"—in so far as these are understood as being laws which are independent of the Word of God and capable of being known "naturally." . . . Thus the central concept of [Christian] ethics is that of "freedom": not understood in contrast to obedience, but as "the freedom of the children of God" which is "the freedom *of* [italics mine—VE] obedience and therefore true freedom." ([1951] Busch, pp. 376-77)

How much of what passes as "Christian ethics" in our day is actually anything more than "natural ethics"—how much shows the slightest interest in the "theological ethics" of which Barth speaks?

4. Eastern Europe and the Cold War with Communism

After having "blown it" during World War II, Karl Barth bounced back to redeem himself during the Cold War by giving us some of his best expressions of Christian Anarchy. Because of personal connections and interests there, he tended to focus upon Hungary.

In a lecture delivered in that country, he pointed out that it is

> a dangerous temptation for the "Christian community" *either* to set itself up in opposition to the new order in principle, by keeping to the old, *or* by identifying itself with the new in an equally partisan fashion. *Or* it could retreat into a false neutrality on an apolitical "inner" line. On the other hand, "the church best performs its service in the midst of political change when its attitude is so independent and . . . so sympathetic that it is able to summon the representatives of the old and new order alike . . . to humility, to the praise of God, and to humanity, and can invite them all to trust in the great change (in the death and resurrection of Christ) and to hope in his revelation." ([1948] Busch, p. 355)

A rather close application of "Jesus and the tribute money," wouldn't you say?

On subsequent occasions:

> A church which is concerned to tread a cautious path between opposition to the new state and collaboration with it—which has clearly come to terms with the question of guilt—[should] for the rest [be] concerned with evangelization and building up the community. . . . Barth felt compelled to write to his friends in Hungary, saying in an open letter that they now seemed "to be going too far in the direction of compromise with the new order." (Busch, p. 355)

Emil Brunner tried to goad Barth into issuing "a call to oppose communism and make a Christian confession"—as he had done against the Nazis. But this time, Barth chose to stick with his Christian Anarchy, pointing out that

> the church of Christ never passed judgment "on principle," but by individual cases, "making a new evaluation of each new event" [which, note, as opposed to automatically following the principles of some party line, is a rather anarchic approach in

itself]. . . . One difference between the former period and the present was that to "deify" Bolshevism was hardly a serious temptation in the West, though this kind of possibility had been very much the case during the time of the Nazi danger. . . . [But] "I am against all fear of communism. A nation which has a good conscience, whose social and democratic life is in order, need have no fear of it. Much less the church, which is sure of the gospel of Jesus Christ." (Busch, pp. 355-56)

I take it that Barth has in mind "fear that the western democracies will fall for communist ideology"; he seems not to consider the possibility of Soviet military expansionism.

In a 1949 lecture, his argument was

that the formation of an Eastern bloc and Western bloc was based on a conflict of power and ideology and that the church had no occasion to take sides in it, either with the East and its "totalitarian abominations" or with the West, as long as it gave the East grounds for just criticism. But today "the way of the community of Jesus Christ in the present" has to be "another, third way of its own," in great freedom. (Busch, p. 357)

Later,

Ilya Ehrenburg, who had wanted to get him "to sign the Stockholm (i.e., Moscow) peace appeal against the atomic bomb, [he dismissed] after a two-hour conversation." "I now react in a decidedly negative fashion to such obvious propaganda moves. . . ." But Barth also refused to identify himself with the other side, and in any case, in the summer of 1950, he learned from a sound source that he was under scrutiny from the American Secret Service. . . . "So one is always between two firing-lines." ([1950] Busch, p. 382)

Christian Anarchy won't make you friends anywhere.

Not that I have any inclination toward Eastern communism, in view of the face it has presented to the world. I decidedly prefer not to live within its sphere and do not wish anyone else to be forced to do so. But I do not see that either politics or Christianity require or even permit the conclusion which the West has drawn with increasing sharpness. . . . I believe anti-communism as a matter of principle to be an ever greater evil than communism itself [presumably because, as "the arky nearest the truth," it makes Christian claims which dupe people into taking it *for* Christianity]. . . . The Christian churches should have considered it their task to influence both public opinion and the leaders who are politically responsible by a *superior* [italics mine—VE] witness, to the peace and hope of the kingdom of God." ([1969] Busch, pp. 382-83)

"Anti-" means *against*. God is not against, but *for* men. The communists are men, too. God is also for the communists. So a Christian cannot be against the communists but only *for* them. To be for the communists does not mean to be for communism. I am not for communism. But one can only say what has to be said *against* communism if one is *for* the communists. ([1958] Busch, p. 383)

Before any reader is too quick to applaud this sentiment, let him ask himself whether he would be just as happy to have Barth turn it around to say that one must also be *for* anti-communist rightists. Can you buy it that Republican presidents are men, too? It is Christian Anarchy only if Barth's formula is read *both* ways—*all* ways.

I hereby nominate the following as the best line in this book— and what should become *the* standard anarchical response to the eternal cry of the zealot, tare-storming activists of arkydom. On a Swiss radio broadcast came the question: "What should we *do*? [italics theirs]—as small, helpless people who seem to have no influence on the present confrontation between the powers." Barth's answer: "WE SHOULDN'T WORRY SO MUCH"—a counsel of "not-doing," note well, which Jesus worded, "Be not anxious; you can't add an iota to God's work in any case" ([1952] Busch, p. 385).

V. The Anarchical Royal Man

After he had read my treatment of Barth on Romans 13, it was Warren Groff of Bethany Theological Seminary who pointed me to Barth's "Royal Man" passage from his *Church Dogmatics* IV/2 (1955). Although displaying an approach entirely different from the *Romans II* passage of 1921, "The Royal Man" stands as a second classic presentation of the biblical concept of Christian Anarchy. It has to be sheer coincidence, but the "Royal Man" passage came seven years before Barth's 1962 retirement just as his "Romans 13" passage came seven years after the 1914 birth of dialectical theology. Anyone who cares to can take these as Barth's Alpha and Omega.

The great advantage of this second statement is that it opens out the New Testament basis of our thought. Heretofore, not only Barth but the rest of our thinkers as well have had us concentrated pretty much on Mark 12 and Romans 13. Now the entire Gospel account of the historical Jesus will be brought into view:

"The conformity of the man Jesus with the mode of existence and attitude of God consists actively in what we can only call the pronouncedly *revolutionary* character of His relationship to the orders of life and value current in the world around Him" (p. 171). That word "revolutionary" (not italicized in Barth's text) is the one we need to watch if we are to understand him. As we read on, it will become obvious he is not using it as he did in *Romans II,* as the principle of "revolution" which—along with the counterpart principle of "legitimizing"—is prohibited and rejected. The word "revolutionary" will read in Barth's sentence *only* if it be taken as "the Revolution of God" which can't even begin to be correlated with any sort of human revolution. Actually, the word "anarchical" (*Christian* Anarchy) is the one that would best express what Barth has in mind. We will need to make this adjustment each time Barth uses "revolution" or "revolutionary" in connection with Jesus.

> Jesus was not in any sense a reformer championing new orders against the old ones, contesting the latter in order to replace the former [which, of course, is what, earlier, Barth and ourselves have been identifying as "revolution"]. He did not range Himself and His disciples with any of the existing parties. . . . Nor did he set up against them an opposing party. He did not represent or defend or champion any programme—whether political, economic, moral, or religious, whether conservative or progressive [this pair, both here and hereafter, can as well be read by our previous terminology "legitimizing or revolutionary"]. He was equally suspected and disliked by the representatives of all such programmes, although He did not particularly attack any of them. Why His existence was so unsettling on every side was that He set all programmes and principles in question. And he did this simply because He enjoyed and displayed, in relation to all the orders positively or negatively contested around Him, a remarkable freedom which again we can only describe as *royal*. (Pp. 171-72)

Every element of our definition of Christian Anarchy appears here.

> On the other hand, He had no need consistently to break any of them, to try to overthrow them altogether, to work for their replacement or amendment. He could live in these orders [namely, Barth specifies, those of the temple cult and the Roman civil regime]. . . . He did not oppose other "systems" to

these. He did not make common cause with the Essene re-
forming movement. He simply revealed the limit and frontier
of all these things—the freedom of the kingdom of God.
(P. 172)

The kingdom, the Arky of God, comes into Barth's picture just
where Christian Anarchy says it should.

Earlier we suggested that the problem of the arkys is not that
they are diabolical but that they are *human*. Now Barth says it:
"Inevitably [the orders', or arkys'] provisional and relative character,
the ways in which they were humanly conditioned, their secret fal-
libility, were all occasionally disclosed" (p. 172).

And this anarchy of Jesus is itself transparent of the anarchy
of God himself:

> In the last resort, it was again conformity with God Himself
> which constituted the secret of the character of Jesus on this
> side too. This is the relationship of God Himself to all the
> orders of life and value which, as long as there is history at all,
> enjoy a transitory validity in the history of every human place.
> This is how God gives them their times and spheres, but with-
> out being bound to any of them, without giving any of them
> His own divine authority, without allotting to any of them a
> binding validity for all men. (Pp. 172-73)

At this point, Barth goes into the small-print section in which
he adduces all sorts of scriptural evidence to fill out his argument.
We will trace the outline of that argument with only the barest hint
of the amount of Scripture he uses: "Attention should first be paid
to what we might call the passive conservatism of Jesus. Rather
curiously, Jesus accepts and allows many things which we imagine
He ought to have attacked and set aside both in principle and practice" (p. 173).

What Barth calls "passive conservatism" could as well be called
"apparent legitimism," what Paul called "submission to the governing authorities," or what we earlier referred to as "God's sufferance
of the arkys." And of course, it is this aspect of Christian Anarchy
which, both in Jesus' day and ours, revolutionary activists simply
cannot abide: "We will not put up with all this wickedness!" Barth,
on the contrary, scripturally documents Jesus' submission to: (a) the
temple cult; (b) the cultural order of the family; (c) the synagogue
and the Jewish law; (d) "the economic relationships and obligations
of His time and background"; and (e) "in respect of political relationships and orders and disorders."

In my words (not Barth's): If the name of the game is "Let's Fight the Evil Arkys"—replacing them with a Christian social order or overhauling them to be part of that order—then "submitting" to their illegitimacy is the worst possible move one could make. If, however, the case is that Jesus already has conquered them and is continuing to actualize that victory, then our "submitting" is the best thing we can do to keep out of the way and let him overcome them with his good. And surely it must be plain that it is only *his* good that can overcome evil. Paul could never have meant to suggest that *our* good ideas, good intentions, and good deeds are sufficient for that task.

Yet Jesus' "submission" is only one, the first element of his anarchism. Barth now:

> It is quite evident, however, and we must not ignore this aspect, that there is also no trace of any consistent recognition in principle. We can describe the attitude of Jesus as that of a passive conservatism in the further sense that it never amounted to more than a provisional and qualified respect (we might almost say toleration) in face of existing and accepted orders. Jesus acknowledged them and reckoned with them and subjected Himself to them and advised His disciples to do the same; but, He was always superior to them. And it was inevitable—we now will turn to this aspect—that this superiority, the freedom of the kingdom of God, should occasionally find concrete expression in His words and actions, that an occasional creaking should be unmistakeably heard in the timbers. (P. 175)

Barth now proceeds to run through his same (a) to (e) list, this time giving scriptural documentation as to how Jesus' "submission" to the arkys is qualified. It should be said that in no instance does that qualification take the form of hinted or threatened attack and revolt. We shall quote only two examples, the first out of the (a) category of Jesus' submission to the temple cult: "When He paid the temple tax for Peter and Himself in Matt. 17:24f., He did not do so on the basis of an unqualified recognition which the disciple was to regard as binding, but ['the children are free,' however we will pay] 'lest we should offend [the authorities]' " (p. 175). Almost: "Yes, I and my followers will submit—but, you should know, we don't *have* to." Or, as in John 10:18, "No one takes [my life] from me, but I lay it down of my own accord. I have power to lay it down, and I have power to take it again." Let's call this "qualified submission." Yet it would seem that Jesus seeks to *avoid* offending the authorities just where Christian revolutionaries seek opportunity *to* offend them.

The second example comes out of Barth's (e) category of Jesus' submission to the *political* authorities:

> Ought tribute be paid to Caesar or not? Well, the coin bears the image of Caesar, so: "Render to Caesar the things that are Caesar's—precisely those things and no more, is the obvious meaning—and to God the things that are God's." There is not a second kingdom of God [namely, one God has appointed to Caesar] outside and alongside the first. There is a human kingdom which is authoritative and can demand obedience only as such [i.e., only as a *human* arky]. And this kingdom is sharply delimited by the one kingdom of God. (P. 176)

This, then, is the second element of Jesus' anarchism: the *style* of his *submission* that qualifies it as being anything but *legitimizing*. But what is clear is that *revolutionary defiance* is far from being the only means of refusing to legitimize the arkys. Jesus knew a better one, "qualified submission."

Barth then finds the third and final element of Jesus' anarchy to be the radical conclusion drawn from the other two—involving, of course, the nature and action of the oncoming kingdom of God:

> But the crisis which broke on all human order in the man Jesus is more radical and comprehensive than may be gathered from all these individual indications. . . . "No man also seweth a piece of new cloth on an old garment, etc." (Mark 2:21f.). For Jesus, and as seen in the light of Jesus, there can be no doubt that all human orders are of this old garment or old bottles, which are in the last resort quite incompatible with the new cloth and the new wine of the kingdom of God. . . . All true and serious conservatism [i.e., legitimizing], and all true and serious belief in progress [i.e., revolutionism], presuppose that there is a certain compatibility [or possibility of transition] between the new and old. . . . But the new thing of Jesus is the invading kingdom of God revealed in its alienating antithesis to the world and *all* its orders. . . . Everything else that we have to say concerning the radical antithesis of the new thing which was actualized and appeared in Jesus to the totality of the old order can be said only in relation to its complete ignoring and transcending of this order. We can merely attempt to see with what profundity He attacked it by this ignoring and transcending. He attacked it—in a way from which it can never recover—merely by the alien presence with which He confronted it in its own sphere. (Pp. 176-77)

In our chapter following, what Barth here calls the attitude of "complete ignoring and transcending" Kierkegaard will more colorfully call "God's infinite indifference" to the "worldly passion of partisanship" which so fundamentally motivates the arkys. But however it be identified, the attitude lies at the very heart of what we mean by Christian Anarchy.

Barth proceeds to at least make a try at going through his (a) to (e) list regarding this third element of anarchy. We, again, will quote from his (e) section—where it is somewhat amazing to find Barth citing those teachings of Jesus which Christian revolutionaries are strong in applying on the level of personal relationships but which they somehow keep in abeyance when it comes to their fight with the political arkys:

> It is exactly the same in relation to the juridical and political sphere. Here, too, we have a questioning of the very presuppositions, *which is all the more powerful in its lack of any direct aggressiveness* [italics mine—VE]. What are all the attempts at reform or overthrow in which Jesus might have taken part or which He might have instigated or directed compared with the "revolution" [quotes mine—VE] which He did actually accomplish in this sphere? He did not oppose the evil which He came to root out. . . . His injunction to His followers, not as a law, but as a free call to freedom, is of a piece with this. They are not to resist evil. . . . If they do not want to be judged, they are not to judge. . . . They are to love their enemies and pray for their persecutors. . . . [Indeed, they are to join Jesus in the prayer of his most abject and yet freest act of submission:] "Father, forgive them; for they know not what they do." (Pp. 178-79)

That is Barth's royal and anarchical commentary on "The Royal (and Anarchical) Man." There is one conclusion Barth does not draw but which I (if I may) will: There is no point in our haranguing the arkys about their illegitimacy. They can't comprehend what we are saying, and no positive results are to be expected on that front in any case. However, it *is* important that Christians remind one another about the illegitimacy of the arkys (the illegitimacy of *all* the arkys, both good and bad)—yet there is no reason to raise our voices (or our gorges) in doing *that*.

VI. From Here to Eternity—with Blumhardt (1955-68)

From here, we follow Barth through his retirement and on to his death.

1. East-West Crisis in the Hungarian Revolt

Of course, the Soviet viciousness in suppressing the Hungarian revolt put Barth under great pressure to desert his anarchical nonpartisanship and join the anticommunists. But he held his ground:
"Barth's view was that communism had 'pronounced its own verdict
on itself' in Hungary and that 'it did not need ours.' Furthermore,
before being interested in the splinters in other people's eyes, people
should take the beams out of their own" ([1956] Busch, p. 427).

In this situation, it was none other than Reinhold Niebuhr
who was sent by some of the Pharisees and some of the Herodians
to entrap Barth in his thought. . . . But knowing their hypocrisy he
said, as per Mark 12:

> The question "Why is Karl Barth silent about Hungary?" has
> been raised against me even from America. But Karl Barth has
> remained silent and knows why. It was obvious that this was
> not a genuine question. It did not arise from the practical
> problems of a Christian who seeks an exchange of views and
> fellowship with another, but from the safe stronghold of a
> hard-boiled Western politician who wanted to lead his oppo-
> nent on to thin ice, either to compel me to accept his primitive
> anti-communism or to unmask me as a crypto-communist—in
> either case to discredit me as a theologian. What could I have
> said in reply? ([1957-58] Busch, p. 427)

Well, he might have said, "Give God what belongs to God"; he
would have had good precedent.

In a postscript to a work by his Czech friend Josef Hromádka,
Barth wrote: "The church on both sides should not let itself be
bound by anything—even by tradition, ideology, or the interpretation of history—other than the task to preach the gospel. This
task was to be undertaken in an utter openness of faith in which
men could start from the view that 'Jesus Christ also died for "Marx-
ists," and he even died for "capitalists," "imperialists," and "Fas-
cists"'" ([1958] Busch, p. 433). Yet, because he still sensed in
Hromádka an ideological bent, Barth had to say, "I could not really
feel at home in the air of the (Prague) All Christian Peace Movement, although I was very sympathetic towards it" ([1964] Busch,
p. 433).

In trying to get across to other Czech friends, he came up with
what might be his most trenchant epitome of Christian Anarchy:
"The gospel puts us in a place 'above the clouds of the conflicting
and feuding ideologies, interests, and powers in the present Cold

War.' [Barth] was therefore 'most allergic to any identification of
theology with social and political thought, and also to any drawing
of parallels or analogies between them—in which the superiority of
the *analogans* (the gospel) to the *analogatum* (the political insights
and views of the theologian concerned) did not remain clear, un-
interchangeable, and visible.' However, Barth did not see a standpoint above the conflict as an excuse for social and political
indifference. Rather, it was the stimulus to a 'resolute attitude in
which we can be of help with our Word, for the sake of God's will.
We must show solidarity with *the man* by showing solidarity with
men—of the left and the right, sufferers and fighters, the just and
the unjust, Christians and atheists—while at the same time being
sympathetically critical towards them' " ([1962-63] Busch, p. 433).

2. Last Words on First Themes
I Stand Alone on the Word of God—the B-I-B-L-E:

> "It is not so much a matter of our encountering the witness
> of scripture as of our encountering the one to whom the tes-
> timony of scripture bears witness. . . ." But in no circum-
> stances may "the freedom of the Word of God . . . be limited
> [by] a sovereignty which we already impose on its testimony:
> it must be allowed its own sovereignty." ([1963] Busch, p. 466)

Scripture shall not be put under the constraints of any of our arky
presuppositions—such as, "it *must* agree with our current political
understanding of 'liberation' "; or "it must *not* express anything of
what we have chosen to call 'sexism' or use language we have defined
as 'sexist.' "

*The Church Dogmatics Winds Up, as it Began, with Christian
Anarchy:* In Busch's précis of that final volume he cites Barth thusly:

> [He] went on to talk of the "struggle for human righteous-
> ness." This, in his view, is directed against the "uncontrolled
> powers." What he means are those powers which come into
> being when the possibilities of human life [break away] from
> man and rule him—just as man [broke away] from God. [Barth]
> cited political absolutism, money, ideology, and also fashion,
> sport, and trade! [He] stressed emphatically that the kingdom
> of God can be neither realized nor even prepared for by man.
> It is "a factor *sui generis*" not only over against the world, but
> even over against the Christian world. ([1960] Busch, p. 444)

3. And so to Sleep—with Blumhardt

In another return to the beginning, within that last segment of the
Dogmatics—in his exposition of the Lord's Prayer, under the phrase
"Thy kingdom come"—"in a long consideration of the two Blumhardts he referred to the [mentors] through whom his understanding
of the kingdom of God had begun to grow at the beginning of his
long career" (Busch, p. 454). Barth concluded the passage with a
hymn that, under inspiration, had come to the elder Blumhardt.

> Jesus is victorious Lord
>   Who conquers all his foes;
> Jesus 'tis unto whose feet
>   The whole wide world soon goes;
> Jesus 'tis who comes in might,
>   To lead from darkness into light.

Karl Barth died in his sleep during the night of December 9,
1968. He had spent the day working on a lecture.

> He was still at work in the evening when he was interrupted
> by two telephone calls, about nine o'clock. One was from his
> godson Ulrich Barth, to whom he quoted a verse from a hymn
> which spoke comfortingly about the Christian hope. The other
> person who wanted to speak to him so late at night was his
> friend Eduard Thurneysen, who had remained faithful to him
> over sixty years. They talked about the gloomy world situation.
> Then Barth said, "But keep your chin up! Never mind!"—
> [signing off with the old Blumhardt motto:] "He will reign!"
> (Busch, p. 498)

And so to bed and to sleep—from which, on "that day," he
(along with Thurneysen, the Blumhardts, and all the rest of us) shall
awake to proclaim: "He reigns, indeed!"

Chapter Six

DIETRICH BONHOEFFER
Almost Persuaded

In our first chapter I named both Karl Barth and Dietrich Bonhoeffer as more-or-less followers of the Blumhardts who, consequently, were themselves more-or-less anarchist. With Karl Barth,
of course, I was dead wrong—there was no "more or less" about
his anarchism. However, with Bonhoeffer, I was right. Nevertheless,
he does have some things to say on the subject that merit attention.

My trouble with Bonhoeffer on Christian Anarchy is the same
I have felt with him on radical discipleship: he is *almost* persuaded
but can't get himself fully consistent. The first three parts of his
Nachfolge (*The Cost of Discipleship,* Macmillan) is undoubtedly the
classic work out of the entire tradition of radical discipleship. Yet
when he comes to Part IV, on the church, he slides back into a
formal, structured, established concept which I (for one at least)
simply cannot reconcile with the disciple community of the forepart
of his book. And it is the same thing again with "anarchy."

I find two major treatments of arky (or "the Sword") in Bonhoeffer. One is in *Nachfolge* (originally published in 1937) and one
is in his *Ethics* (Macmillan), written between 1940 and '43. As we
have found regularly to be the case with our anarchists, he goes
directly to Mark 12 and Romans 13. His *Nachfolge* treatment is a case
of Christian Anarchy, clearly of a piece with what we already have
seen. He is discussing the passage (1 Cor. 7:20-24) in which Paul
counsels Christians to stay in that station of life in which they were
called, specifically instructing the slave not to undertake all-out efforts to get himself freed (counseling against revolt, if you will):
"As a slave he is already torn from the world's clutches, and become
a freedman of Christ. That is why the slave is told to stay as he is.
As a member of the Body of Christ he has acquired a freedom which
no rebellion or revolution could have brought him" (pp. 290-91).
Christian Anarchy, as we have seen, is dedicated to the cause of

human freedom. But, as a good anarchist, Bonhoeffer sees that true freedom, true liberation, is not served by fighting the arkys, by rebelling against or trying to revolutionize them.

> It is not as though St. Paul were trying to condone or gloss over a black spot in the social order. He does not mean the class-structure of secular society is so good and godly an institution that it would be wrong to upset it by revolution. The truth of the matter is that the whole world has already been turned upside down by the work of Jesus Christ, which has wrought a liberation for freeman and slave alike. A revolution would only obscure that divine New Order which Jesus Christ has established. It would also hinder and delay the disruption of the existing world order in the coming of the kingdom of God. . . . To renounce rebellion and revolution is the most appropriate way of expressing our conviction that the Christian hope is not set on this world, but on Christ and his kingdom. And so—let the slave remain a slave! It is not reform the world needs, for it is already ripe for destruction. . . . Therefore let not the slave suffer [even] in silent rebellion, but as a member of the Church and the Body of Christ. He will thereby hasten the end of the world. (Pp. 291-92)

Bonhoeffer is powerful in showing that Christian Anarchy derives from the eschatological orientation of the gospel. Just as far as he is from blessing rebellion and revolution, so far is he from legitimizing the established arkys—and that combination is precisely what we mean by Christian Anarchy. When he says that revolution would "obscure the divine New Order," I take him to mean that revolution's strident assertion, condemnation, threat, challenge, and rage simply cannot be transparent to the kingdom of God. Such represents too contrary a spirit. For Christians simply to answer worldly politics with more politics, adding worldliness to worldliness—this can but hinder God's program of having worldliness wither away as it is overcome by *good*.

 " 'Become not the bondservants of men.' This [enslavement] can happen in two different ways. First, it may happen by a revolution and the overthrow of the established order, and secondly by investing the established order with a halo of spirituality" (p. 292). Either joining the arkys or fighting them spells enslavement to them; the only freedom is to ignore them and go with the Arky of God.

 "The world exercises dominion by force and Christ and Christians conquer by service" (p. 293).

Regarding Romans 13, then, Bonhoeffer says:

> [St. Paul's] concern is that the Christians should persevere in
> repentance and obedience wherever they may be and whatever
> conflict should threaten them. He is not concerned to excuse
> or to condemn any secular power. No State is entitled to read
> into St. Paul's words a justification of its own existence. . . .
> St. Paul certainly does not speak to the Christians in this way
> because the governments of this world are so good, but be-
> cause the Church must obey the will of God, whether the State
> be bad or good. (P. 294)

Bonhoeffer makes it clear that the contextualist question about how
well the state may or may not be behaving at the moment has nothing to do with Paul's counsel regarding it.

> The whole of Paul's doctrine of the State in Romans 13 is
> controlled by the introductory admonition: "Be not overcome
> of evil, but overcome evil with good" (Rom. 12:21). It is im-
> material whether the power be good or bad, what matters is
> that the Christian should overcome evil by good. The question
> of the payment of taxes to the Emperor was a point of temp-
> tation with the Jews. They pinned their hopes on the destruc-
> tion of the Roman Empire, which would enable them to set
> up an independent dominion of their own. But for Jesus and
> his followers there was no need to be agitated over this ques-
> tion. "Render unto Caesar the things that are Caesar's" (Matt.
> 22:21—or what we have been identifying as Mark 12), says
> Jesus. "For this cause pay ye tribute also" (Rom. 13:6), says St.
> Paul at the end of his exposition. So, far from contradicting
> the precept of our Lord, the Pauline charge is identical in
> meaning—the Christians are to give Caesar what belongs to
> him in any case. . . . To oppose or resist at this point would
> be to show a fatal inability to distinguish between the kingdom
> of God and the kingdoms of this world. (Pp. 295-96)

I understand that last to mean: if a person thinks that withholding taxes—namely, a political power-play challenging the world's
evil—bears any sort of relationship to the coming of God's kingdom, he is confused as to which kingdom-spirit he is representing.
But for Bonhoeffer to join his fellow anarchists in centering precisely
on those tax passages, and for him to agree completely that the issue
is the disallowing of revolution as a Christian option—well, this
gives Bonhoeffer as good credentials as any of the Christian anarchists we've seen.

If Bonhoeffer had had the sense to stop writing at that point, Christian Anarchy would still be where he stands. However, when we turn to his counterpart section in *Ethics,* things have changed. Bonhoeffer has lost his fine sense of balance between legitimization and revolution and slid to one side. And—would you believe it?— although in point of time he is approaching the moment when he voluntarily will choose actually to join a violent rebellion against the state (the plot to assassinate Hitler), his theological slide is the other way, namely, into an interpretation that is strongly legitimizing both of church and state.

In that long treatment, he is still very strongly opposed to any sort of disobedience to either church or state—but I find virtually nothing to balance that up, no recognition that these arkys may themselves be as illegitimate and ungodly as all get out. I quote just one passage (the *Ethics* discussion of taxes) and assume you will be able to sense Bonhoeffer's change of attitude.

> Disobedience can never be anything but a concrete decision in a single particular case [which case, he will tell us, is when the state in question can with certainty be identified as the apocalyptic Antichrist of the end-time]. Generalizations lead to an apocalyptic diabolization of government. It would, therefore, not be permissible to refuse to pay taxes to a government which persecuted the Church. Conversely, the fact of obedience to government in its political functions, payment of taxes, acceptance of loyalty oaths and military service, is always proof that this government is not yet understood in the sense of the apocalypse. An apocalyptic view of a particular concrete government would necessarily have total disobedience as its consequence. (P. 343)

Notice that Bonhoeffer here has moved entirely beyond Jesus' argument that taxes are a special case of what the Christian owes to the state—this, for the fact that the coins bear the image of Caesar, proving that they do indeed belong to him. On the contrary, Bonhoeffer's argument would seem to say that anything Caesar demands is legitimately owed to him: military service and, presumably, the pinch of incense, the silencing of the gospel, you name it. He comes close to saying that, because the state is God's instrument, Jesus' "Give to God the things that are God's" intends that you are to give to God by way of his intermediary Caesar—a rather clear case of legitimizing.

I read Bonhoeffer to say that *any* disobedience is allowable only if a person is fully convinced that we stand at the *eschaton* and that *this* state is actually the particularized embodiment of Antichrist, which is to say totally of evil, the very incarnation of the demonic (which, by the way, is a judgment I would think sinful human beings are hardly qualified to make). And, Bonhoeffer continues, if that state *is* Antichrist, then Christians dare not render it obedience *in anything*. If the state is not Antichrist, total obedience; if it *is* Antichrist, total disobedience—these are the only options Bonhoeffer considers. Thus he leaves himself no room for the other biblical command about our obeying *God* rather than man.

That makes for problems. Both Jesus and Paul tell their followers to pay taxes to the Roman Empire. For Bonhoeffer, this would have to mean that that state was not yet the apocalyptic Antichrist—in spite of its idolatrous worship, its crucifying of Jesus, its persecution of the church, its exorbitant taxation and actual enslavement of entire populations, its gross immorality, and its military cruelty culminating in the devastation of the Holy Land. Presumably, then, even *that* state legitimately claimed the *total* obedience of Christians. But how, then, would Bonhoeffer handle Paul's selective *disobedience* in refusing to stop preaching the gospel when that legitimate state ordered him to?

Bonhoeffer, of course, wrote this passage at the very time Nazism was at the height of its evil and at the very time *Bonhoeffer was himself involved in a plot* of ultimate rebellious disobedience against the state. (In 1941, two years before his arrest for complicity in the attempted assassination of Hitler, Bonhoeffer "travelled to Switzerland on a secret mission for the counter-espionage department. 'At that time Bonhoeffer spoke to me [namely, Karl Barth] of the plan to form a military government which would first of all halt the German troops'" [Busch, pp. 314-15].) So what did he mean to be telling his readers? Was he (1) exhorting them to be totally *obedient* to Nazi Germany? Or was he (2) setting that state up as the apocalyptic Antichrist and exhorting them to be totally *disobedient* to it? Bonhoeffer himself, of course, is not consistent with either of those options—and neither of them makes very good sense.

I am not surprised to find a conservative, legitimizing tendency surfacing in Bonhoeffer's thought. Whether or not his churchly Lutheranism had anything to do with it, he never showed any of the *hilaritas* of needling arky balloons that is so conspicuous in Kierkegaard and Barth and evident in other of our anarchists as well. Bonhoeffer often recognizes a certain "resident holiness" in the

structures of church, state, and society that our other anarchists
never see at all. For instance, taking simply Barth as representative
of the entire anarchist group, he is entirely committed to the holiness
of God. Consequently, when it is a matter of this holy God being
present with his gathered people, obviously something holy is transpiring there as well. In this sense (but only in this sense) Barth fully
accepts the holiness *of the church*. But that this somehow carries over
into a resident holiness within the human, arky power structures
into which the church has organized itself—this Barth (and all true
Christian anarchists) would fundamentally deny. Yet I am not as
certain Bonhoeffer would.

So I am not surprised at Bonhoeffer's conservative legitimizing; it is the *sequence* of his positions of which I can make neither
head nor tail. If, under the growing evil of Nazism, he had gone
from conservative legitimizing to Christian Anarchy to violent revolution, that would be quite understandable. But, under the growth
of Nazism, to go from Christian Anarchy *then* to conservative legitimism and *from that* to violent revolution . . . well, I don't know.

During the summer of 1943, from the prison where he was
under detention, Bonhoeffer wrote a paper addressed to the judge
advocate of his case. In it he defended his actions and his relationship
to the government. He cited his Christian-Anarchy treatment of
Romans 13 from *Nachfolge* but not his legitimizing treatment from
Ethics—which, of course, would have been the piece showing him
the more strongly committed to total obedience to the state. Strange!
(*Letters and Papers from Prison* [Macmillan], p. 60).

Bonhoeffer's participation in the plot plainly is at odds with
his stated positions regarding government—but I don't know that
this inevitably creates a *theological* dilemma. We have spotted a similar contradiction in Barth (and probably could in almost any thinker).
However, regarding Bonhoeffer, Barth, and any similar instances,
perhaps our rule ought to be: Inconsistencies are not to be read as
signaling theological change unless accompanied by explicit ratio-
nalizations and explanations indicating the same. Under the pressure
of events, any of us can wind up acting below the level of our best
understanding. I contend that Barth and Bonhoeffer show up as
true proponents of Christian Anarchy in spite of all.

This book set out to be a study of Christian Anarchy. It was no part
of its design, nor did I foresee, that it would also address the issue
of tax-withholding. I take no responsibility for the fact that that has

happened. The fault lies squarely with Jesus—and with Paul for
having followed his lead. It was they who chose tax-withholding as
the symbol of the revolutionist arky faith their Christian Anarchy
was intent to reject. That is why later anarchists *can't* develop the
biblical bases of their position without running into the issue. However, now that we are well into it, we might as well finish the job.

To this point, we have encountered the exegeses and exposi-
tions of Jacques Ellul, Martin Hengel, Karl Barth, and Dietrich
Bonhoeffer. These people show remarkable agreement upon a quite
original line of interpretation. But, lo and behold, it may have been
that ancient anarchist Søren Kierkegaard who founded the school
of thought. His word comes in *Training in Christianity* (Princeton
University Press, 1944), pp. 169-70:

> What could [Jesus] do with kingly power who was the most
> indifferent of all men with respect to everything worldly? The
> small nation to which he belonged was under foreign domi-
> nation, and naturally all were intent upon the thought of shak-
> ing off the hated yoke. Hence they would acclaim him king.
> But, lo, when they show him a coin and would constrain him
> against his will to take sides with one party or the other—
> what then? Oh, worldly passion of partisanship, even when
> thou callest thyself holy and national [patriotic]—nay, so far
> thou canst not stretch as to ensnare [shake] his indifference.
> He asks, "Whose image is this that is stamped upon the coin?"
> They answer, "The Emperor's." [Says he,] "Then give to the
> Emperor what belongs to the Emperor, and to God what is
> God's." Infinite indifference! Whether the Emperor be called
> Herod or Shalmanezer, whether he be Roman or Japanese, is
> to him the most indifferent of all things. But, on the other
> hand—the infinite yawning difference which he posits between
> God and the Emperor: "Give unto God what is God's!" For
> they with worldly wisdom would make it a question of reli-
> gion, of duty to God, whether [or not] it was lawful to pay
> tribute to the Emperor. Worldliness is so eager to embellish
> itself as godliness, and in this case God and the Emperor are
> blended together in the question, as if these two had obviously
> and directly something to do with each other, as if perhaps
> they were rivals one of the other, and as if God were a sort of
> emperor—that is to say, the question takes God in vain and
> secularizes him [by implying that whether God does or does
> not get what belongs to him is a question of the kind as to
> whether or not the Emperor gets the tax coin belonging to
> him]. But Christ draws the distinction, the infinite distinction,

and he does this by treating the question about paying tribute to the Emperor as the most indifferent thing in the world, regarding it as something which one should do without wasting a word or an instant in talking about it—so as to get more time for giving unto God what is God's.

"Thus Kierkegaard doth make cowards of us all." He not only said it *first;* he said it *best.* Why, for instance, should he get the honor of seeing that the Mark 12 passage belongs in the revolutionary setting of first-century Palestine and deals with the issue of revolution—when, in his day, the science of biblical studies wasn't even far enough advanced to tell us that finding the historical setting is the way one is *supposed* to go about understanding a text? Why should a rank amateur get to make that discovery, when it was something that should have been left for the likes of Martin Hengel?

"Oh, worldly passion of partisanship [which leaves my phrase "human arky faith" looking pretty weak], even when thou callest thyself holy or patriotic—nay, so far thou canst not stretch as to shake his indifference." Surely, "infinite indifference" beats even Barth's as the very term for describing Jesus' unarkyness. Kierkegaard also beat Barth to the punch in his refusal to bridge between God and the emperor, theology and politics, divine activity and human activity, God's arky and human arky. He saw that the tax-withholders' sanctifying of their political revolution as being *of God* is just as much "worldliness embellishing itself as godliness" as is the legitimizers' sanctifying of the political establishment as being *of God.* Well put, that! He also sees that it is "to take God in vain and secularize him" whenever we suggest that he *must* stand on one side or the other of our political quarrels. No, on this one, ours is a God of infinite indifference. So let Caesar have his coin without even taking time to talk about it. Rather, from you, the word should be: Takes all a' my time to praise my Jesus—all a' my time to praise my Lord. If I don' praise him, the rocks goin' a cry out, Glory and honor! Glory and honor! Ain't got time to die.

I am not offering to research the matter, but my guess is that, under the total and long-time impress of arky dominance, the as-much-as-unanimous interpretation of Mark 12 and Romans 13 has been a legitimizing one. Jesus' and Paul's counsels to pay one's taxes, therefore, undoubtedly have been seen as entirely obvious and unexceptional—to the point of actually being superfluous. The state and church being holy arkys of God, nonpayment and revolution would, of course, be unthinkable. What else could Jesus or Paul conceivably have told us, except to pay our taxes?

Our anarchist tradition, then, has come along to break that earlier interpretation wide open and stand it on its head. Jesus and Paul are not out to legitimize the arkys but to argue God's illegitimizing of them. Suddenly, this has the effect of making their commands to pay taxes surprising, unexpected, and hard to understand—this, instead of reasonable and obvious. "If the established arkys are illegitimate before God, then surely we good Christians *should* be out resisting them, challenging them, fighting them, replacing them, transforming them." But, "NO!" come back Jesus and Paul, "if God has illegitimized the establishment arkys, he has illegitimized the revolutionary arkys in the same move. He is not about to take political sides. Rather, he is calling his people to stay completely out of that power contest—that contest of which tax-withholding is just as much a part as tax-legitimizing is."

It strikes me that, on every count—whether technical exegesis of the texts, historical probability, congruence with the total gospel, or theological consistency—the anarchistic interpretation is completely superior to and more accurate than the classic, legitimizing one. But a third exegesis—which I have frequently heard *claimed* but never seen *produced*—is one that would meet all the above tests and come out showing that Jesus and Paul would want to be understood as actually *recommending* that we withhold taxes from the current U.S. Government.

Although I do not find them offering any particularly original exegesis of our texts, we might take a moment to put the Anabaptists into the picture. A number of years ago, as part of an official Church of the Brethren position paper on the subject, I researched the entire Brethren history (from 1708 on) regarding its views on tax-withholding. The results then won the approbation of Donald Durnbaugh, the acknowledged expert on Brethren history. Some Brethren scholars have said they thought they *could* document that some Brethren individuals withheld taxes during the Revolutionary War, though I have not seen where any *did* so document. Yet, that matter quite aside, what is plain is that, up until very recent times, every official Brethren statement and every statement by a Brethren official has understood the Scriptures as opposing tax-withholding rather than encouraging it.

I cannot speak with the same authority regarding the various

Mennonite and Hutterite bodies. Yet my impression is that the case would be the same there as with the Brethren. However, regarding Anabaptist *origins*, I do know that—in *Anabaptism in Outline* (Herald Press), the most comprehensive survey of early Anabaptist writings yet done—Editor Walter Klaassen, without hesitation, says: "Because the government was instituted by God and acted in God's stead, it had to be obeyed. Taxes and dues should be paid without resistance. (Only the Hutterites refused to pay taxes for war or the executioner)" (p. 244). My guess is that, by the time we get into official institutional positions, these groups would show up as consistently opposing withholding as have the Brethren.

I do not mean to imply that the Anabaptists already possessed the same interpretation of Mark 12 and Romans 13 that we have found in our scholars. My guess is that it rather has been the case that the Anabaptists (a persecuted people, remember) existentially sensed the illegitimacy of the arkys and so intuitively resisted any legitimizing interpretations of the texts. For the rest, the sheer desire to be biblically obedient would have them paying their taxes—without even trying to think through all the whys and wherefores. They were Christian anarchists, not by thinking out a theological position, but simply in the process of being as biblically obedient as they knew how to be.

It is indisputable, then, that among the Anabaptists of both Brethren and Mennonite background, the greatest pressure, promotion, and argument for tax-withholding has come just exactly *now*. There is no evidence that it is a result of new biblical insight. That third, pro-withholding exegesis of the texts has not been forthcoming. What, then, does this about-face in the Anabaptist position signify? The only way I can understand it is that we are trading our Christian-anarchist tradition for a contemporary liberal Christian-revolutionist one. I would be happy to hear another explanation.

Chapter Seven

ANARCHIC THEOLOGY
AND ARKY POLITICS

In his book on Karl Barth, George Hunsinger set out Barth's basic premise thus: "Only if the two [theology and politics] are not confused—with each retaining its own integrity—can either have anything to say. Theology must not be politicized, nor politics theologized." Certainly we found Barth himself confirming and carefully *observing* this principle.

Ellul makes the point just as strongly in reference to his own career and authorship:

> Here was my approximate intellectual path from 1940 to 1959: Could I bring all of history, all of human invention into a Christian perspective? In other words, was synthesis possible? . . . Neither synthesis nor accord was possible. Should we then give in to this other fault frequent in Christianity? Since synthesis is impossible, since antithesis is obvious, shall we exclude, condemn, damn? . . . So I also had to accept that laws, morals, and political systems have their value outside of Christianity. (*Season,* pp. 173-74)

Elsewhere in that book (p. 213) he speaks of "the irreconcilability of the revelation and the world."

It should be recognized that this is not simply a theoretical proposition on Ellul's part. His field of professional expertise is the history of institutions and politics (as well as biblical theology). If anyone would have been able to bring off the marriage of theology and politics, he is the one. And he had made the big try. His negative conclusion comes out of hard-wrought experience.

Yet long before, Kierkegaard could have told (and did tell) Barth and Ellul *why* the merger was forever impossible: "Politics consists of never venturing more than is possible at any moment, never going beyond what is humanly probable. In Christianity [on the other hand], if there is no venturing out beyond what is prob-

able, God is absolutely not with us—without of course its following
that he is with us whenever we venture farther out than what is
probable" (quoted in my Kierkegaard book, p. 304).

That makes sense. If things are happening simply according
to human possibility and probability, if nothing is going on that
cannot be explained sheerly in human terms, then also to claim that
God is present and active is meaningless. God's presence is either
that which takes things *beyond* the merely human or it is nonsense
to speak of it as *God's* presence at all. Given the fact that, by definition, politics deals solely in human possibilities and probabilities,
it has no way of recognizing any reality beyond that human limit.
And given the fact that, by definition, theology deals solely in the
difference made by the presence of God, it has nothing to say if
forced to speak from within the political limit where God is not
recognized.

What it comes to is that theology and politics are controlled
by two different orders of truth. Theology is *true* only to the extent
that it is faithful to the gospel, faithfully communicating God's self-
revelation in history (history with the divine difference) as that has
been recorded and interpreted in Scripture. On the other hand,
politics is *true* only when its proposals and actions are truly realistic
and workable within the limits of sheer human possibility. Either
order of truth is valid. Neither Kierkegaard, Barth, nor Ellul has
any intention of putting down politics. Both theology and politics
have complete validity as long as each stays within its own presuppositions. Yet every attempt at mixture creates complete confusion.
At any given moment, a person must be clear and make it clear
whether he means to be faithfully proclaiming the gospel of what
difference God makes in the world or whether he means to be proposing what are the purely human possibilities of a situation. If it
be assumed that these two come to the same thing, then the person
is not speaking of God—who must make a difference, else there is
no reason to bring him into the picture at all.

Ellul sees a further implication of Kierkegaard's distinction:

> It was not a question of giving Christian responses or solutions
> [to the world's political problems] which would be absurd.
> How can we propose solutions derived from our faith to peo-
> ple who live outside the faith? But more important, the Bible
> is not a recipe book or an answer book, but the opposite: it
> is the book of questions God asks us. (*Season,* p. 73)

To recommend to an unbelieving world the ways and means of God
as being the solution to its political problems makes about as much

sense as selling people gasoline as the answer to their transportation problems when they've never seen an automobile.

The intent of this chapter is to demonstrate the sort of galimatias that results when we ignore the foregoing counsel of our wise Christian elders and try to speak theology and politics with the same voice. Our specific example is the *theology* of peace and the *politics* of peace. Our point is that they are not the same thing. Each is valid—but only when we keep absolutely clear as to which is being done when. Theology will not translate into political terminology, because that would force it to be silent about God. Politics will not translate into theology, because it *can't* talk about God.

At this point, it gives me real satisfaction to be able to report that I have found this distinction between theology and politics—even between "the theology of peace" and "the politics of peace"—to have first and best been formulated long antedating the efforts of Ellul, Barth, and even Kierkegaard. The case is, regularly, when I get a good idea, I later discover that I had subconsciously cribbed it from one of these three. It is satisfying now to know that, as often as not, those fellows had cribbed their good ideas from Scripture (from where all the best cribbing is done).

The original thinker in this case was the Old Testament prophet Isaiah. Actually, he admits that he is cribbing from the Lord; but his chapter 30:1-5 reads thus:

> "Woe to the rebellious children," says the Lord, "who carry out a plan, but not mine; and who make a league, but not of my spirit, that they may add sin to sin; who set out to go down to Egypt, without asking for my counsel, to take refuge in the protection of Pharaoh, and to seek shelter in the shadow of Egypt! Therefore shall the protection of Pharaoh turn to your shame, and the shelter in the shadow of Egypt to your humiliation. For though his officials are at Zoan and his envoys reach Hanes, every one comes to shame through a people that cannot profit them, that brings neither help nor profit, but shame and disgrace."

Then, in verse 15, God reveals what *his* alternative plan would have been: "For thus says the Lord God, the Holy One of Israel, 'In returning and rest you shall be saved; in quietness and in trust shall be your strength.' But you would not."

Isaiah, here, was speaking to a political situation very like the one in which we find ourselves today. The impending Assyrian invasion threatened as complete an end of Israel's world as nuclear holocaust threatens the end of ours. And the inevitability of the

Assyrian calamity was of a much higher order than nuclear calamity today. The Assyrians were actually on the march, and there was nothing Israel could possibly do to deter them. Conversely, in our situation, no party shows any serious intention of launching nuclear attack, and "mutually assured destruction" does constitute a strong deterrence of such.

Yet, for Isaiah's Judah as for us, there was frantic need for a "peace plan" (in our case, "disarmament"; the equivalent in Judah's terms being "how to make it when we have no arms"). The plan Judah hit upon was to sign a mutual defense pact with Egypt. The agreement was to be that, if Assyria attacked Judah, Egypt would be committed to come to Judah's aid. No doubt the hope was that the very existence of the pact would be a deterrent sufficient to keep the Assyrians from invading.

Isaiah presents the Lord, of course, as being politically critical of this political peace plan—although I am going to argue that the much more fundamental criticism comes at a different point. Yet the Lord does point out that, sheerly as *politics,* the plan is completely *unrealistic,* giving no attention to the actual human probabilities involved. *Egypt* cannot be counted upon to rescue Judah. Indeed, why should she even want to?

Making the parallel application to our own situation, then, do we seriously think the Lord would consider it *more* realistic for *us* to count upon the Soviet Union's doing the right thing if we decided upon the political solution of unilaterally disarming? From any calculation of human probabilities, is not the one expectation about as equally unrealistic as the other?

Yet, note carefully that God's primary criticism is not that Judah is making a poor political choice. He gives no hint of any superior peace plan—nor does he even suggest the possibility of one. No, what he criticizes is Judah's assumption that *political* reality is the only reality there is, that human probabilities are all we have to work with, that the only possibility of solution will have to be a *political* one. Rather, no one has given a thought to the fact that there is a God around whose counsel might be sought, who might have a word on the subject or a plan more realistic and promising than the one the politicians have devised. Judah is condemned for thinking *politically* where she should have been thinking *theologically,* for leaving God out just where he should have been counted in. Are we, in our peace efforts, doing any better?

And when, in verse 15, God reveals *his* peace plan—"In returning and rest you shall be saved; in quietness and in trust shall be your strength"—it turns out to be totally *theological* in character and not *political* at all. From the standpoint of sheerly human probability, God's is the most unrealistic proposal yet. However, as a theological faith in the power of the living God, it is the only realistic solution possible.

So, Isaiah has set the stage for Kierkegaard, Barth, Ellul, and now ourselves to consider "the theology of peace" and "the politics of peace" as two different orders of truth which must be treated independently and separately in light of their differing premises and frames of reference.

In the earliest version of this chapter, written before I knew I was a Christian anarchist, the opening sentence read: "I am a committed *pacifist.*" I now see it is impossible for one to be both a "pacifist" and an "anarchist" at the same time—this because "pacifism" identifies simply one more human arky toward which an anarchist must be "un-arkycal." The way in which the word "pacifism" most frequently and most consistently is used among us has it referring to that arky faith which is convinced that human piety can be so organized, directed, and empowered through techniques of nonviolence and reconciliation as to pacify society and eliminate its recourse to militarism and war.

When *Christian* pacifism is specified, this usually adds only that Jesus of Nazareth is looked to as our greatest proponent and teacher of pacifistic ethics and method. Such, of course, hardly amounts to "the active presence of God" as being absolutely essential for spelling the difference between war and peace and so must still qualify, not as a theology of peace, but simply as a politics of peace.

Now it is also true that, in the earlier manuscript, I insisted that I was "at odds with the great majority of 'pacifists' both within and outside the church." That may have been sufficient to make the distinction; but now, as a Christian anarchist, I feel the need to identify my position as completely separate from that of arky, political "pacifism." My best suggestion is "anarchical nonresistance"—though much more important than finding a label is the making of the distinction.

As a Christian anarchist, I cannot buy the assumption that the problem of war can be solved by the holy arky of pacifist politics operating within the limits of the humanly probable. I do not find human history ever even having demonstrated this possibility. More importantly, I do not find my Bible ever promising or foreseeing it.

My faith, then, needs a *theology* of peace in which peace becomes a possibility only through the intervention of an active presence of God that does indeed make all the difference. Let's work first, then, at such a "theology of peace." I already have devoted an entire book to the effort (*War and Peace from Genesis to Revelation*, Herald Press) and have no desire to duplicate it here. What follows, then, is a minimum, bare-bones version of that fuller theology. Yet this, as that, focuses on the very real and necessary difference the presence of God makes. It is, then, very much a *theology* of peace that makes no claim at all of having any practical, worldly, political relevance.

I take very seriously the apostle Paul's statement in 1 Corinthians 15:22 that "in Adam" all *die*. And I understand him to mean that humanity—in its Adamic determination to perform the God-function for itself, to achieve justice and righteousness through its own arky powers of moral suasion (which, to put it biblically, is the presumptuous appropriation of the fruit of the tree of the knowledge of good and evil)—that in this way humanity invariably proceeds into death.

When, then, Paul's sentence goes on to speak of all being "made alive," his thought is the furthest from anything akin to human moral achievement. "To be made alive," here, certainly can be taken as synonymous with finding "life," "salvation," "shalom," "justice," "total freedom from violence," call it what you will. And Paul's verb must be taken as deliberately *passive*. Being "made alive" obviously is nothing dead people can do either for themselves or to themselves. Their only hope is that somebody—and it must be said, a very special, much-more-than-human Somebody—do it to them. Paul, of course, specifies that this Somebody is: *with* Christ, *by* the One who made Christ himself alive after he also in Adam had died.

Paul elsewhere not only establishes Jesus as the *agent* of our resurrection into shalom but presents Jesus' personal experience as the paradigm of how—whether individually or societally—the transition from violence to shalom must take place. Jesus of Nazareth, plainly, was both the greatest model and the greatest teacher of love, pacifism, and nonviolence that the world has ever seen. Yet that most exemplary moral teaching and behavior won him not one convert but eventuated rather in the total rejection signified by his crucifixion. As a holy political arky, his "pacifism" didn't work so well.

Clearly it is not the biblical intent to suggest that, although Jesus was unfortunate enough to run into a bunch of particularly hard-nosed characters, we have the right to expect that *our* pacifism will have much greater success in turning violent enemies into lovers.

There long has been an argument as to whether the Jews or the Romans were primarily responsible for Jesus' death. That, I think, represents a misunderstanding; the biblical opinion is rather that of *universal* responsibility. Both the Jews and the Romans are guilty, yet those receiving the most explicit condemnation are *the disciples*. Judas betrayed him, Peter denied him, and the rest fled from him. (And always, in the Gospels, the disciples are emblematic of the Christian community *en toto*.) Even the spectators—the women who looked on and wept over what was happening to Jesus—were condemned, precisely for wanting to play the "spectator" instead of facing up to their own involvement in his rejection.

If it had turned out that Good Friday marked the end of the story—unreversed by God's unwarranted, undeserved, uncalled-for action of Easter—there is no reason to think that Jesus' pacifist witness would ever have been remembered or recorded. This greatest peace demonstration in history had a positive political effect of exactly zero and a negative moral result of universal guilt and thus universal death. Jesus does not turn out to be too good an example of how pacifism is supposed to work.

"As in Adam *all* die." The fate of the pacifist Jesus shows us that, by nature, the tendency of the race—far from that of reform and revolution toward rectitude—is to crucify life and choose death. As I see it, the cross is the theological emblem posted as marking the dead end of any trust in holy arky, the self-realizing piety and moral educability of humanity. And Paul makes it plain that, on the cross, it was not only the one individual Jesus who died. No, as his crucifiers, all the rest of us were there found guilty, were sentenced, were crucified with him. For that matter, it was also in the cross that God went dead; from all that could be discerned, he too had died. Humanity had found Perfect Love more threatening than any military invasion and had responded by triggering more death and destruction than any number of nukes (which can kill only the body) could accomplish. "As in Adam [and on the cross] *all* died."

". . . So also in Christ shall all be made alive." Humanity's is the way of death; but fortunately, Humanity is not the only player on the stage. Easter, now, does not signify simply the one individual Jesus being made alive. No, with Easter, God is the first to come alive again—to become once more discernible, accessible, and active on the scene. Then, in addition to Jesus, Paul speaks of "all" being made alive again in him. I, for one, am ready to take Paul for what he says—the only qualifier being that "all" have not yet heard, accepted, or waked up to the fact that they have been resurrected. Christ has done everything he needs to do or can do; yet "resurrection" hardly is in effect until the individual does his part by getting up out of the coffin and doing something to indicate that he is no longer a corpse.

However, I propose, there was at least one other resurrection on Easter morning as well. The story and reputation of Jesus as moral instructor in pacifism (which, without Easter, would have stayed completely dead and lost) has also been returned to life. Yet this "pacifism," now, is part and parcel of the resurrection-faith and thus totally "theologized"—the presence of God in resurrecting the dead making it entirely distinct from a political program of sheerly human possibility. After Easter, there is no way of understanding Jesus' "pacifism"—which, on its own, had led to nothing but death—as being simply wise counsel to (or even a demand made of) the arkys of worldly politics. No, at Calvary, that world had already registered its final verdict on Jesus and his teaching.

It seems obvious, then, that the *theology* of peace, the gospel of shalom, is a word "hearable" only by those who themselves have "with Christ been made alive." It is a resurrection word for resurrected people and affords no sense, meaning, or relevance outside the context of resurrection. It is a word of shalom; yet the only shalom it knows or can envision is that of this Prince of Peace. It is through his resurrection that shalom is created and in his parousia that he, in fact, *becomes* our shalom. But, as to how far human violence might be mitigated through good politics within the limits of human probability—here, the *theology* of peace has absolutely no wisdom or counsel to offer. It knows and can speak only of the difference *God* makes—having no basis for even an opinion outside that.

Thus, proceeding to put this theology into the form of theological *ethics,* or biblical *injunction,* I would propose something as follows: In the power of his resurrection (and only in that power), you have now been made able and can afford to renounce all violence, whether self-assertive or self-defensive. You can venture just that far, secure in the faith that—even if making yourself vulnerable leads to your death or the death of your nation—the God who, out of death, already has made you alive with Christ, can, according to his own choosing, resurrect whatever needs resurrecting time and time and time again.

Notice that we here have duplicated the regular (if not universal) pattern of the Bible's ethical injunctions. These are two-part statements. There is, of course, a "command clause," the imperative regarding what the agent is to do. However, there is also an "enablement clause" explaining what God has done or offers to do that will make it possible for the agent to obey the command. And it is, of course, the enablement clause that is the explicitly theological statement of the difference God's presence makes in the case. St. Augustine's prayer is perhaps the best generalized version: "Command, Lord, what thou wilt—and *give* what thou dost command." Consider, then, these biblical examples.

"Now the Lord said to Abram, 'Go from your country and your kindred and your father's house to the land that I will show you' " (Gen. 12:1). The command to go away from everything you hold dear makes sense only because of the enabling clause, the promise that "I will show you"—which is to say, "I will be there with you, showing the way; only that will make your going even a possibility."

The Ten Commandments should never be read beginning simply with the First Commandment. That is to miss the enabling clause and make the commandments themselves very bad news indeed. No, Exodus 20:1-2 reads: "And God spoke all these words, saying, 'I am the Lord your God, who brought you out of the land of Egypt, out of the house of bondage.' " That is to say, "If I already have exercised such grace and power in your behalf, you can be certain that I also am committed to continue that exercise in enabling you to meet these admittedly impossible commandments."

In Romans 12, where Paul is ready to shift from proclamation of the gospel to ethical injunction, his transition reads: "I appeal to you therefore, brethren, by the mercies of God, to present your bodies. . . ." In effect, he has two enabling clauses there. The little word "therefore" actually says: *because* God has done for you all that I have just been talking about, it now is a realistic possibility for you to present your bodies and what all. Then, even more explicitly, he tells us that it is "by the mercies of God" (not by the power of our piety) that we will find ourselves able to live out such impossible counsels as "repaying no one evil for evil," etc.

A final example gets us back to our "peace" theme. In Isaiah

2:1-5, notice that what there amounts to a *command* for us to beat
our swords into plowshares is most explicitly preceded by the *enablement* of the nations in coming to God to learn his ways and to
be judged (i.e., made right) by him. The theology of peace we are
developing differs only in Christianizing the idea by specifying the
enablement as being God's resurrection-capability revealed in Christ.

Such a theology of peace, obviously, is slanted toward a particular audience and meant especially for it. In the first place, it is
the audience of one's brothers and sisters of the faith—those who
already have heard and accepted the gospel but who always need
their understanding broadened, deepened, and made more obedient.
In the second place, the theology of peace certainly should be presented as an integral part of the gospel one presents in the evan-
gelistic endeavor of winning new Christians. In this respect, the
theology of peace *is* proclaimed to the world, although certainly not
as good advice to the world *as world*—but rather, as proclamation
designed to bring people *out* of the world as world. Then, too,
Christian evangelism can proceed only individual by individual; the
arky idea of Christianizing populations *en bloc* has proved a fatal
one. So the "right" audience for the theology of peace is the faith
community and individuals on the way to becoming part of it.

Perhaps no harm is done in (occasionally) proclaiming the
theology of peace in the political milieu of secular government and
statecraft; yet we need to be clear about the economy of such a
situation. Statements regarding the difference made by *God's* presence cannot be accepted as relevant to conversations committed to
considering only *human* probabilities. So if, as inevitably must be
the case, the theological proclamation falls upon deaf ears, the pro-
claimer is entirely out of order and showing a most un-Christian
spirit in berating and denouncing the politicians for rejecting his
Christian truth. No matter how Christian any of those individual
politicians might be in their personal commitment, as politicians
they are prohibited from operating theologically—and *ought* to be.

For instance, if the members of Congress were to vote the
armed forces out of existence and, in explaining their action, testified
that they were trusting the power of God to resurrect the nation if
it came to that, they would quickly be impeached—and *ought* to be.
If those members personally happened to be Christians, fine. But it
was not *as Christians* they were elected to office but as politicians
completely committed to finding the best actions possible *within the
limits of human probability* and to justifying those actions upon the

same premise. All the documentation concerning their office, role, and function—from the U.S. Constitution on down—assumes that the state is a secular, political, human institution and not a Christian, theological one.

It can no more be tolerated that a Christian politician justify his decisions by appealing to a religious faith not shared by the body politic than it can be tolerated that a Christian physicist propose theories that explain phenomena at given points by conjecturing miracles of God. Politics is just as much a science within the bounds of human probability alone as physics is. So, not only *will* the Christian theology of peace fall on deaf ears with the government—it *ought* to. Let government once become the debating society for all the different theologies and theories of God and it would be rendered completely useless for its true task. As Barth, Ellul, and Kierkegaard have insisted, politics has a chance of being good politics only if it stays entirely away from theology.

Perhaps there is no harm in occasionally challenging the political world with the gospel—although certainly there is nothing positive to be expected from doing so. *Perhaps* there is no harm in occasionally reminding the government that it is *godless*—although its perfect retort would be: "True! That's by design. If we are to have any chance of governing a pluralistic and secular citizenry, we will need to be godless and theologically ignorant."

Jesus apparently understood this very distinction between theology and politics. When he had his chance before Pilate, his actions confirmed the irreconcilability of their respective viewpoints rather than being an attempt at establishing communication. He made no effort to convert Pilate or to engage him in theological discussion; rather, he suggested that the two of them belonged to two totally different worlds of discourse. Yet neither did Jesus make any effort to denounce the Roman state and curse Pilate for being who he was; it is not the task of theology to sit in judgment upon politics. Theology is to be judged theologically and politics politically. So, quite the contrary, Jesus showed a profound understanding, almost sympathy, for Pilate's situation. In the account of John 18:36, Jesus says, "My kingship is not of this world. If my kingship were of this world, my servants would fight. . . ."

Jesus' word—the complete contrary of the word of many of his modern, pacifist followers—is not the angry denunciation of Pilate's continual fighting. Rather, in effect, "You know, Pilate, it is only the fact that my experience of reality is open to God instead of being limited to this world of the humanly probable as yours is—it is only this that frees me from having to fight the way you always have to be doing. Indeed, if my government had to be confined to the same horizon as yours, I would find myself having to fight just as you do." There is no point in castigating Pilate for being a fighter; under his circumstances, the poor guy has no alternative.

It follows that what any sort of violence on any level then indicates is that the perpetrator—at that moment and in that act— is "outside of Christ." In one sense, this makes the violence of the world more excusable than that of Christians, in that the world has never claimed to be "in Christ."

It would seem to be in following this lead that Ellul, Hengel, and perhaps others have insisted that violence turns out to be entirely *necessary* to a secular government's self-preservation and functional existence. It is of no help at all, then, for Christians to butt in with the glib suggestion that any government could be peaceful if it only chose to be so. That shows no understanding whatever. Jesus is much nearer the mark in implying that liberation from violence can be found only in the shalom *of God*. Thus Jesus could feel true compassion, not just for a particular praetor, but for a miserable Roman Empire and an entire secular world that, in failing to know God, had gotten itself locked into endless rounds of fighting: "they know not what they do." There is *sin* here, of course— but it is the essential sin of choosing to go without God (of which many of the pacifists may be just as guilty as the secular world they berate). Yet, in face of the tragedy of this loss of God, the shrill screams of "Why don't you be peaceful like we good pacifists are?" show a particular lack of perception and sensitivity.

So, the *theology* of peace is what it is, God's word for the ears of faith that can hear—but nothing of much use as *political* counsel to a secular world that knows not God. Indeed, this may have been what Jesus had in mind when he said, "And when you hear of wars and rumors of wars, do not be alarmed; this must take place [as long as the world remains a world closed to God's shalom], but the end is not yet [when God shall come to open that world to himself and resurrect it out of its grave-clothes of violence]" (Mark 13:7).

Yet arky pacifism has not heard Barth's anarchical dictum that theology dare not be politicized nor politics theologized if either is to retain its validity. So what we get here is a religio-political voice that tries to speak both ways at once and thus winds up in an incoherency that is neither good theology nor good politics. Under its own terms, the theology of peace is *realistic* in putting its faith in a *real* God of proven resurrection capability. The secular world's mainline political tradition also is *realistic* in confining itself to the *real* limits of what is humanly possible and in wrestling with the *reality* of being forced into violence when resort to God is not a live alternative. Yet religio-political pacifism turns out to be incapable of realism on either front.

Pacifism's normal mode of operation, it strikes me, is something as follows: The biblical theology of peace, we have seen, proclaims, "Because you have experienced what it means to be made alive in Christ and so have total confidence in the resurrection capability of God, you now can afford and are enabled to renounce all violence and live defenselessly."

Pacifists, however, because many are themselves not that concerned about theology and because they sense that the first, enabling clause truly is quite irrelevant and "unhearable" on the scene of secular politics, have a tendency simply to *drop* the enabling clause and go with the command clause as their party line. They simply command, "You (individual, community, corporation, or nation) certainly can afford and are well able to renounce all violence and live defenselessly if you will simply choose to."

Of course, dropping the enabling clause eliminates any reference to the difference made by God's presence—thus reducing the proposition from theology to the sheer politics of immediate human possibility. It frequently is attempted to rectify this reduction (to a degree) by making the statement read: "*Jesus teaches us* that we can and should renounce all violence and live at peace." However, this does *not* restore the statement to the status of theology, because it still does not recognize any need for enablement by God and it treats Jesus simply as a secular moral teacher and nothing more.

Besides that, the statement is now false and unbiblical. Jesus never taught anything as sheer secular counsel; he taught *everything* with constant reference to the necessity of our being enabled by God. If you want Jesus' real opinion on the world's possibility of making itself peaceful *apart from* God's enablement, then hear him say to Pilate: "If my kingship were of this world—as yours *has* to be—why then even my own people would have to be out there fighting, just as yours have to be."

So, even though the pacifist position sees itself as "religious," claiming the support of Jesus, the Bible, the churches, et al., it offers very little in the way of a *theology of peace*. The theology has been reduced to politics.

Well, then, does pacifism represent a good *politics* of peace? Not very. As Barth and the others have suggested, the only way of getting either good theology or good politics is to keep each distinctly within its own frame of reference, working from its own distinctive presuppositions. Taking even a very good theology and trying to reduce or remold it into a political program simply does not make for good politics. As Ellul put it, "Giving Christian responses or solutions [to political problems] would be absurd. How can we propose solutions derived from our faith to people who live outside the faith?"

As Ellul further hints, the greatest problem with the politics of the "pacifism" of the Christian Left is its total lack of *realism*. If politics is the art (or science) of the humanly probable, then no political proposal is of any help or value unless there can be demonstrated a high probability, first, that it will be acceptable to the citizenry and, second, that implementing the proposal would produce the actual benefits claimed for it. And the proposal, of course, must be shown as workable within the realistic limits of human finitude, self-centeredness, moral weakness, nationalism, lust for power, and general sinfulness.

How, then, is it of any help to anyone for pacifists belligerently to demand that a secular society, on its own, in a secular world, proceed to pacify itself in a way the gospel suggests is possible only to a God of resurrection capability? It certainly is anything but proclaiming the gospel (good news) to a sick world simply to demand that it heal itself—and then damn it in no uncertain terms when it rejects such impossible counsel. Pacifism of this sort is hardly a following of Jesus in the attitude he took toward Pilate. And, sheerly as politics, the pacifist approach strikes a truly expert politician like Ellul as off-the-wall, romantic utopianism—spinning dreams of what we *wish* might be, as though that were the equivalent of presenting a realistic plan for getting there. Here is political thought that betrays little or no comprehension of the realities of human existence and world affairs. Here are "doves" who are probably not as "harmless" as the ones of which Jesus speaks but who also are no wiser than doves, when Jesus wants them "as wise as serpents."

The root difficulty, of course, is just what was suggested at the outset. The arky faith regularly identified as "pacifism" can manage to be neither honest theology nor honest politics—failing, as it does, to recognize the incompatible frames of reference, the necessary distinctions between, and the respective limits of the two. Consequently, its "theology of peace" becomes *unfaithful* by dropping the God-reference (which was the only thing that made it theology)—this in the effort to make that theology more commensurate politically. Its "politics of peace" also becomes *unrealistic* by demanding that the world do for itself what is only a *theological* possibility. The attempt to be both theology and politics prevents it from being either.

"But is there, then, a valid *Christian politics of peace?*"

The question is worded wrongly and so must be answered no. Recall how adamantly Barth objected to any political program or party taking the adjective "Christian," or "religious," and then trying to use that as a recommendation of its truth and superiority. Christian political programs are as impossible as Christian mathematical formulas or Christian cookbook recipes.

Let's try again: "Is there, then, a valid *politics of peace* in which Christians can conscientiously participate?"

Most certainly! There is no reason to deny, even, that it can be the Christian's *theology* of peace that moves him to participate in the political effort. Yet, while engaged in that effort, he is obligated to act simply as a *citizen* (a political entity) and not pull rank as a *Christian*. Every proposal offered will need to be justified on political grounds, as humanly credible in the achieving of particular human results—not on the grounds that God commands it and promises to do thus and so. This in the same way that a Christian may be a physicist, but he still must keep his physical theories within the human limit and not try to enhance them with resort to miracles of God. The limits of discourse must be respected: when doing theology one *must* speak of God; when doing politics one *must not* speak of God.

In order to keep the distinction between double-mouthed "pacifism" (which tries to be both theological and political at the same time) and single-mouthed politics, let's give the latter a new label, "peacemaking." In the first place, I would think, this politics of peace, this effort at peacemaking, ought to show much more understanding of and compassion for the world and its rulers than is commonly the case with the pacifists. We need an appreciation for the kind of bind in which a secular society—a world that does not know God, remember—finds itself when there are no good answers,

when apparently the best option is the admittedly poor one of violence. We need to be able to put ourselves in the shoes of rulers
who have the responsibility of keeping a show on the road and
populations viable when all occasions do conspire against that. Conversely, we need to sense the irrelevancy of simply dismissing all
these officials as being "bad people" and the futility of glib arid easy
solutions (such as total, unilateral disarmament) in the face of un-
manageably complex problems.

In our peacemaking, we need to realize that the sciences of
politics and statecraft require expertise of the same order that med-
ical science does—and a person's "Christianity" is no substitute for
political wisdom. The top-of-the-head opinions of rank amateurs
are of no more help regarding national policy than they are regarding the treatment of cancer. The peacemaker who volunteers to
counsel the government on what it should do had better be properly
credentialed in political science.

For instance, regarding a political complexity like Nicaragua,
I find much more enlightening and helpful a scholarly article in a
secular journal, written by a political scientist who knows the history
of the country, has been there in government service or as a trained
political observer, and who knows politics—such an article I find
much more helpful than one in a religious magazine by a sincere
and dedicated Christian whose observations are limited and whose
political expertise is nil. If high-level peacemakers intent on being
government advisors expect to be heard, they will have to show
some high-level political savvy at the same time.

The above would seem to imply that, regarding the politics of
peace, Ellul's maxim definitely applies: "Think globally; act *locally*."
Locally (even below the level of political structure, for that matter)
is where all of us politically amateur peacemakers have a chance of
making a contribution. We might help a neighbor find peace with
God, help someone get at peace with himself, bring peace within a
family and prevent a divorce, and so on up the line. And do not for
a moment scorn this level of peacemaking as being peanuts in comparison to international peacemaking. Politics being based upon the
humanly probable, the probabilities of making a significant difference are much greater locally than internationally. At the level of the
local, the apparently small efforts of a great many people just might
add up to a lot more peace than will ever be produced by the efforts
of a few experts at the intractable top. And who knows but that

God's will for peace might be meant to work from the bottom up rather than the top down.

Yet, even regarding the peace of the nations, a practical, constructive politics of peace will stand in some contrast to the customary pacifist effort. Because peacemaking, now, is the practical attempt to ameliorate the conditions of tension, conflict, and military confrontation *in the world and under the terms of the world's political limits of human probability,* peacemakers will have to recognize and accept the impossibility of a secular world's renouncing all dependence on violence. Otherwise, if the peacemaker becomes "holier than thou" and refuses to consider any move other than total, unilateral disarmament, he will only make himself irrelevant and of no use to anyone.

Notice that, in a *theology* of peace, God *can* call his people, the believers, to become completely defenseless. However, in a *politics* of peace, *we* have no right to call a secular state to become defenseless—as a humanly prudential move. For that matter, what right does a Christian have to demand that a secular state produce in itself an order of peacefulness that the demander himself has not been able to attain within his own marriage—or a church to demand, when it can't even pacify its own Christian constituency?

When the goal of peacemaking is to help the world in preventing injustice and forwarding justice, the pacifist denial of secular society's right to self-defense and self-liberation cannot come across as anything other than totally irrelevant or even subversive. Remember, the world does not have a God it can trust to take care of survival, justice, peace, and all those things we look to God for. So a secular society should hardly be expected to venture the sort of nonresistant risk-taking Christians can afford.

Consequently, the parameters of realistic political peacemaking will have to be stated thus: Granted the secular world's felt necessity for the options of both self-defense and just revolution against tyranny, how can we best scale back and tone down military preparation and threat without, in the process, jeopardizing either national security or the possibility of just revolution. This, I would contend, is a realistic goal which good human politics might have a significant probability of achieving. To scorn this one in favor of the truly "Christian" vision of a world that neither needs or wants arms would succeed only in making the proposers feel righteous about themselves, without being of any help anywhere.

Stating the issue this way has the immediate effect of giving peacemaking an entirely different complexion from that so common today. No longer is it possible to make the simplistic and polarizing distinction between "we moral pacifists" and "those (everyone else) immoral warmakers." Now, it would seem, proponents from virtually every point on the political spectrum can buy the thesis that, as long as security is preserved, it is altogether right and proper for us to seek every possible means of scaling back militarism. Yes, there will be differences of opinion about what level of armament represents "military security"; but that is a question that can be debated and perhaps even settled without casting moral aspersions on anyone.

Peacemaking, now, need no longer be a battle between the righteous and the unrighteous but a common dialogue by those seeking the same end but having differing ideas about how to get there. Accordingly, the situation is "relativized"—i.e., each strategy proposal from whatever cause group can be accepted as honest and well intentioned, yet relatively (but only relatively) right or wrong, wise or unwise, practical or unrealistic, contributory or distracting. Now, even such a proposal as that of the Reagan Administration— that presently to proceed with the development of our nuclear technology will actually enhance future chances for mutually scaling-back with the Russians—that proposal can be accepted as an honest effort at peacemaking, even while arguing that it is not the wisest or most promising approach (which is not at all the same thing as its being damned as an expression of the president's *desire* for nuclear war).

Perhaps the first obligation of wise political peacemaking, then, is to depolarize and defuse the process of peacemaking itself—opening it to include all citizens of goodwill (and being generous in that attribution), building mutual respect (rather than nurturing dark suspicion), welcoming every proposal (rather than defending one's own as being God's truth and dismissing other people's as being of the devil). The world that peacemaking must address and with which it must work is one caught in the very difficult and complicated predicament of needing to preserve national security and, at the same time, back away from superfluous and dangerous militarism. There is no easy solution; peacemakers who imply that they (or the Bible) can provide one are not being very helpful.

No, for peacemaking, the order of the day is calm, dispassionate, reasoned, politically savvy debate—a meeting of minds to address a common problem in search of a mutually satisfactory solution. This will call, first, for complete mutual respect and then for the most deliberate and careful sort of speaking and hearing, giving and taking, negotiation, arbitration, compromise, and political creativity. But what peacemaking neither wants nor needs is simplistic slogan-eering; mutual accusation, denunciation, and recrimination; raging passion; stiff-necked inflexibility; or the demanding insistence of "We aren't going to put up with any more of this stuff. We want this thing solved—and we want it solved *now.*" Peacemaking never has been known to be well served by tantrum.

What we have come to, then, is that a *faithful* theology of peace can be a wonderfully moving and inspiring proclamation of promise and grace—on its own terms. Likewise, a *realistic* and prac-tical politics of peace can be a humanly helpful bit of business—on its own terms. However, what we don't need is a holy arky (i.e., one asserting *theological* authority) to come on claiming that it has the *political* ways and means of creating a totally peaceful world. For that, I am afraid, we still must await the work of God when he decides the time is right.

To point out, then, what I hope is the obvious: We have here spoken only of "peace." Yet the essential principle of keeping the-ology theology and politics politics would apply similarly, regarding whatever issue might come to hand.

It seems to me that most of the current, widespread discussion re-garding religion and politics has been less than helpful for the failure to make clear what we mean by "religion"—or "politics," for that matter. Allow me this opportunity to clarify at least what *I* mean.

1. "Should Christians be active in politics?" Of course—if that is where their gifts and interests lead them. At the same time, how-ever, I must say I know of no scriptural or gospel arguments indi-cating that *political* channels offer such unique possibilities for serving one's neighbors and doing good for the world that *all* Christians have a sacred obligation to be politically active. Nevertheless, any Christian is also a *citizen* and so holds the very same political status as any and all other citizens. Christian and non-Christian citizens alike have the same *freedom* to participate or not participate politi-cally—and the same civic *responsibility* to do so. I cannot see that being a Christian affects the matter one way or another, neither privileging nor hampering one in the political arena.

2. "Is it proper for Christians to use political means to promote their particular religious values and morals within a pluralistic so-ciety?" Sure; it is as proper for Christians to promote their values

as for any and every other faith-system (or nonfaith-system) to promote its. My problem comes, rather, when we identify any of these
as being "Christian" (or "religious") values and morals.

As with all faith-systems, there is not the slightest doubt that
Christians *derive* from their gospel particular standards of values and
morality. Even so, it strikes me as grave error for us ever to identify
any such derived morality as being "*Christian* morality." Contrary
to the way in which it often is treated, the Christian-biblical gospel
is *not* just a superior moral system among other moral systems (i.e.,
it is much more than simply wise counsel as to what constitutes
good human behavior). No, the gospel is essentially an account of
God's actions in history, not moral instruction as to how nice people
should behave.

That there is no such thing as "*a* Christian-biblical morality,"
which, if followed, would spell social health and salvation, I find
indicated in two ways: (a) If there is such a unified Christian-biblical
moral system, the faith-community of the church has never been
close to a consensus on what it is. (b) Every moral system ever
claimed to be the "Christian" one probably has been duplicated in
other faiths (including wholly secular faiths). If there is anything
unique about Christianity, it obviously does not lie in the moral
systems derived from it. What sense, then, does it make to restrict
a particular system by specifying it as "Christian"—when the fact
that one *is* a Christian doesn't make him any more likely to accept
it and the fact that he is *not* a Christian makes it no less acceptable
to him?

The fact is that any number of different moral systems can be
and have been derived from the biblical gospel—with each having
about as good arguments, documentation, and support as another.
Nothing is to be gained (and a great deal of Christian charity is to
be lost) by the church splitting up to battle over whose is "the truly
Christian moral system." I am quite confident, for example, that the
liberal Left's is not true Christian morality and the conservative
Right's is actually *immorality* (or vice versa). Doubtlessly the Left is
reading its Bible correctly on some points and wrongly on others—
and the Right likewise. I would be happy to have it said either that
both represent Christian moralities or that *neither* does (good arguments either way). But what the evidence will not allow is any party's
claiming that what it represents is "Christian morality" while any
party else represents "un-Christian immorality."

What this says, then, is that Christians of any and all persuasions have a perfect right to promote in the political arena whatever morality they have derived from their Christian faith. Of course, that morality is what *they* take to be the "Christian" one—yet they would be smart to leave the adjective at home when going out to offer the morality for public, political consumption. They should consider that, although the term "Christian" gives that morality divine sanction *for them,* it will prove nothing but a handicap with anyone else. Other Christians who happen to "know" that their own is the one really true Christian morality will hardly be impressed by the party of the first part claiming divine sanction for its screwball ideas. And to denominate any one position as "Christian" certainly will hinder Jews, Hindus, secularists, atheists, and whoever from accepting it. No, even if a person's moral views are derived from the gospel, when he takes them into the political arena for promotion there, those ideas will need to stand on their own (untheological) feet, being sold on the basis of a sheerly human wisdom that can appeal pluralistically, quite apart from any considerations of religious commitment. Thus President Reagan was right in saying that he prefers we approach abortion as a *moral* problem rather than a *religious* one.

Religiously derived moral ideals are welcomed and needed in the political marketplace—although not in the form of *religious* claims. So, how about it?—*Christians* with their *Christianly* derived values active in the public arena? Yes. But, *divine sanction* introduced as *political* recommendation in a secular, pluralistic setting? Inviting the secular public into an intramural squabble over which Christians represent the true Christian morality and which an immoral perversion? This is where I have been insisting that religion and politics must be kept strictly separate, each within its own particular framework, operating out of its own distinctive presuppositions.

So you tell me which side of the "religion in politics" debate I am arguing. My opinion is that the commonly presented either/or—namely, either "religion freely mixing in politics" or "religion kept strictly out of politics"—is poorly put and much too simplistic to handle the complexities of the matter.

3. "Should particular *political* entities (systems, parties, programs, agencies, cause groups) include the word 'Christian' in their titles or be publicly identified as 'Christian'?" That political entities of whatever origin or ideology should *exist* goes without saying. That they should label themselves in such a way as to imply some sort of divine sanction, God's endorsement of their moral superi-

ority, or super-political authority—that practice is highly questionable.

Although, admittedly, Karl Barth did join more than one political party that was denominated "Christian," it is plain that he played no part in naming them so. He is perhaps the thinker who has been most adamant against coloring and biasing the human search for political truth by injecting extraneous, nonpolitical, non-human, faith considerations. To do so is a crime against God in dragging him down to the level of partisan politics (see Mark 12) and a crime against man in confusing and messing up his effort to come to the highest political wisdom of which he is capable.

4. "Should church officials or official church bodies (pastors, congregations, district administrations, denominations, ecumenical bodies) make edicts implying that certain political proposals mark a degree of Christian fidelity and obedience that others do not?" This is a tricky one. It strikes me as proper for such bodies to speak in terms of general, inclusive, long-range political goals but improper to designate any particular, detailed, and exclusive political strategy as being the one Christian means of getting us to a goal.

Thus: Yes, it is proper for the church to call us into the search for world peace. But no, it is not proper to specify a "nuclear freeze" as the one true Christian proposal for getting there. Thus: Yes, it is proper for the church to raise a Christian concern regarding the right of the unborn to life. But no, it is not the place of the church to specify, regarding abortion, what is the only law of the land that will be acceptable as moral and right. (Thus, for myself, I am convinced that the most truly moral law regarding beverage alcohol would be prohibition. Yet, knowing it to be unworkable, I am not even interested in promoting that politically as the right law for a pluralistic society. The church has to give the world room to find the moral options that are most workable in its own worldly situation.)

The moral alignment which leads me to my conclusions regarding these questions is this: The essential fact to be noted is that all political ideas, proposals, and options are creations of fallible and sinful human beings, done under the limitations of a quite morally intractable social environment. This is to say that no political proposal (no matter how Christian it is claimed to be) can guarantee very much, if anything, in the way of good results. At the very best (regarding, say, peacemaking) some proposal might result in averting certain disasters and alleviating certain conflicts—yet certainly not transform society into the peaceable kingdom of God. At next best, this proposal could prove entirely ineffectual and unworkable—yet not do any particular harm. At worst (even with the most Christian of intentions) it is quite possible for it to backfire and bring results the exact opposite of those desired. In a word, politics is a chancy business.

So, on a moral scale from zero to one hundred, the righteousness of God would lie at one hundred (the top), and all the human righteousnesses of our political morality would scatter themselves at the bottom—from zero, say, up to three. Now, politics properly done within its own horizon would operate out of a close focus upon that bottom cluster and thus find appreciable, worthwhile, and important moral distinctions between, say, a 3.0 proposal and a 2.75 one.

However, let the church try to get into the act by dragging in theological considerations (God, Christian or not, the will of God, the righteousness of God) and the reading of the scale is immediately transformed. Now, with the righteousness of God in the 100 spot, *all* the options of human politics are seen to be under God's judgment as unrighteousness—and the difference between a 3.0 and a 2.75 is as much as indiscernible.

This would result in an entirely accurate picture—*if* the church were ready to confess that *its* solemn political decrees and counsels (even if 3.0s) are actually of a kind with and as much as indistinguishable from the 2.75 political decrees and counsels of the heathen; *if,* in its pronouncing righteous judgment and damnation against the politics of the state and world, the church were willing to put its own politics under the same condemnation.

Yet, by officially designating its chosen politic as being the "Christian" one—the will of God, the expression of his righteousness—the church gives the impression that its place is at the 100 level, the top of the scale, as much as infinitely removed from all the un-Christian options clustered at the bottom. And that, obviously, is a totally false picture of the actual moral alignment involved.

Of course, what this designating of particular political opinions as "Christian" actually accomplishes is to introduce into the body of Christ wrath and division where none needed to happen at all. Clearly, the church *does* have to meet and cope with theological and spiritual divisions in the body; these have to do with the integrity of the gospel the church is committed to protect. Yet I find no suggestion anywhere in Scripture that the church has also been delegated to protect the political orthodoxy of the world. I'm confident there are any number of Christians who consider themselves great ecumenists but who, rather than serving Christian unity, actually are shredding the body of Christ by insisting that *their* political opinions be recognized as the "Christian" ones, thus impugning the Christianity of whatever brothers and sisters see otherwise.

Thus we do great and totally unnecessary damage to the body of Christ whenever we move to politicize the church and the gospel. Why, for instance, should we jeopardize Christian unity for the sake of a matter as problematic as the Nestlé boycott? Grant, for an opener, the complete justice of wanting to correct Nestlé's misuse of its infant formula; there were still hard questions that should have been faced. (a) By what rationale did we focus all our power against Nestlé, while showing no concern at all regarding the much greater damagers of human welfare, the tobacco and liquor industries, which we not only fail to oppose but fail even to discourage our own Christian constituents from patronizing? By what sort of moral selectivity is it we pick our political targets and marshall our fighting spirits for justice? Indeed, I would be happy once to find the church as concerned about the misuse of its own product (biblical theology) as it was about Nestlé's misuse of its.

(b) No matter how evil Nestlé's practice, the question should have been raised as to whether the amassing of the church's partisan political power *forcibly* (by economic clout) to impose our virtue on the company was a means consonant with the gospel counsels of suffering love. (The church's opinion of the rightness of economic boycott reverses dramatically as soon as it is a question of local congregations withholding financial support from denominational programs they find to be Christianly unworthy.)

So why could not the churches—in the interests of preserving both Christian truth and their own Christian unity—have been content to raise the moral issue of Nestlé's practice. The church then could have recognized the Christian integrity of (1) those led to join the boycott *and* (2) those preferring the more loving, *persuasive* approach of talking things out with the Nestlé executives *and* (3) those feeling called to make their moral witness on issues other than the Nestlé one? Speaking thus, the churches could have been heard by their total constituencies as having a word from God. But no, what we like to credit as being "Christian courage" must take the form of infallible edicts as to which political option is "the Christian one"—leaving stand the implication that whatever church members fail to agree are not the true Christians their morally dogmatic breth-ren are.

If this is what "religion in politics" is to mean, I find it truly contributive to neither politics nor religion. It distorts political real-ity by implying that one political position stands outside the judg-ment of God, 97 points above all others. And it is actually destructive of religious reality, namely, the mutual recognitions of love obtain-ing between head, hands, and feet—all the various members of the body of Christ.

Religion and politics? I think I am saying that there are senses both in which they belong together and in which they must be kept clearly distinct. That of which I am certain is that political-religious-moral dogmatism is of absolutely no help.

Chapter Eight

CHRISTIAN ANARCHY
AND CIVIL DISOBEDIENCE

Although the authorities in this book were chosen for what they could tell us about Christian Anarchy, they have gone regularly to the Scriptures that address the issue of tax payment. We have collected a number of expert opinions but will now turn to a biblical-theological analysis of our own. From this biblical base, then, we can broaden the focus to a consideration of civil disobedience in general—of which, clearly, tax-withholding is but one (though perhaps the prototypical) example.

Now, at each point where Scripture advises against the withholding of taxes it includes a rationale to back up the advisory. That rationale is different in each case. It is most important for us to understand how each ties in directly to the concept of Christian Anarchy.

Mark 12:13-17

We have seen that, in Mark 12, the argument is that Caesar's image on the coin is proof enough that the stuff is his; that it came from him; that, in essence, it is nothing we even should want or value, being the godless mammon of the Evil One. Caesar's "money" was never anything that either *did* belong or even *should have* belonged to *us*—and God denies that it was ever anything of his, either. When Jesus says to give to God what *belongs* to God, he obviously is exempting the mammonish coinage which he already has specified as belonging to the caesar who created it.

Our care and concern, then, dare not focus on this arky power-struggle over who gets to say how the filthy tax lucre is to be spent. How Caesar spends *his* money is his responsibility. There is no suggestion that God has appointed us Christians to try to take over as Caesar's comptroller—although, admittedly, Scripture never speaks about what responsibilities we may have as *citizens of a democracy*. (I would suggest as a rule of thumb that civic responsibility is a proper obligation only insofar as it does not threaten our prime responsibility of giving God what belongs to God.)

In any case, Jesus makes it plain that the arky involvement of fighting Caesar over money can only be a distraction from that prime responsibility. The battle of the arkys—whether it be the "good ones" or the "bad ones" who seem to be carrying the day—has absolutely nothing to do with the coming of the kingdom of God and *his* redemption of the world. So, Jesus tells us, rather than fighting him for it, let Caesar take his cut—so that you can continue to *ignore* him. The stance can be described as nothing but "unarkycal."

Romans 12:14–13:8

We will need to give more detailed attention to Romans 13—in that I have come to realize how firmly we are in the grip of the passage's traditional "legitimizing" interpretation. The support for this reading falls into a most interesting alignment. Of course, the Christian Right (along with conservative evangelicalism in general) welcomes this theological view of Romans 13 as confirmation of its own *politically* conservative commitment to political establishment as being God's chosen means for governing the world.

Yet curiously enough, the Christian Left also accepts, if not welcomes, the legitimizing interpretation—although under an entirely different rationale and for a totally different purpose. In some cases the argument runs: Mark 12 shows *Jesus* to be strongly *illegitimizing* of Caesar. Romans 13 has *Paul* coming out just the other way. In this showdown, Jesus obviously should take precedence over Paul; therefore, we aren't obligated to give particular weight to Paul's counsel about paying taxes and honoring the authorities. Alternatively, the argument runs: Yes, Paul does legitimize established government; yet certainly he must intend this regarding only "good" governments. Accordingly, his counsel about paying taxes must apply only to governments worthy of our tax dollars; when he says to pay taxes to those to whom they "are due," he must mean to those who, in our opinion, are morally deserving. Thus, it would follow that Paul had in mind paying them only to the "good" Roman Empire of his day and not the "Evil Empire" of ours.

As a way out of the political sophistries of both the Right and the Left, I propose an anarchical reading of Romans 13 that has Paul *illegitimizing* the political world as a whole—and thus entirely bypassing the dispute about his legitimizing anything, whether of the Left or of the Right, whether judged to be politically good, bad, or indifferent. If I may, I will call mine: "A Reading of Romans 13 Under the Premise that Its Author Was a Student of the Old Testament." (I disdain to argue this premise, because anyone undertaking to challenge it is manifestly belated, bewildered, and benighted.)

1. If we respect Paul's context by examining the total passage of Romans 12:14–13:8, it is plain that his purpose in introducing "the governing authorities" is in no sense to argue their "legitimacy." His main topic is the Christian obligation to love *any person whatever* and live peaceably *with all*. Check it out; he opens this inning by placing his hit: "Bless those who persecute you; bless and do not curse them" (Rom. 12:14). He extends that run to second base (13:1), at which point he introduces his "governing authorities" illustration. This he closes off neatly at third (13:7). He then proceeds to make his home-plate score by ending up where he started: "Owe no one anything except to love one another" (13:8). Pretty slick, I would say.

The "governing authorities," then, are brought in as Paul's example of those to whom it will be most difficult to make the obligation apply—but whom God nevertheless commands us to love, even when our natural propensity most strongly urges us to hate, resist, and fight them. As he elsewhere states the offense even more pointedly, "Why not rather suffer wrong? Why not rather be defrauded?"—which, of course, is not the easiest thing in the world for human beings to do.

Thus—just as with Jesus' praying, "Father, forgive them, for they know not what they do," and his teaching about "turning the other cheek," "going the second mile," and the like—Paul is using the governing authorities as a test case of our loving the enemy—even when doing so is repugnant to our innate moral sensibilities (which sensibilities we ought never, never, never equate as being the very will of God; but which we regularly do go on to equate so anyhow). If this "indiscriminating love" reading be correct, then verse 7 (the final word of the "governing authorities" section) ought to agree with Paul's overall love theme.

This it most beautifully does *if* "pay all of them their dues—taxes, revenue, respect, honor" advises against our withholding *any* of these items from *whatever* governing authority claims them as due. If, however, the verse is taken to mean that we are to allow these things only to nice governments who are known to be deserving of them—then we have gone from "indiscriminating love" to "highly discriminating love," and Paul has undercut his radically Christian argument merely to mouth the trivial and obvious ("For if you love those who love you, what reward have you?" [Mt. 5:46].)

Yet that absolutist interpretation is made as much as unimpeachable when Paul proceeds to wrap up his entire disquisition on "indiscriminating love" with verse 8. He drops the "governing authorities" illustration and universalizes the principle: "Not just the taxes and honors claimed by the governing authorities, we Christians ought not resist or try to withhold anything justly (or even unjustly) claimed from us. No, the only unpaid claim that dare be found outstanding against us is that we have not given anyone as much love as God would have us give."

2. We ought not interpret Paul's Romans-13 words without also considering what he has to say about the Roman Empire elsewhere. Elsewhere, of course, he talks about principalities and powers, rulers of the present darkness, and things of that sort. I don't know that any of these is to be understood in direct reference to Rome; yet there is every reason to believe Paul would include Rome in that passel. And if you want the Old Testament angle, it would be this: As a well-educated rabbi, Paul would be entirely cognizant of the scriptural opinion regarding pagan oppressors of Israel from the slavemasters of Egypt through to the Seleucid tyrants of Syria. I can't imagine anything that would lead him to exempt the current Roman regime from that long-established judgment. This in itself should warn us against a too easily legitimizing reading of Romans 13.

3. The history of Paul's own relationship to and knowledge of Rome should also warn us against that reading. In an earlier chapter we already suggested what Paul's previous experience must have taught him. He would have known that Rome's was a pagan domination and military occupation of the Jewish homeland. Under the likelihood that it was as a small child he had come to Jerusalem for rabbinical training (Acts 22:3), Paul would have been fully informed about the growing Jewish restiveness and Rome's cruel, mass deportation-enslavement-crucifixion suppression of the same. Along with the rest of the church, Paul's prime name for Rome would have been "Dealer of Death to the Author of Life" (Acts 3:15). He would have known that, only a few years earlier, the Christians of Rome (to whom he was writing), under the edict of Claudius, had had their congregations broken up and dispersed. Paul himself, of course, could point to a number of instances in which the empire had disrupted his ministry and abused his person. Thus, to read

Romans 13 as a legitimizing of *that* government should be held off as our last possible alternative of interpretation rather than welcomed as our first.

4. In the opening line of his "governing authorities" section (13:1a), Paul tells us to "be subject" to them. I found Barth most convincing (in our earlier chapter) that "be subject to" has absolutely no overtones of "recognize the legitimacy of," "own allegiance to," "bow down before," or anything of the sort. It is a sheerly neutral and anarchical counsel of "not-doing"—not doing resistance, anger, assault, power play, or anything contrary to the "loving the enemy" which is, of course, Paul's main theme. Then, just as any good writer would do it, Paul's *final* reference to the authorities (v. 7) becomes a simple repetition of his opening one: "Pay all of them their dues" says nothing different from "Be subject to them."

5. Romans 13:1b-3 proceeds to speak about government's being "instituted of God." When it is a noted Old Testament scholar who is talking so, I consider the original institution of Israelite monarchy to be our best help in understanding him. In that paradigm (1 Samuel 8), it is made entirely clear, explicit, and axiomatic that the people's demand for worldly government amounts to a *rejection* of God and his government. (And if even an *Israelite* monarchy signified a rejection of God, how much more so a *Roman* one?) But did God therefore conclude: "That being so, Samuel, what you and I need to do is resist that government with everything we have in us. We should work at subverting Saul's government so that, in its collapse, we can convince the people to give up this crazy idea of worldly government and come back to the true government of my direct rule"?

That, surely, would pass as good *human* logic—and, I think, *is* the essential logic of today's Christian Left. However, it is not the *divine* logic. God and Samuel, of course, helped set up the very government they so strongly disapproved. No, the word is, rather: "Samuel, if these knuckleheads insist on having a worldly government, we had better get in there with whatever influence we have left and try to limit the amount of damage such an outfit can do, see whether there is anything at all worthwhile we can manage through it."

God and Samuel accept (and honor) Israel's (bad) decision *as accomplished fact* and proceed to live with it rather than try to reverse it. God *accepts* (I didn't say *approves*) worldly government—with its taxation and conscription and all the rest—as being absolutely necessary once humanity has rejected *his* government. If you won't have *him,* you are going to have to have *it* (and thus the sheer naivete of a recent proposal from the Christian Left that "now we should challenge worldly government to give up its evil taxation and conscription"). Although Scripture never ever gives an inch on government's essential illegitimacy before God, neither is the possibility ever raised that human piety might be capable of ridding itself of worldly government and returning to him. God never even hints at any move of the sort—and undoubtedly would find such to be just as serious a usurpation of his power as the original move *to* worldly government was. What God has *accepted* we would be wise not to try to *reject.*

So, is Paul correct in saying that the fact that a government exists shows that it has been instituted of God? Yes—if he be read *dialectically,* as with his Old Testament source. Paul knows that worldly government is an illegitimate usurpation of God's power—knows it as well as God and Samuel did. However, what his well-justified-in-hating-Rome readers need also to know is that God *accepted* his own rejection as accomplished fact and thus proceeded to accept (yet hardly "legitimate") worldly government as a "given," a human necessity through which he just might be able to prevent some damage and perhaps even gain a bit of good. So Paul is warning his Christians against thinking they can go God one better: if God has shown himself willing to put up with a monstrosity like Rome, your *unwillingness* to do so turns out to be, not moral heroism, but an arrogant bucking of what God has instituted (instituted by his *accepting* it, not *approving* it).

6. In verse 4, then, Paul calls these governing authorities "servants of God." Within his dialectical framework, he can do this with the best sort of biblical precedent. In this regard, the prophet Isaiah has Yahweh say the following about the bloodthirsty Assyrian hordes poised to sack Israel:

> I have given my warriors their orders
> and summoned my fighting men to launch my anger;
>   they are eager for my triumph.
> Hark, a tumult in the mountains, the sound of a vast multitude;
> hark, the roar of kingdoms, of nations gathering!
> Yahweh of Hosts is mustering a host of war,
> men from a far country, from beyond the horizon.
>   It is Yahweh with the weapons of his wrath
>   coming to lay the whole land waste.

>   Isaiah 13:3-5

Here we have caught Isaiah—in cahoots with Paul—calling the representatives of a pagan conqueror "warriors (and to that extent 'servants') of God." However, in another passage the prophet makes it plain that this carries absolutely no implications of "legitimizing":

> The Assyrian! He is the rod that I wield in my anger,
> and the staff of my wrath is in his hand.
> I send him against a godless nation,
> I bid him march against a people who rouse my wrath,
> to spoil and plunder at will and trample them down like mud
> in the streets.
> But this man's [i.e., the Assyrian's] purpose is lawless,
> lawless are the plans in his mind;
>> for his thought is only to destroy
> and wipe out nation after nation.

> When Yahweh has finished all that he means to do on Mount
>> Zion and in Jerusalem, he will punish the king of Assyria
>> for this fruit of his pride and for his arrogance and vain-
>> glory, because he said:
>> By my own might I have acted
> and in my own wisdom I have laid my schemes.

Isaiah 10:5-7, 12-13

What is here cited as the sin of the Assyrian is likewise the essential sin of all human arkydom—the pretension that it is the actions of our own might and the wisdom of our own schemes which are determining the course of human history. We use even the banner of active Christian love and discipleship to cloak this denial of the truth of God's sovereign lordship: In the vainglory of the Assyrian, *we* say, "By my own might. . . . In my own wisdom. . . . My strength is as the strength of ten, because my heart is pure."

Later, with Deutero-Isaiah and the pagan *Persian* conqueror Cyrus, the dialectic contradiction becomes even more extreme:

> Tell me, who raised up that one from the east,
> one greeted by victory wherever he goes?
>> [or for that matter, the one from the west that Paul knows]
> Who is it that puts nations into his power
> and makes kings go down before him? . . .
> Whose work is this, I ask, who has brought it to pass?
> . . . It is I, Yahweh.

Isaiah 41:2-4

Thus says Yahweh to his anointed
   [that's the word "messiah," or "christ"!],
to Cyrus, . . .

For the sake of Jacob my servant
and Israel my chosen
   I have called you by name
and given you your title,
   though you have not known me.

I alone have roused this man in righteousness,
   and I will smooth his path before him;
he shall rebuild my city
and let my exiles go free—not for a price nor a bribe
[but simply because I commanded my servant],
says Yahweh of Hosts.

                                                              Isaiah 45:1, 4, 13

When Paul calls the Roman governing authorities "servants of God," it makes no sense at all to take him as meaning they are good Christians whose deepest desire is to obey and serve God. However, read him along with his Old Testament prophetic mentors and his entire passage makes perfectly good sense. If God can make such use of Assyrian warriors that Isaiah calls them "God's boys"—and if God can make such use of a Persian emperor that Deutero-Isaiah calls him "God's messiah"—then we better consider that God may be using Roman no-goods in the very same way.

7. The Old Testament parallel holds throughout verses 2-5. About as much as Paul can see as a possible godly use for God's Roman "servants" is that (precisely as with the Assyrian warriors) they are quite adept in punishing bad people. (If this is Paul's "legitimizing" of Rome, it is a most backhanded compliment.) Just as with the Assyrians, the Romans always go overboard on the punishing bit—and God will have to take up that little matter with them, just as he did with the Assyrians. Yet this does not change the fact that God can use Roman punishment in the service of his own justifying of humanity.

Therefore, Christians of Rome, here is what all this means for you: (a) You should take care not to be an evildoer whose governmental punishment represents the just anger of God you have brought upon yourself. That God's "servant of punishment" is himself "bad" is no evidence that you are "good" and your punishment therefore undeserved. That the U.S. Government is divinely illegitimate is no evidence at all that its punishment of the Berrigans' "civil disobedience" is wrong and outside the will of God. The expose of Assyrian evil does not amount to an argument for Israelite innocence. Rome does punish many innocent people (and God will hold it accountable for that: " 'Vengeance is mine, I will repay,' says the Lord" [Rom. 12:19]). Yet this does not prohibit Rome from being used "in God's service" to punish some who really need it for their own good.

(b) Then consider verses 4-5 in particular. Just because you Christians can see that the Roman Empire is obviously godless and wicked, don't draw the simple, human-minded conclusion that it must be God's will for you to resist, contest, and fight it.

Paul, yes; Isaiah, yes; but Jeremiah is the one most insistent that the pagan oppressor is *not to be resisted*—precisely because that rod of punishment may be acting in the service of God: "Bring your neck under the yoke of the king of Babylon [Paul words it 'be subject'], and serve him and his people [Paul words it 'pay whatever they claim as their due'], and live. Why will you and your people die by the sword, by famine, and by pestilence, as the Lord has spoken concerning any nation which will not serve the king of Babylon [as actually happened to the Jewish nation that ignored Paul's counsel of nonresistance, fought the Romans, and died]?" (Jer. 27:12-13).

You could find yourself resisting the particular use God has in mind for that empire; at the very least, you definitely are trying to take over and do God's work for him, pulling up the tares he told you to leave for *his* harvesting. When God wants that empire overthrown, he is fully capable of doing it on his own.

And if, in your fighting the empire, you happen to get yourself killed, the fault is not necessarily that of the Evil Empire; it does not automatically follow that yours was a heroic martyr's death in the service of God. It could as likely represent God's righteous anger against those who are just as guilty of wanting to be "lord of history" as the Romans themselves are.

8. So, in verses 5-8, Paul asks us again to "be subject"—always loving; never resisting, contesting, trying to impose our own wisdom and will. This is why you pay taxes (better: do not resist their being collected), so as not to have Jesus accuse *you* (as Paul got himself accused) of "kicking against the goads" (Acts 26:14)—i.e., trying to obstruct God's *Roman* servants as Paul had been trying to obstruct his *Christian* ones. Never owe anybody—*anybody*—anything except love.

No one ever said loving Assyrian warriors was going to be easy; but when you are obeying God by loving instead of resisting them, don't let any holy-joes try to make you feel guilty by telling you that you are actually approving and supporting Assyrian evil. There is not one word in Romans 13, or anywhere else in the New Testament, implying that to "not resist one who is evil" (Matt. 5:39) is tantamount to legitimizing him—this no more than Isaiah's nonresistance legitimized Assyrian militarism, Jeremiah's Babylonian, Deutero-Isaiah's Persian, Paul's Roman, or a modern Christian's American militarism.

Finally, notice that this interpretation of Romans 13 reads as *anarchically* as all get out. It carefully declines to legitimize either Rome or resistance against Rome. It will give neither recognition nor honor to any political entity whatever—nation, party, ideology, or cause group. There is only one Lord of history—and that is God. He shows no cognizance of our commonly accepted distinction between the holy arkys he supposedly sponsors and the unholy ones he opposes (though this is not to deny that he acknowledges a degree of relative difference between the moral performance of one arky and another). Yet, after the model of the Israelite original, *every* arky starts out under the sinful illegitimacy of messianic pretension, claiming for itself recognition as world savior and a true lord of history. Nevertheless, though the arkys all be under judgment (as all of us individuals are, too), God will *use* as servant whatever arky he chooses (when he chooses and how he chooses). He will also *punish* these servants the same way—even while *loving* each and every human individual involved the whole time. That's Christian Anarchy.

Matthew 17:24-27

In Matthew 17, we find a third tax advisory—with a still different (and most powerful) rationale to back it up. In this instance the tax in question is named as "the double drachma." That rather clearly identifies it as the tax dedicated to the operation and upkeep of the Jews' own "temple of the Lord." However, there are three points to note.

1. The Matthew author gives no attention at all to the tax's "temple" aspect, not so much as using the word in his argument. Indeed, he was writing for a post-temple, perhaps largely non-Palestinian, non-Jewish audience that would have no more inkling

that he was talking about a particular "temple tax" than the rest of us would.

2. He wrote this incident into his Gospel *after* the temple already had been wasted by the Romans. *If,* at the time Matthew's intended audience read this instructional passage there was in effect a "temple tax," it would have been going to the upkeep of pagan, Roman temples (F. F. Bruce tells us that the temple-tax—for at least some period in some areas—outlasted the temple itself in just this way).

Thus, what is totally incredible is that Matthew might explain: "I wrote this whole passage only to keep the record straight that *Jesus, in his day,* did himself pay *the temple tax*—which I am aware doesn't even exist for you folks. So I wasn't meaning to suggest that the incident has anything to say *to us.* Not at all; precisely because our tax situation is different, we might fairly conclude that he would teach *us* to *withhold* some of our taxes."

3. Just as with Mark 12 and Romans 13, the Matthew-17 passage obviously is dealing with a *general theological-ethical principle.* The texts contain not the slightest hint that they are meant as contextualist, particularist case studies. Some argue that these texts teach only that first-century Christians were to pay particular taxes because they were comparatively *benign*—leaving us free to assume that Jesus would want *us* to withhold the *vicious* sort of taxes we face. However, if this method of turning Jesus' and Paul's words completely upside down is obedient "biblical scholarship," it is a much more reprehensible method than the fundamentalists' unscholarly, universally castigated "proof-texting."

In the Matthew-17 passage, the apodictic, completely open and unqualified question is put: "Does not your teacher pay the tax?" The answer is just as unqualified: NOT "Well, that's hard to say. Some he does and some he doesn't—it all depends. You'll have to be more specific." No, quite the contrary, Peter's answer is a totally unambiguous "Yes."

Well, that clear-cut, abrupt, and quite surprising an answer (as though tax payment poses no problem for Christians at all) certainly calls for a bit of explanation and rationale. So Jesus comes on the scene to give it: "What do you think, Simon? From whom do the kings of the earth take toll or tribute? From their sons or from others?" And when he said, "From others," Jesus said to him, "Then the sons are free."

Follow this thought carefully; it is the best-ever argument for tax-withholding—and straight from the mouth of Jesus. In Romans 13, Paul advises us to "pay taxes to whom taxes *are due.*" The withholders regularly pounce on this phrase to mean "pay taxes only to those regimes you decide are good enough to *deserve* them"—and we already have argued that this is a misreading. However, the Matthew-17 Jesus cuts through all this relativistic contextualizing about which regime does or does not deserve what—and cuts through it in a word: "You and I, Peter, we have but one ruler, we recognize the claim of but one lord, know only one caesar as *deserving* anything of us—namely, the Lord God Almighty, our Dear Daddy *(Abba).* And *He* doesn't charge his own kids any taxes at all! As *his* children, Peter, we don't *owe* any taxes to anybody—least of all that bum Caesar. We are free!"

That Jesus is some anarchist! Revolutionary or establishment; left, right, or center; good, bad, or indifferent—name what arky you will—and Jesus says, "I belong to my Daddy. I am not bound to any arky, owe no allegiance (or anything else) to any of them, want nothing from them, recognize no claim by them, deny that they deserve anything of me. God's children are free!" In this, Jesus was way ahead of the withholders: *If* (as they would have it) tax payment is to be premised on the moral merit of the government presenting the bill, then they ought not be paying any taxes to anybody. How disobedient to Jesus to be paying taxes where he clearly decrees that they are *not* deserved—in effect to be *denying* that we children are indeed free.

What this means, of course, is that when, in his very next sentence, Jesus says that, nevertheless, he and Peter are going to pay the tax, he will be making payment for reasons entirely extraneous to the recognition of any arky, honoring its power, admitting its claim, affirming its rights, acknowledging its merit. Pay his taxes he will; but he is not in any sense legitimizing the arkys and their behavior in the process. Neither is he abrogating his freedom. He pays the tax not because he *has* to but because he *wants* to—for reasons that have to do entirely with his relationship to *God* and not the arkys.

What seems the case with all three tax passages is most clear and apparent in this one from Matthew 17. The argument is *dialectical* in nature—that is, it operates in the tension between two different ideas, neither of which dare be ignored, even though neither will neatly correlate with the other. Thus dialectical thinking is directly counter to any simplistic moralism in which the difference between right and wrong is as obvious as black and white. But catch the movement of Matthew 17:

STEP ONE (Yes, he pays): "Does the Master pay the tax?" To which Peter responds with an unequivocal, "He does!" But that can't be the whole truth. Something more just has to be said; things simply are not that quick and easy! Peter's answer creates more of an ethical dilemma than it resolves.

STEP TWO (No, he doesn't): So Jesus comes on to argue that, actually, he does NOT *pay* the tax (in the sense of recognizing himself as under obligation to the assessing party—which is what "pay" normally is taken to mean). No, given the essential illegitimacy of each and every caesar, Christians are under no constraint and, in effect, never owe and thus never *pay* a Caesar anything. The children are free!

STEP THREE (Caesar gets his money; but Jesus is guilty neither of *paying* it nor of *withholding* it): Now Jesus says to Peter: "That we are *free* means we are free to let Caesar take his coin without it representing any 'paying' of him. We are free to love our enemy and practice what Barth called the 'not-doing' of NOT being angry, NOT assaulting, NOT demolishing, NOT causing offense. Be free then, Peter, to let the man have his tax money—without your being made feel guilty by those who accuse you of collaboration with evil. Be free to 'resist not one who is evil,' knowing that that is the very way of God."

This argument from Matthew 17 probably should be seen as one instance of the great ethical dialectic that pervades Scripture. Its two poles can be defined as follows: POLE NEGATIVE is the fact that all the principalities and powers bent on governing human society do so in competition with, and defiance of, God. In his eyes, they are all illegitimate and under judgment (as they should be in our eyes as well). However, because *God's* judgment is always one of grace, POLE POSITIVE is the fact that, even to these rebellious powers, he responds (as we *should*) "by some strange 'not-doing' precisely where men feel themselves most powerfully called to action" (to use Barth's wording again).

The dialectic is indeed a strange one—the *decree* of God's judgment *against* the arkys being guilt worthy of death; and the *action* of his judgment *for* the arkys being justification toward life. But, in God's grace, it works. Throughout the biblical history, God never legitimizes Israel's monarchy; yet never does he fight against it or try to revolutionize it, either. He doesn't even make it his business always to be rubbing that arky's nose in its own illegitimacy, forever asserting *his* holiness in contrast to its unholiness. No, his is the wonderful patience and love of NOT being angry, NOT assaulting, NOT demolishing, NOT causing offense.

Consequently, this one must be seen to be believed! Doing things his way, God was able to use that God-rejecting, illegitimate arky of David to produce for us the one true son of David, the one legitimate King who (in *his* way, not *ours;* in *his* time, not *ours*) will take away all necessity for arky-government with all its taxation, conscription, and what all. Hallelujah! There's gonna be a great day.

The "strange work" of God's NO always is in the service of the "proper work" of his YES. Yet whenever we humans try to evade or deny that NO in our effort to go directly to the YES, the inevitable result is the blocking-out of the YES itself.

Whether, then, in the large with this overall dialectic or in the small with Matthew 17, we come out at the same place. We dare never be guilty of legitimizing the arkys God has illegitimized; neither dare we ever be guilty of resisting the arkys (the *same* arkys) God lovingly is trying to help. So no more than Jesus will *pay* taxes (in violation of Pole Negative), no more will he *withhold* them (in violation of Pole Positive). He is careful not to cause offense against God in the first instance—and not to cause offense against the arkys in the second.

We are still talking about Matthew 17 and *why* Jesus would have us pay taxes even to governments that manifestly do not deserve them. In Mark 12, the stated reason was "Let Caesar have his coin so he will get off your back and leave you alone to be giving to God all that belongs to him." In Romans 13, it was "Let Caesar have his coin so that you won't be drawn into the disobedience of failing to love him." Now, in Matthew 17, it is "Let Caesar have his coin so as not to be guilty of causing 'offense.' "

That's a funny one. Who is this Jesus who can tell *us* not to cause offense (thirteen times in seven different books of the New Testament such wording is found) when much more frequently the scriptural word "offense" is used to report the offense he himself causes—to the point that both Romans and 1 Peter name him as "the Rock of Offense"? Scripture must have in mind two different sorts of "offense," and I think the concept of Christian Anarchy can help us sort them out.

Our frame of reference will be this: CHRISTIAN TAX PAYMENT (by which we intend an allowing of Caesar to take his taxes—although doing that as a free action which in no way grants legitimacy to his claims) is the model of all the offense-causing actions of Jesus. Such payment is an entirely *theological* and *anarchical* action. It is theological in that it is purposed totally as obedience to *God,* having only him in view and nothing or no one else. Conversely, it is anarchical in its total disregard of the arkys. The action has no intention that relates to them. If they happen to be there and become offended at what Jesus does, that's their business. It was never any part of his purpose to get them offended. He had absolutely nothing in mind except to obey God.

CHRISTIAN TAX WITHHOLDING, on the other hand, is an entirely *political* and *arky-faith* action. It is political in that, without reference to any particular difference the presence of God makes, it would use offense as a tactic for influencing events within the public sphere of human possibility and probability. It is of arky faith in that it is a good-arky action directed specifically against the bad arkys in the confidence that they can be powered into improvement. The "offense," now, is deliberate and desired—is seen as the very means for achieving political gain.

Notice, then, an interesting asymmetry that is significant regarding the difference between these two ways of offense-causing. Even though, in Mark 12, Jesus winds up paying the tax (or at least recommending that it be given to Caesar), and although he is not *trying* to offend anyone, he does manage to offend every arky around, the Establishment on the right just as much as the Revolution on the left. And of course, all parties—including the disciple community itself—in one way or another became offended to the point of finally colluding in his crucifixion. Jesus' is an entirely *accidental* (he was not *trying* to offend anyone) yet entirely *universal* offensiveness. The arkys *en bloc* are offended that he gives all his attention to God and none to them—in fact, refuses to acknowledge them as even being "of God" (as each knows good and well it is). And the moral significance of the arkys' offendedness is this: it is a confirmation of Jesus' *truth* and a judgment of their *wrongness* in being offended by him. The judgment of the arky is that He came to the world and the world knew him not—choosing rather to be offended.

On the other side, the offense-causing of tax withholding is structured quite differently. In the first place, it is *deliberate* rather than accidental, a strategy designed precisely to get a bad arky offended. Secondly, it is strictly *unilateral* rather than universal in its effect. The idea is that the action be *applauded* by one's own and all other holy arkys and be offensive only to the bad ones. The offense-causing is actually a weapon (an instrument of force) in arky warfare. Yet apparently the conviction is that the moral significance is still of a kind with those offended by Jesus—i.e., the bad arky is self-condemned by its taking offense at the *truth* of the good arky.

Given, then, these two utterly different varieties of offense-causing, it should be plain that, when Jesus told Peter to pay the tax so as "not to give offense to them," it was nothing of his concern that the arkys be protected from becoming offended. They are going to be offended soon enough—and there is nothing at all wrong with that happening. Rather, Jesus is counseling Peter to remain "anarchical" and not enter the arky struggle that uses offense-causing as an instrument for establishing the righteousness of one's own arky and bringing judgment upon the opponent's. This distinction between, on the one hand, the offense-causing that must happen whenever God's truth encounters the arkys and, on the other, the offense-causing sought out by one arky to be used against another—this seems to be the key for making sense of all Scripture's "offense" talk. "For what credit is it, if when you do wrong [i.e., set out to cause offense] and are beaten for it you take it patiently? But if when you do right [i.e., show no desire to offend anyone] and suffer for it you take it patiently, you have God's approval" (1 Pet. 2:20).

Although we are continuing our argument, it is at this point we need to open out the topic from "tax-withholding" to "civil disobedience in general" (the former being simply a particular case of the latter). By "civil disobedience" I now have in mind any deliberately illegal action (the breaking of a law) done in the service of the witness and protest the Christian feels called to make against a particular evil of the state or society. In due course, we will discover that there are other forms of Christian lawbreaking that do not fall under this definition; but, for now, our concern is solely with "civil disobedience" so defined.

"Witness and protest" constitutes the operative term here. The two words are not quite synonymous but are so closely related that we will always want both in saying what needs to be said. "Protest" (even though the etymology of the word signifies "testify *for*") normally identifies the complaint *against* the perceived evil—while "witness" is the more positive affirmation of the good alternative being proposed. In itself, of course, the action of disobedience inevitably communicates more of protest than of witness—though even

here, there has to be some verbal, cognitive accompaniment if ob-
servers are to have any knowledge of *what* is being protested. Thus,
when we find a sidewalk blocked with angry bodies, we can conclude
that a protest is going on. Yet no real protest or witness is taking
place until someone, somehow, *tells* us what it's all about. In any
case, "witness" and "protest" are so closely related in "civil disobedience" that we ought not speak of either without thinking of both.

Let us proceed, then, to analyze and explore "political offense-
causing" (civil disobedience)—particularly when that is used as a
means of Christian social witness and protest. What is its economy?
What is it meant to accomplish? What is its moral significance and
effectiveness?

Would it be correct to say that the goal of Christian social
witness and protest is "to force people to face up to the truth about
themselves in the hope they will repent and change their ways"?
Let's use that as our talking point—although a stricter wording
would have it stated: "to force supporters of a particular arky [say,
"peace through nuclear strength"] to face up to the evil of that arky
and so repent and change their ways [to those of the arkys of disarmament, nuclear freeze, or whatever]." Is that a fair enough statement of the matter?

Let us postpone for a bit our consideration of the phrase "*force*
people to face up to the truth" and for now have it read "*present* to
people the truth." Clearly, ahead of our witness and protest's "force-
fulness and compellingness," the top priority is that its *content* be
"of the truth." And if it is indeed "of the truth," the witness and
protest should concentrate upon presenting that truth so as to be
as clear, reasoned, and intellectually convincing as possible. "Persuasion" is the goal of any true witness and protest. And for the presentation of persuasive content, the best media, I suggest, are those
that allow room for much information, full exposition, and extended
argument. Thus, the best sort of witness and protest will take the
forms of informal conversation, formal discussion, phone calls, letters, letters-to-the-editor, articles, pamphlets, speeches, sermons,
books, films—whatever is most appropriate to "thoughtful content."
If our content is "the truth" (which we ought never simply take for
granted, just because it is "ours"), and if our target-audience does
truly become offended *over that content,* then that offendedness fairly
may be taken as a judgment against those who heard the truth and
rejected it.

But what do you do when, even if your audience is offended,

it fails to convert? This is the hard one. I propose that the only thing to do is to admit you do not yet have the votes and (hardest of all) admit that, even when you know for a certainty that what the voters are doing is bad wrong, it still is right that the majority rule. If the national majority of this country (i.e., majorities in the citizenry, legislature, and administration) feel that increased defense expenditure is what is needed, then—hard as it is to agree—that is what *ought* to happen. Undoubtedly (undoubtedly?) we would be better off if (say) the board and staff of the National Council of Churches were to take over and run things in their Christian wisdom—yet it would be bad wrong for that gang (or any other communion of the saints) to take office against the will of the majority. No matter how frustrated they may be at having their truth rejected, Christians dare never pursue their political objectives by trying to subvert or bypass the democratic process. Obviously, that process is in no way infallible—but anything else is worse. Or, as Barth put it, "The acknowledged shortcomings of democracy are not improved by its abolition."

No, "persuasion" is the only power truth has, the only power consonant with it. So if persuasion isn't working, there is no alternative but to go on being persuasive—there is nothing else to do. (It is at this point, by the way, where it is most helpful to have a faith that God is the ruler yet, that it is the Father's good pleasure to *give* us the kingdom. Then we can know that the salvation of the world, the triumph of right, doesn't hinge upon our persuasiveness in any case.)

We have proposed what *should* happen when our best efforts at rational persuasion fail to win the votes; but what *does* regularly happen at that point? Well, particularly if we are convinced that it is only the truth of *our* witness and protest that stands between the world's life and its nuclear death, then we have real trouble accepting that there is nothing to do but keep on being rationally persuasive until, if and when, we *might* possibly win the vote. There may not even be enough time for that. We find it morally unthinkable to stand powerlessly by and watch evil take its course. We *have* to try something that might work.

The most common move at this point is to try to strengthen our witness and protest *by turning up its volume.* As we move from rational persuasion into anger, stridency, accusation, denunciation, abusive language, what Ellul called "dramatization," propaganda, demand, placard (I consider it manifestly impossible to get a persuasive argument about anything into a five-word slogan), demonstration—whatever lies outside "speaking the truth in love"—any and all of this is what I mean by "turning up the volume."

This brings us back to our earlier phrase, "*forcing* people to face the truth about themselves." "Rational persuasion," of course, does not come under that head, in that it is always careful of—even protective of—the opponent's right to disagree and not change his mind until he freely chooses to do so. It could be argued that a certain "forcing of people to face the truth" is the prerogative of God, Christ, and those prophets who have been licensed to use the phrase, "thus says the Lord." But I have grave doubts whether Scripture ever suggests that any Christian body has the moral authority to *force* people to face up to what *we* take to be the truth—or to make "thus say we" the equivalent of "thus says the Lord." *Our* "truth"—particularly our political counsel—dare never be authoritarianly forced upon people but always tentatively advanced ("This is what seems right to us in the situation, though we *could* be wrong").

Notice that "turning up the volume" does not in any way serve the *content* of our Christian witness and protest. The chances of that content being right and true are maximized at the stage of "rational persuasion," where the emphasis is upon thought and dialogue. Making the witness and protest "loud" only makes it the more difficult to hear, sort out, and think through.

Neither does turning up the volume serve the interests of the *persuasiveness* of our witness and protest. Getting loud marks an effort to overpower the hearer, not persuade him. And the world has every right to tell us, "I'm not going to listen to you until you stop screaming." "For the anger of man [or even his righteous indignation] does not work the righteousness of God" (James 1:20).

Why, then, this turning up of the volume? What purpose of Christian witness and protest does it serve? The answer is "offense-causing." It irritates people. Causing offense is one of the most effective ways of getting attention, of goading a bad arky into making some response. And, as already noted, we take a bad arky's becoming offended as an indication of its refusal to face the truth about itself and thus as a judgment upon its wrongness.

The problem with this answer, of course, is that the offense caused by turning up the volume does not call attention to the truth content of the witness and protest but to the offensive behavior of the witness-protester. The persuasive content of the witness and protest has been completely drowned out by the noise of the behavior and so is no longer even a factor. And if the issue is now the

offensive behavior of the witness-protester, then the bad arky's offendedness is not a moral judgment against *the arky* but against the
witness-protester. "For what credit is it, if when you do wrong
[deliberately set out to offend someone] and are beaten for it you
take it patiently? But when you do right [make a Christian witness
and protest by speaking the truth in love] and suffer for it you take
it patiently, you have God's approval" (1 Pet. 2:20, again).

With this we come to the high end of the volume control,
namely, the making of one's Christian witness and protest through
the vehicle of "civil disobedience"—"illegal activity," "a deliberate
breaking of the law," or whatever. Questions about the Christian
economy of civil disobedience have puzzled me for a long time:
What is the aspect of illegality supposed to add to Christian witness
and protest? Why is it assumed that one's witness and protest is
truer and more Christianly faithful for including illegality? What is
it about illegality that presumably makes the witness and protest
more effective? The only answers I can find have to do with offense-
causing.

I have been particularly puzzled about this move into lawbreaking upon realizing that, in almost every case, the law that is
actually broken is an innocent one which all parties would agree is
perfectly just and which no one could claim reasons of conscience
for violating. The peace movement's tax resisters are not questioning
the state's right to legislate and collect an income tax. What they are
protesting is *the use* to which a great deal of that money is put—
regarding which, obviously, the IRS carries no responsibility or influence at all. Actually, the quarrel is not with any "law" (unless it
be that of majority rule) but with the mind of Congress, the Administration, and ultimately the civil majority of the nation as a whole.
Yet the lawbreaking and the witness and protest are lodged with an
agency that isn't even in that line of command.

Similarly, of course, the justice of the law against breaking and
entering is not what is being challenged by those who invade draft
offices; or the law against trespassing or obstructing traffic or blocking access to a place of business by those whose demonstrations
make them guilty of such infringements. The law that is broken has
nothing to do with the issue being contended—nor does the breaking of *that* law have any bearing on the truth or falsehood of the
witness and protest that supposedly is being made. What, possibly,
could be the end and goal of such action except being offensive for
the sake of causing offense?

And let's look for a moment at the why and wherefore of the offendedness that comes in response to civil disobedience. Our democratic process does include the rule that the majority shall call the shots—yet this is not its only rule. Along with it goes the rule that, before the vote (and for that matter, *after* the vote, in preparation for the next one) anybody, no matter what the cause he finds important, shall be given every opportunity to get his witness and protest heard and his hearers rationally persuaded. "Libel" and "the fomenting of armed rebellion" may be the only limits. Perhaps no other nation in history has done better at this freedom of expression, of dissent—at giving a hearing to every possible point of view, at making the media and all levels of government accessible to the citizens and their various opinions. Neither the Christian peace movement nor any other cause-group can complain that it has been denied the opportunity of exercising its witness and protest to win whatever voters it can persuade.

Yet, within this freedom, there is a limit set by our social contract, a gentleman's agreement if you will: "I agree to exercise *my* witness and protest within these bounds and restrain myself from going further, if *you* will agree to do the same." In the present case, "these bounds" is the understanding that illegal activity shall not be used as a means of amplifying one's witness and protest. And, I contend, the essential offendedness that meets *any* exercise of civil disobedience (whether the *content* be good, bad, or indifferent) is: "No fair! You are claiming for your witness and protest a special privilege which we would never think to use in pursuit of our own political objectives. Why, if we were to grant the legitimacy of civil disobedience to every witness and protest that thinks itself important, lawbreaking would become the order of the day and our whole democratic society fall apart. And for sure, we aren't about to grant you exemption on the grounds that your witness and protest is *Christian*."

It is as if, during a convention debate, with delegates lined up at a mike awaiting their turns to speak, some guy were to come barging in to take the floor with the excuse, "But what I have to say is *important*. I will be speaking the Christian truth—not playing around with trivialities like you jackasses." You think that might not result in a bit of offendedness? It was this fellow's deliberate strategy to break the law of "wait your turn" in order to get special attention for *his* witness and protest. How different is that from grabbing the P.A. system ("public address system," recall) of civil disobedience out of the conviction that my pet cause is so important that the rules of fair play can be suspended?

If this is not the rationale that legitimates Christian civil disobedience, what rationale does? The suggestion that, within our democratic tradition, civil disobedience is an honored means of doing politics is indefensible. In that case, is the name of the game now to be "Grab the Mike Free-for-All"? Who has the privilege of taking over the microphone and who not?

I read the newspaper account of a Quaker lady who said that she had tried writing to government officials and doing everything she could think of in the way of a peace testimony—but, because nobody had listened to her, she was now ready to move to the civil disobedience of tax-withholding (as though the failure of other people to accept her truth somehow justified her recourse to questionable methods). I don't think she quite understands the democratic process. She *is*, of course, guaranteed the right freely to make her witness and protest—which right she had freely exercised. Yet nowhere was it ever guaranteed her that, because she knows her witness and protest to be true, other people (and the government as a whole) are under obligation to agree with her. There had been a fair vote, and her side lost. She is guaranteed only the right to go out again and win whatever votes she can for the next round.

Neither in the Bible, in the Constitution, nor anywhere else do I find the rule that, just because a team knows itself to be "the best" and yet is losing the ballgame, it has the right to ignore the regulations and resort to unfair tactics—simply to ensure the triumph of the good, the true, and the beautiful. The offendedness with which civil disobedience invariably is met would seem to be wholly justified—and without implying anything one way or another about the moral status of those who became offended.

Granted, the evil arky of government (Congress, Administration, and public majority) is very good at simply ignoring any minority witness and protest with which it happens to disagree. Yet, like it or not, that is its democratic right. I suppose legislators and administrators—and perhaps even the populace—have some obligation to read the letters and listen to the speeches of the peace people (particularly if those be respectfully addressed); but they are under no obligation to agree with them.

Granted, too, an act of civil disobedience can often serve as "a punch in the nose" to get the arky offended enough to give the witness-protester some attention. Yet consider that the punch in the nose, the act of lawbreaking in itself, carries no *content* of its own, sends no message of rational persuasion. No, it is only after the brute has come awake that the witness-protester has opportunity—in the courtroom or to the press—to explain the message of peace, goodwill to men the dastardly poke in the nose was meant to communicate. "It was an act of love—for their own good, to force people to face up to the truth about themselves—you must understand."

However, through his chosen tactic, the witness-protester has not created the best possible climate for the gentle persuasions of reason and love but actually the very worst. It isn't easy to get the ear of a brute you've just given a throbbing nose. For some reason, he tends to see the figure before him as a cheat and a rascal rather than hear him as the messenger of peace he actually is. The situation has degenerated into a political brawl with any and all moral significances totally confused.

There is now absolutely no way of sorting out how much of the brute's offendedness is actually the responsibility of the witness-protester, the brute's justified reaction to the offensively intended action of subverting fair play and the democratic process—and how much is the truly judgmental offendedness of the brute's refusing to face the truth. So, for example, to my mind a trial of the Berrigans is of no moral significance, no revelational/evil-exposing value at all—certainly nothing akin to the trial and crucifixion of Jesus in which the world clearly proclaimed its own judgment and condemnation. Quite the contrary, in the politics of civil disobedience I can see only two worldly arkys condemning each other. "A plague on both your houses," as Christian anarchists would inevitably say.

The above is my own honest and best effort to understand the economy of and rationale behind strategic civil disobedience. I am not happy about the results. If anyone can instruct me and propose a more accurate interpretation of the phenomenon, I would be eager to hear it. I am quick to grant that most Christian tax-resisters are conscientiously convinced they are acting solely out of the desire to be obedient to God. However, I can't see that they have much in the way of biblical or theological support for that conviction. And when they do undertake to explain and defend their action, it most often is done in the political terms of a forceful witness and protest against the arkys of evil.

My guess is that their logic runs something like this: Very correctly, they believe that Christians dare not be guilty of granting legitimacy to establishment evil. But they take this to mean, then, that anything less than joining the revolutionary opposition *does* amount to such legitimization. They can't see the third option of Christian Anarchy, because they don't really believe there is a kingdom truly "not of this world" which God is perfectly capable of establishing in his own time and in his own way. Thus, they have no alternative except to join and support those holy arkys which, to their minds, show the greatest potential as vehicles of God's kingdom. Their fundamental error, of course, is in assuming that humanity's social destiny is limited to the *politically* possible rather than being controlled by a *theology* of unlimited (even "resurrection") possibility.

Yet with this, does it not make sense that the Rock of Offense—whose kingdom is indeed "not of this world"—would say to Peter: "It is true that we do not owe either tax money or anything else to any earthly ruler. The Real Ruler's children are free. Nevertheless, Peter, let the collector have the tax he asks and don't try to withhold it. That would be a deliberate 'seeking to offend' and would only suck us into the political, offense-trading brawl of the arkys. At the same time, it would lose us all the moral, revelational, judgment-bringing power of Evil's *true* offendedness at Innocent Truth."

You don't suppose Peter was remembering that conversation when he wrote, "For what credit is it when you do wrong [by intentionally breaking tax laws or other just laws] and are beaten for it you take it patiently? But if when you do right [by going out of your way not to cause offense, even to the point of paying taxes that aren't actually owed] and suffer for it you take it patiently, you have God's approval" (1 Pet. 2:20, one last time).

NOTE: We need to be clear about the varieties of "Christian lawbreaking" that have NOT come into consideration here. The *theological* action of obeying God even when that must involve disobeying an unjust law—such as Paul's refusing to stop preaching the gospel when there was a court order for him to do so—this is entirely different from using lawbreaking as a political power-play. Such belongs on the "Jesus" side of our distinction between the two forms of offense causing. Paul's action wouldn't even have been addressed to the government, as an effort to expose and condemn it. In fact, he would have had no concern about whether the government became offended or not, he being arkycally disinterested. This sort of Christian lawbreaking ought not even be called "civil disobedience." Obedience to God is the only end in view, with any disobedience to the state being entirely accidental.

In fact, let me offer one litmus test for making the distinction: If an action of lawbreaking is done solely as obedience to God, then, plainly, whatever media exposure occurs is entirely incidental to the purpose. If, however, media exposure is *sought* and valued, the action must have a political, arky motivation that goes far beyond simple obedience to God.

Although the evidence is that Jesus disapproved the tax-withholding civil disobedience of the Zealots, it is not even cases of this sort that we have been considering above. The Zealots were oppressed and subjugated people who, except for illegal actions, had absolutely no means of witness and protest open to them ("protest" against the Empire that was crushing them or "witness" to the Messiah they expected to come save them). Their "civil disobedience" was the spontaneous cry of faith out of the midst of their pain.

As the One who himself uncomplainingly suffered the greatest injustice ever perpetrated, Jesus, of course, has the authority to judge the actions of even these desperate sufferers. I don't. I certainly am not in position to give a moral opinion regarding situations of this sort, and the foregoing has not presumed to do so. We have here been speaking *only* of those civilly disobedient Christians who already enjoy the world's greatest freedom of witness and protest but who can't be content with that. No, out of frustration in not being able to persuade the world that they're "right," they have seen fit to go further and claim for their cause the special privilege and exemption that even worldly politicians deny to themselves.

Chapter Nine

THE MODUS OPERANDI OF HISTORY
Arky and Anarchy

Corresponding to our basic concepts of "arky faith" and "Christian Anarchy" are two completely different understandings of how human history is directed and the economy by which it transpires. In particular, we will now address the matter of society's moral progress and ethical achievement: How do we expect that "the good" shall become the character of social reality?—this whether, at the moment, we are thinking of that "good" in terms of world peace, justice, social equity, the elimination of poverty, racial harmony, family life, or whatever.

In this regard, the goal of the chapter is to show how completely Scripture is committed to an anarchical rather than an arky view.

First, the very concept "arky faith" as much as dictates what its theory of history will have to be. It is the faith that social good becomes actual as those arkys we perceive to be good either displace the established arkys of evil or convert them to good. The political, human contest of good arkys against evil ones is precisely history's *modus operandi* for things being made right. Or, in Christian terminology, it is by this means that God's will shall come to be done on earth as it is in heaven.

The *vehicle* of "the good" certainly is understood as being these God-serving arkys, but let me try some other terms to describe the *economy* of that good's victory. We could call it *gradualism*. That is (in the Christian version, now), God, through his word, tells us what goal he has in mind for us and sets us to the organizational, arky task of *gradually* learning, practicing, promoting, and enforcing the ways of (for example) "peace" until, in time, peacefulness becomes the order of the day. The gradualism, of course, is that of moral nurture

and growth, our becoming more and more adept until we finally
achieve what God has in mind for us. If we were to express the idea
with a chart, it would be a line starting at a low point of morality
and then—likely with some ups and downs, losses as well as gains—
gradually rising toward the goal of high-level morality.

The process could as well be termed "progress" as "gradualism." (I do not necessarily have in mind doctrines of automatic or
inevitable progress.) The idea is still that of making incremental
gains until the goal is attained. The principle, again, might be identified as "continuance"—since, rather than that of any sort of radical
disjuncture ("social revolution" not even being radical enough for
what we have in mind), the concept is one of unbroken passage
from starting point to end goal. Finally, the term "triumphalism"
would be appropriate—indicating the upward movement of good
arkys winning out over the bad ones (the powers of peace over the
powers of war, for example).

Now, because, in the world (i.e., in secular society), it is hard
to conceive what means of moral accomplishment there could be
other than this gradualistic triumph of good over evil, I think most
Christians have simply taken for granted that this must be the understanding of Scripture as well.

Our natural tendency is to start from the assumption that "God
has no hands but our hands to do his work today." Accordingly, we
believe that, if God's will is to be done on earth, it will have to be
done in the way we go about seeing that our own wills get done
there. So we proceed to read and use our Bibles as manuals of arky
triumph through moral progress—never once noticing that Scripture isn't with us in any of these assumptions. It understands the
modus operandi of history in completely different terms. I hope the
following study comes as something of a shock to you—as it did to
me.

The very term "arky faith"—we have seen—as much as *says*
that progressive triumph in the arky struggle is its means of moral
accomplishment. The term "Christian Anarchy" is different in that
the term itself gives no hint as to what its positive way and method
will be. The term is accurate *negatively,* however, in telling us that
Christian *anarchy* will make no use of the arkys, will not so much
as recognize their presence, will accordingly be "unarkycal."

Also, here as previously, Christian Anarchy is going to go
entirely with the Arky of God and with the Jesus Christ who—
Colossians 1:18 tells us—is THE ARKY. And of course, it is precisely

because Jesus is The Arky that Christians must be anarchistic toward whatever other powers claim arky status.

The anarchical principle now to be expounded as the theme of Scripture we will identify as *death and resurrection*. Our term could as well be *grace,* in that resurrection, being nothing that humans can either work or merit for themselves, can come only from God and that never as anything other than a gift of his grace. In this regard, arky faith clearly is a doctrine of human *works.* It can, I suppose, evade the accusation of works-righteousness by claiming the grace of God to be that which elects and hallows our arkys and gives them the victory. But arky faith certainly never can rate as a "doctrine of grace" in the way Christian Anarchy does.

As the theme statement for our study of death and resurrection, we turn (again) to 1 Corinthians 15:22: "As in Adam all die, so also in Christ shall all be made alive."

When Paul speaks of our being "in Adam," he rather clearly intends "Adam" to be symbolic of the universal human tendency to want to dispense with God and his authority and determine the course of life and history for ourselves. We do this by depending solely upon our own apple-wisdom from the fruit of the tree of the knowledge of good and evil, convinced that that makes us morally competent (no question but that we *know* what is good and what is evil) and qualifies us to engineer the triumph of the good.

Yet the apostle states flatly that the Adamic principle never can be expected to produce growth, maturity, and moral development but only deterioration and death. Our "being made alive," then (or what we have been calling humanity's achievement of moral probity), Paul tells us can come about only through that gracious intervention of God which, because of our being "in Christ," *resurrects* us into "newness of life" right along with Christ himself.

Thus, the graph of "death and resurrection" will be one entirely different from the continuous and gradual ascent of arky triumph. Now the line on the chart will mark a deterioration and fall to the low point of Good Friday. It was there humanity died morally when our vaunted apple-knowledge had us so confused as to wind up *murdering* the very Arky (the beginning, the primal source) of All Good, the Incarnation of God's Grace, the One who was to have been our "Peace." It was in that death, Paul tells us, that we ourselves died, were co-crucified with Christ. Clearly, his thought is that the cross marks the spot where, in Adam, *all* died. From that point, it is not through any sort of continuity or gradualism but as the completely radical disjuncture of an Easter reversal that God intervenes to suddenly jump the line up to the ultimate level of all being made alive.

Keep this graph before your eyes, for it is now our purpose to show that this death-and-resurrection pattern does by no means either begin or end simply with Jesus' Good-Friday-to-Easter experience. That, of course, is the high point of the development. But the pattern itself dominates the Bible from beginning to end. In a quick run-through, we will now spot seventeen different variations on the theme—with the hope that the whole message of Scripture will consequently take on this anarchic coloring.

1. No sooner are we off the blocks than we encounter our first instance—in the third chapter of Genesis. Adam decides he can handle life on his own and wants the fruit of the tree he thinks will enable him to do it. God tells him that if he eats the fruit he will die. Adam eats it and promptly dies (it didn't take long for that line to hit bottom). His death in relation to God is signified by his effort to hide from God. His death in relation to himself is signified by the burning shame over his own nakedness. His death in relation to others is signified by the fact that the beloved wife, whom (just thirteen verses earlier) he had addressed as "bone of my bones," is now referred to as "that blankety-blank you stuck me with, she did it." His death in relation to his world is signified by his being kicked out of Eden. End of story. Well, yes, it would be—except for the fact that there is a little resurrection text tucked in there, verse 21: "And the Lord God made for Adam and his wife garments of skins and clothed them." He picked up the dead and provided them what they needed in order to be made alive again. The story can and does go on, but the graph is plainly that of God's gracious resurrecting of the dead.

2. In Genesis 7, there is a flood that drowns the human race in its own sinfulness. As verse 23 has it, "Only Noah was left, and those that were with him in the ark." End of story. But no, the first verse of the next chapter reads, "But God remembered Noah and all the beasts and all the cattle that were with him in the ark." I once heard a sermon in which the preacher argued that the point of the Noah story is that the human race always comes through. Baloney! The point of the Noah story is that God always remembers. The only hope for any of us who are either drowned by or cast away upon the flood of our sins is that God might remember us as he did Noah. The pattern is death and resurrection.

3. In Genesis 22, the command that Abraham should sacrifice his son Isaac spells the end not only of that one individual but of the entire promise regarding Abraham's descendants. End of story. But suddenly God intervenes to save the situation. And "Abraham called the name of the place, *The Lord Will Provide*." He distinctly did not call it, *We Can Make It*. The pattern is that of death and resurrection.

4. The name "Jacob" means "the Supplanter." As long as Jacob insisted upon living up to his name, his graph was a downward skid that came to its low point when he was forced to agonize over what would happen when he faced the brother he had so badly cheated. It is at that Gethsemane, then, in wrestling with God, that, in effect, "Jacob the Supplanter" had to die in order that the new man "Israel" (the one who strives with God until God's will is done) might be made alive. This is a very powerful picture of death and resurrection.

5. The story of Joseph graphs as a downward track from being rejected brother to being sold into slavery to being carried away into Egypt to being jailed as a slave in far-off Egypt. It is only at this low point that God intervenes to give Joseph the dream interpretation that will suddenly spring him into being made alive as a ruler in Egypt and savior of his own people. The pattern is not that of gradual human betterment but of death and resurrection.

6. In 2 Samuel 12, King David sins with Bathsheba. In response to Nathan's hooded parable, David's own judgment is "As the Lord lives, the man who has done this deserves to die." To which Nathan comes back, "You are the man." And this would be the end of the story—except for the fact that verse 13 reads, "The Lord has put away your sin; you shall not die." David's is the way to death—until God reverses it with his gracious resurrection.

7. The Assyrian invaders are ready to destroy Jerusalem, and in Isaiah 10:33–11:1 the prophet describes how the Lord will come in judgment to level that whole forest (Assyrian and Israelite trees alike). End of story . . . until, in 11:1, "there shall come forth a shoot from the stump of Jesse"—of course, the tree of the Messiah in whom eventually (as Paul has it) *all* will be made alive. Here, perhaps for the first time, we have death and resurrection as the social pattern of world history rather than just isolated instances concerning individuals.

8. Deutero-Isaiah, then, in the great fifty-third chapter of the book, portrays the Suffering Servant of Yahweh who gives his life for the many, then to find himself restored and vindicated, even out

of death itself. Here—perhaps for the first time—we encounter death as the voluntary giving of oneself, rather than committing suicide through one's own sin. Yet the pattern is still very much that of death and resurrection. The servant does not save himself, even by his perfect love and obedience; he is resurrected by God.

9. In his thirty-seventh chapter, Ezekiel has a spectacular picture of broad-scale death and resurrection (that of an entire nation) in his vision of the valley filled with dry bones. What is so very apparent is that dry bones have absolutely no potential for making themselves alive again. Only a God of wonderful power and grace has any chance of bringing off this one.

10. As we come into the New Testament, we find our pattern being presented in some quite subtle but very relevant ways. Mark 8:34-35 reads: "If any man would come after me, let him deny himself and take up his cross and follow me. For whoever would save his life will lose it; and whoever loses his life for my sake and the gospel's will save it."

Jesus' "whoever would save his life" probably has reference to human moral triumphalism—and he says that the method won't work. On the other hand, the voluntary losing of one's life only to find it saved just has to imply the involvement of something on the order of a resurrection. How, apart from a resurrection, can losing one's life be made to produce a saving of it? Here—perhaps for the first time—death and resurrection is presented as the deliberate principle and model for Christian ethics, for the whole of Christian behavior and action.

11. This brings us to the Gospel accounts of Jesus' own Good Friday crucifixion and Easter Sunday resurrection. It is significant that Mark devotes nearly half his Gospel just to this event and the Passion Week that forms its context. This death and resurrection is, of course, the paradigm to which all earlier variations point and from which all the following variations proceed. Here lies the pivot of our whole thesis and study.

12. Paul uses *baptism* as the connector for making Jesus' own death and resurrection the model and motive of our own. In Romans 6, he says:

> Have you forgotten that when we were baptized into union with Christ Jesus we were baptized into his death? By baptism we were buried with him, and lay dead, in order that, as Christ was raised from the dead in the splendour of the Father, so also we might set our feet upon the new path of life. For if

we have become incorporate with him in a death like his, we shall also be one with him in a resurrection like his. . . . For in dying as he died, he died to sin, once for all, and in living as he lives, he lives to God. In the same way you must regard yourselves as dead to sin and alive to God, in union with Christ Jesus. (vv. 3-5, 10-11)

Think about it. In choosing to be baptized into union with Christ Jesus, you renounced any and all faith in gradualistic triumphalism and signed into the pattern of death and resurrection.

13. In Ephesians 2, Paul brings the pattern over from our personal (baptismal) experience and into the experience of society at large. He relates death and resurrection to the broad-scale social accomplishment of the reconciliation of Jews and Gentiles into the one body of Christ. Given the depth of that animosity, the reconciliation marks a feat of "revolutionary social change" such as arky methods simply cannot touch.

Paul makes it clear that this was not a case of some dedicated Christians taking courses in conflict resolution and then putting their skills to work in negotiating a settlement. Essentially it was the gracious work of the God who "loved us with so much love that he was generous with his mercy . . . bringing us to life with Christ . . . raising us up with him" (vv. 4-6). God did it, but he did it through the Christ who himself *is* our peace (v. 14). For in his own person he killed the hostility (v. 16) by restoring peace through the cross (vv. 15-16). Thus, you who were once far off have been brought near through the shedding of Christ's blood (v. 13) so as to create out of the two a single new humanity in himself, thereby making peace (v. 15).

Here is death and resurrection as God's way even to social reconciliation, equity, justice, and peace.

14. A great advantage of the book of Revelation (and what makes it most appropriate as the concluding book of the Bible) is that it portrays the death-and-resurrection pattern in a larger frame of reference than we have seen anywhere else. It is presented now as the pattern of universal history, the procedure through which the kingdom of the world is to become the kingdom of our Lord and of his Christ, the means by which the whole of creation is to find its destiny in the kingdom of God.

In Revelation 12:10-11, John describes this victory and tells how it is won: "This [the time of Jesus' resurrection] is the hour of victory for our God, the hour of his sovereignty and power, when his Christ comes to his rightful rule! For the accuser of our brothers is overthrown, who day and night accused them before our God. By the sacrifice of the Lamb they have conquered him, and by the testimony which they uttered; for they did not hold their lives too dear to lay them down."

We are talking now, of course, of God's final victory in which Satan himself is conquered and all evil—individual, social, natural, supernatural, and cosmic—is forever done away. Here is achieved humanity's ultimate state of justice, peace, and righteousness. How is it accomplished? Not by our gradual growth in morality, obviously. It is accomplished by "the sacrifice of the Lamb," his death and resurrection. Nevertheless, John is clear that we humans have our own part to play in this triumph. And what is that? We are to testify and bear witness to what the Lamb has done. And, the text specifies, that can truly happen only when it is with us as it was with Jesus, that we do not hold our lives too dear to lay them down. The pattern of our witnessing is to be that of death and resurrection, just as it was for the One to whom we witness.

15. In his eleventh chapter, the Revelator gives the pattern an application to which we should pay most careful attention. As we saw earlier in this book, it has been, perhaps, in the life of the institutional church that there has been the strongest tendency to go the way of arky power and prestige. The customary understanding of the call of the church has been that it should grow in size and influence—gradually winning the status and following through which it can "Christianize" society and lead the world in moral development.

However, Revelation 11 gives an entirely different picture. In this vision, the faithful church is portrayed in the form of two witnesses who, dressed in sackcloth (not velvet), make their humble testimony in the face of a profoundly hostile world. They are olive trees (fruit bearers) and lamps (light bringers) in the service of their Lord. Their way—far from leading to glory and acceptance—leads directly to a self-giving martyrdom, from which they are raised up to victory through an explicit resurrection by God. The way of the church through the world, John tells us, definitely is meant to be that of death and resurrection.

16. The Revelator then specifies (20:6) that a Christian's personal salvation, his hope of eternal life, lies not in any built-in immortality but in a resurrection as real and as bodily as that of Jesus himself: "This is the first resurrection. Happy, indeed, and one of God's own people is the man who shares in this first resurrection!

Upon such the second death has no claim; but they shall be priests of God and of Christ."

17. Finally, in the opening of his twenty-first chapter, John makes death and resurrection the very *modus operandi* of God's New Creation: "Then I saw a new heaven and a new earth." (He could as well have called it a *resurrected* heaven and earth, because he obviously is thinking of renewal rather than a complete junking of the old in order to start all over from scratch.) Again, "Now at last God has his dwelling among men!" A little later, "He will wipe every tear from their eyes; there shall be an end to death [and how could that happen except through *resurrection*?] and to mourning and crying and pain; for the old order has passed away!" Once more, "Behold! I am making all things new! [*resurrection* again]." And finally, "A draught from the water-springs of life [*resurrection* life, no less] will be my free gift [of *grace*] to the thirsty."

Can there be any doubt that Scripture sees the completely anarchical (arky-ignorant) grace of resurrection from the dead as being THE *modus operandi* of universal history? Is it not obvious that it puts no faith at all in the possibility that humanity's sincere arky efforts might win the day for God and for the good?

Allow me now to get my conclusion in here—before you jump to a wrong one. No more than, in a previous chapter, the emphasis upon the Christian *theology* of peace was meant to prohibit any secular *politics* of peacemaking—no more, here, is God's way of history meant to prohibit the human, arky way of moral development.

After all, for a world that has chosen not to know God—and thus cannot know, either, his gracious willingness or his total capability to resurrect whatever wants resurrecting—for this world there is no moral option at all except the one of using our poor apple-wisdom as best we can manage, sorting out what we decide is "good" and "evil," encouraging the one and discouraging the other. And, of course, it is *this* lost and needy (though scheduled to be resurrected) world the Master has sent us to be *in,* even while warning us not to be *of.*

No, the issue is not that of accepting the one mode of history and rejecting the other. The issue is—as Barth had Paul putting it regarding tax payment—that Christians need to know what they are doing when they do it. You *are* involved in the arky contest for the moral betterment of the race. But do you know *how* you got there,

why you're there, and *what* you're supposed to be doing while you
are there?

The paramount caution, surely, is that Christians remember
they are Christians and not worldlings. Worldlings, obviously, *have*
to put their faith—their mouths, their moneys, their energies, their
enthusiasms, their hopes, their dreams, their confidence, their ex-
pectations—either in the human potential for moral progress or
nowhere at all; they are left with no other option.

Christians, in their turn, must have sympathy for the world
caught in this plight and also an understanding of why it always
must be making such big claims for its preferred arkys. These are as
much in the way of *gods,* a hope of salvation, as the world can
muster. Yet, let Christians once begin falling for this bill of goods
and downplaying their Christianity (their faith in the lordship of a
gracious, resurrection-capable God)—this in the hope of better
identifying with and being of help to the world God so loves—once
start this, and they actually are betraying their assigned role, are as
doctors rushing off to comfort and cheer the patients while leaving
their vital medicines behind. Christians must love the world and be
of active service in it—yet without ever once buying the world's
understanding of itself or affirming the faith it proclaims.

So, not, of course, the totality of Christian concern and effort,
but surely the totality of faith and confidence must center, not where
worldlings center theirs, but where we have found Scripture centering, in the grace of a God of resurrection capability. If the world
is ever to be saved, it will have to be God who does it. If God's will
is ever to be done on earth as it is in heaven, it will have to be God
who sees to its being done. As Ellul put it, "Man can't do God's
will without God." If the kingdom of God is ever to be our human
reality, it will be only because it is the Father's good pleasure to *give*
us the kingdom.

The idea, of course, is common Christian doctrine. My concern is that—as modern Christians speak and write about loving the
world through political involvement, social action, moral development, *et al.*—very little of the biblical faith and a great deal of the
world's arky faith are heard. Is there not good reason to suspect that
the Christian priority about what God must do and what man can
do is being reversed?

Our study has shown Scripture fully committed to the idea
that God's gracious resurrection constitutes the one way of salvation
(for individuals, for church, for society, for the cosmos). Conse-

quently, the arky struggle for morality must be relegated to some lesser function. The world, of course, has things just the other way around: the Christian faith is now the optional factor which may (for those who feel they need such support) even steel and motivate them for the social struggle in which the salvation of the world actually lies. I am not bothered that this contradiction in faith priority exists. I am profoundly bothered to find people thinking they are being *Christian* simply in joining the world. We need, most of all, to know what under the sun we're doing.

If, however, according to the Christian understanding, the world's arky struggle toward moral betterment is *not* the way of salvation, then what (if any) positive significance and function does it have?

Regarding this question, the great need of Christians is to become what Ellul calls "realistic," seeing things as they actually are rather than as we wish they might be or as per the propaganda claims made for them. Thus, it is not simply biblical theology that refutes arky faith; an objective, unbiased view of social history refutes it as well. At this, of course, Ellul is the expert; I'm not. As we saw earlier, he is explicit that, from his expert observation and experience of a lifetime, in spite of all the highly touted messianic movements that have been on the scene, he cannot discern that society is making any significant moral progress and, least of all, that it is well on the way toward getting itself saved and set right.

Further, I understand that Ellul and other realistic historians like him consider that the entire history of the race fails to show anything like large-scale, long-term moral progress. (Technological, cultural, intellectual progress, yes; but nothing that truly could be called "moral.") The moral state of humanity seems to be pretty much of a low-level constant all the way through. Certainly, there is movement within the constant parameters. We may seem to be making progress on one front—although, at the same time, retrogressing on another. Moral gains made at one time don't last; things slide back into their former state. In short, our graph of gradual moral triumph is a dream; the historical social data don't support it.

From the viewpoint of Christian realism, then, we need to be skeptical of the continually repeated yet always excited predictions that humanity is moving into a new age, that we are on the verge of a renaissance of justice and righteousness. Such predicters have the very same track record as those predicting the second coming of Jesus—nobody's ever been right yet.

Especially, Christian realists should be leery of the messianic claims made by every newest and brightest arky to come along: "Yes, we thought the Maccabean Revolt was it—but it wasn't. We thought the Zealot Revolt was it—but it wasn't. The Christianizing of the Roman Empire—but it wasn't. The Enlightenment—but it wasn't. The Bolshevik Revolution—but it wasn't. The Student Free Speech Movement—but it wasn't. The Sexual Revolution—but it wasn't. The Viet-Cong Revolution—but it definitely wasn't. The Here's Life America campaign—but it wasn't. President Kennedy's Great Society—but it wasn't. Admittedly, we have been wrong in the past. But not this time. This is the one that will turn things around. You can take it from us that this one is the real thing. The Feminist Movement is the one that will make it. Or Liberation Theology is the one that will make it. Or whatever Harvey Cox next tabs is the one that will make it."

Christian realists need to know what is going on here. These are the confessions of faith, the glorifying of god—on the part of those who, not believing in the true God, face total despair for the world's future unless they can find something in which to hope. The common name for the action is "whistling in the dark," or what Isaiah calls "praying to a god that cannot save." Christians, of course, should feel great sympathy for people caught in such a bind—even while steering completely clear of their enthusiasm for the arkys *they* take to be inspired by the god they look to for salvation.

But if the arkys cannot save, does that mean the whole human arky struggle for moral betterment has no significance, no value at all?

By no means! Actually, it turns out that Lewis Carroll's looking-glass chessboard is an entirely accurate picture of humanity's moral universe. As the Red Queen explained to Alice, *"Here,* you see, it takes all the running you can do, to keep in the same place."

The human race is just that—a "race." Humanity is not racing toward the kingdom, certainly. It is racing to hold its place, to keep itself held together where the Father can find it when comes the time for him to give it the kingdom. And this, we should know, is a *desperate* race. I don't think most people appreciate how precarious is the status of humane existence and human morality. And I do not have in mind particularly the nuclear threat. My opinion is that there are moral threats that could be just as devastating and are even more imminent than that physical one. For what shall it profit us if we gain the whole world (by preserving its physical existence) and forfeit its moral life?

So, Christian realists don't have to accept the arky rhetoric about this or that messianic cause turning the world around and leading it into a new age—in fact, they had better not. They do, however, have a Christian calling ("As thou didst send me into the world, so I have sent them into the world"—John 17:18) to be in there among the arkys, doing whatever can be done (like holding fingers in dikes) to prevent the whole schmeer from flooding out and turning to mud. Christians need to be there. But, just as important, they need to know what they are doing while there. They are not there to join the worldlings in their arky faith but to ignore the arkys in the service of God and neighbor.

Take me, for example. I am what is known in the trade as "an educator." I have put in my time and am currently a minion in good standing of that Grand Old Arky EDUCATION—of which they don't come any more arkyish in claiming primacy for the salvation of society. In education, I am a professor, a doctor of theology, author of the world's only book on Christian Anarchy, which you likely have seen (here being the only place I can safely make that statement), and no end of other such dignities—with all the rights and privileges thereunto pertaining throughout the civilized world, as the president put it so neatly upon granting me my B.A. When it comes to EDUCATION, I am—as it might but probably ought not be put—one of the boys.

However, given to that arky though I be, I consider that I am still quite *anarchical* in my attitude thereunto pertaining. I am *in* the arky but in no way *of* it. To my mind, I have not let the world of education push me into its arky mold but have been transformed by a renewal of my mind to prove what an unacceptable worship EDUCATION is. Rather than its molding me, I have been out to make a few gaps and fissures (or to expose the gaps and fissures) in its structure. Above all, I try to view the educational endeavor *realistically*.

For instance, although both an alumnus and a longtime professor, I have never for a moment bought the propaganda line (public relations department) that La Verne is the greatest little college in the world. It is not. It is no better, and, I hope, not a whole lot worse than any number of other colleges of its sort—and neither love nor money will get me to say anything different.

I do not share Walter Rauschenbusch's turn-of-the-century social-gospel faith that education inevitably spells growth in moral
understanding and that, therefore, the establishment of the American system of universal public education would be the making of
a godly nation. I don't buy the commencement-address idea that
what this old professor has been doing all these years is influencing
young lives toward the purity and goodness he himself represents.
The greater likelihood is that the kids have corrupted me. I don't
accept the college's mission statement as earnest money. I laugh at
the thought that, out of these portals, we are sending a new generation destined to claim the world for truth and right. If that is
what education is supposed to do, why didn't it work any better for
the generation of student volunteers that went out singing *I Would
Be True; Follow the Gleam; True-Hearted, Whole-Hearted, Faithful,
and Loyal;* and *Lord, We Are Able.* If moral idealism is what makes
it, that would have been the generation. This one isn't even interested in such sentiments.

I hold no illusions. I could point out any number of students
for whom an education has done nothing—except enable them to
make more money. I could point out students who would have
better been left uneducated; their added "smarts" only make them
more dangerous. I don't claim to have turned any lives around,
made any students "better persons" than they already were on the
way to becoming on their own. Our educated world of today is in
no way morally superior to uneducated worlds of the past. It may
even be that education has created new moral problems of its own.

Yet in no way do I regret having given my life and energies to
education. My hope is that things may not be quite as bad as they
would be if I had not been there with my finger in the dike (even
if, like as not, it turns out to have been the wrong dike, the dry dike,
anyhow). But that's all right. I'm convinced I've been where God
wanted me. I have no problem in confessing myself the unworthiest
of servants, because neither my self-worth, my salvation, nor my
hope of the world's salvation have ever been attached to arky performance. I have run the good race—not the race to get anywhere
but only to keep things in place and not lose any more ground than
we have to, which is as much as can ever be expected from the arkys.
And if this assessment is *realistic,* I am much happier with it than
with what is bound to be the extravagant unreality of my retirement
dinner.

Something of this sort, I contend, describes the Christian's

role among the arkys—an important role, yet one completely anarchical and not at all according to the arky's own terms. So *I* have
been in education; but my *faith* has never been in EDUCATION.
It doesn't have to be, because I've already got a better God than
that. I have one who *can* save. So, regardless of what my arky service
comes to, I am with my anarchist brother, Ellul: "I may have had
opportunity at times to bear witness to Jesus Christ. Perhaps through
my words or my writing, someone met this savior, the only one, the
unique one, beside whom all human projects are childishness; then,
if this has happened, I will be fulfilled, and for that, glory to God
alone."

Chapter Ten

ON WAYS MORE THAN ONE OF SKINNING CATS OR ACCOMPLISHING OTHER GOOD ENDS

I think I understand why so many Christians find some sort of arky faith to be absolutely essential to their creed. The logic, heard on every side, runs thus: If the good people (we Christians, of course) don't organize (as holy power blocs) to bestow (read: "impose") our goodness upon the world, no improvement will ever take place and society will simply continue its slide into hell. The argument assumes there is only one possible way social good can happen.

It may come as a surprise to hear that I am quick to agree that this is the correct and, indeed, inevitable conclusion—if we are supposing that *political reality* (i.e., that of human probabilities and possibilities) is the only reality there is; that God has no hands but our hands; that ours is not a God who takes it upon himself to intervene in humanity's public affairs. If God is left out (or edged out) of the picture, then it undoubtedly is correct that our one and only hope of social salvation is for good people with their messianic arkys to struggle against the forces of evil in order to install a new and just regime.

If this is indeed our only hope, we ought at least to be honest enough to recognize just how forlorn a hope it is. As we have seen already, from a theological-biblical perspective Karl Barth has shown how presumptuous and wrongheaded it is for any crowd of human beings to claim they have such mastery of, and such facility with, "the good" that they can power it into place as the society of peace and justice.

Also, we have seen that the idea of a just revolution of the saints is by no means an invention of the late twentieth century but has been tried time and time and time again. And yet, whether such revolution succeeds or fails, more often than not the social gain is zilch—or less! The direct-action method of messianic arkys is hardly recommended by its track record.

Finally, we have heard the personal testimony of Jacques El-lul—a saint as qualified as any, both as a biblical theologian on the one hand and a socio-political scientist on the other—who labored for years in different attempts at the Christian transformation of society and came away with the opinion that the method is unrealistic and unworkable.

Nevertheless, if this be the only possible way of getting the cat skinned, we will have to go with it—no matter what. Yet honesty would compel us to admit that our hope, now, is little better than no hope at all.

However, for at least the last couple of chapters, I have been trying to bust us out of this closed, constricted, no-option system that says, "There is only one way; if it's going to be done, we are the ones who will have to do it out of our own resources." Hear then the gospel, the liberating word of God: "There *is* more than one way to skin a cat" (I'm certain it's in there somewhere; my concordance must be faulty).

Politics is not the truth, the whole truth, and nothing but the truth. There is also *theology* that can speak of actual, socio-political differences made by the presence of God. There is a *modus operandi* of history different from that of the human-bound method of gradual increments toward moral triumph—that, of course, being resurrection made possible by the grace and power of one who is Wholly-Other-than-Human.

In this chapter, I want to describe how another way can and did work in a matter of radical, broad-scale, structural social change usually thought of as being the special province of revolution and the class struggle.

We already have heard but need again to be reminded that Christians can do and have done a great deal of good in the way of social service and action—and that without at all forming political power blocs, without taking an adversarial stance toward any government or social institution, without presuming to condemn or fight anybody. Modern liberationists are wrong in sneering at these efforts as being insignificant compared to their big push to turn the world right-side-up.

In fact, although the results are neither quick nor spectacular, it may be that social service has a better record in effecting even structural change than has revolutionism. Not through pressure and imposition, but simply through modeling, the service presence cannot but have some ameliorative effect upon the social structures around it. Would it be correct to say that—no matter how bad off some of these nations may be at present—there is no country into which Christian missionaries and service workers have gone that is not now better off in the way of social justice than would be the case if that Christian presence had never been there? Revolutionary liberationism is *not* the only method of effecting helpful social change. There *is* more than one way. . . . However, the case study here presented speaks of a way that is a much more direct action than simply Christian modeling.

In another of my books (*Towering Babble,* pp. 169-79) I developed what I called "voluntary self-subordination" as being the uniquely Christian way—not necessarily for skinning cats but for accomplishing many other good ends. Just the *verbal* contrast between this phrase and "arky contest" is, of course, conspicuous. But as the rubric of this concept—its most fundamental and essential statement—I cited Jesus' solemn decree from Mark 8:34-35: "If any man would come after me, let him deny himself and take up his cross and follow me. For whoever would save his life will lose it; and whoever loses his life for my sake and the gospel will save it." Although we haven't time to say more here, that book develops the idea in depth and demonstrates that it does indeed characterize the whole New Testament.

Now it is my observation that a goodly number of modern Christians are willing at least to consider voluntary self-subordination as a method of operation for their personal, one-to-one relationships with other individuals. However, when it comes to political reform, radical social change, human liberation, the accomplishment of social justice, or whatever you choose to call it, they don't see the method as having relevance or applicability at all. On this level, they believe "justice" can only be spelled "political contention for equity."

In this regard, then, Jesus and the New Testament become something of an embarrassment to the liberationists. According to their view, Jesus (and the New Testament believers proceeding from him) *should* appear in the role of modern-day reformers out demanding and contesting for the just society. The trouble is they don't fit the mold and can't convincingly be made to do so.

The embarrassment, then, becomes acute with the realization

that the early church lived in a society where the terrible injustice of human slavery was common practice. Yet, rather than fighting or even protesting this evil, the church apparently condoned it—and that not only in the life of the larger society but even within its own circles. And it follows that Paul's little letter to Philemon may represent the greatest embarrassment of all. Here, circumstances as much as force the apostle into a direct confrontation with the institution of slavery—and he appears to poop out completely. He makes no move to protest the injustice of the practice, speaks not one word in condemnation of Philemon's being a slaveowner, makes not a hint of a witness to social justice and human rights.

However, I read Philemon quite differently from what the liberationists do. So I now undertake to establish this minuscule missive as the very model of social justice accomplished through distinctively Christian self-subordination. It is a picture of liberation and social change so radical that the proponents of arky justice haven't had a glimmer of what it's all about.

Philemon is a most frustrating book—a brief personal note that doesn't begin to tell us what we need to know in order to understand it. As much as we do know is this: Paul is writing to his friend Philemon regarding Philemon's slave, Onesimus. Yet, although he belongs to Philemon, Onesimus has just spent time with Paul and is now carrying the letter from Paul to his master.

Philemon lives at Colossae and is a leader in the church there. Whether there or somewhere else (the book of Acts never places Paul at Colossae), Paul had apparently converted Philemon and become his close Christian brother. There seems little doubt that Colossians—Paul's letter to the *church* at Colossae—and this note to *a private individual* in Colossae belong together. Most likely, Tychicus, one of Paul's lieutenants, delivered the letter to the church, while Onesimus delivered the note to his master (Col. 4:7-9).

At the time of his writing, Paul is in prison—although he isn't thoughtful enough to tell us where. Because the matter has something to do with the rest of the story, we are going to guess that he is in Ephesus. (Acts never has Paul in prison in Ephesus, but it does have him spending enough time in the city that an imprisonment would not be incredible. It is not like Paul to stay out of jail for two years in a row.) What makes Ephesus a good guess is that it is the major metropolitan (and Pauline) center nearest the little town of Colossae, about a hundred miles off. It is, accordingly, by far the likeliest spot for a Colossian slave to try to lose himself—as well as have a chance of coming upon Paul. Then too, it is the most likely spot from which Paul would write that he hopes soon to be released and would Philemon have a guest room ready for him (v. 22).

Onesimus, we know, is Philemon's slaveboy ("my child, whose father I have become" Paul calls him in v. 10, which could make Onesimus as young as a teen-ager). The name "Onesimus," by the way, is based on the Greek root meaning "beneficial," "of benefit," or "useful." It is a name an owner might well give to a slave in the hope of its influencing his character. Paul does word play with the name in both verses 11 and 20.

Onesimus is Philemon's slave. Yet he has just been with Paul in Ephesus rather than Philemon in Colossae. Paul opines that he has been "useless" rather than living up to his name "useful" (v. 11). And Onesimus's returning to Philemon raises questions as to how he will be received. Only this much the letter actually tells us, but it can hardly add up to anything other than "runaway." We don't know whether Onesimus knew (or knew about) Paul and so sought him out through the Ephesian church, or whether he just happened to be thrown into the same jail cell with him. In either case, he is now not only a spiritual son but even a working colleague of the apostle.

In the note Onesimus delivers, Paul is probably asking three things of Philemon: (1) At the very least, he is asking that Onesimus be received with kindness and forgiveness rather than with the treatment customary for a runaway slave—legally, anything up through torture and death. (2) Surely, he is also asking that Onesimus be released from slavery ("no longer as a slave but more than a slave, as a beloved brother"—v. 16). And (3) there are strong hints that Paul wants Onesimus released to come back and serve with Paul at Ephesus (vv. 13, 20: "I want some *benefit* (some 'Onesimus') from you").

This is as much as the epistle itself can tell us. So let me now try an interpretation.

In running away from his master, the slave Onesimus was doing precisely what modern revolutionism says he should do. He was moving to effect his own liberation—get out from under terrible oppression and claim the equity of being a freeman alongside Philemon. Although it was a slave revolt of only one person, it was an entirely praiseworthy one—a blow against gross injustice and a move toward a truly just society. This is liberation theology—and a model of what all slaves should do. So, far from feeling any sort of guilt, Onesimus should have been proud of what he had done.

Of course, I don't know how Onesimus *did* feel, but let's assume he felt good about his thrust toward freedom. Yet the evidence would indicate that, particularly after he became a Christian and began to learn from Paul, he started to have second thoughts. His way of getting liberated did not leave him as free as he had expected. Running away, he must now have sensed, left something to be desired as a freeing action. Being a runaway slave is neither as secure nor as relaxed a position as one might hope. Always to have to be looking over your shoulder to see who is coming to get you can hardly be the truest sort of freedom. And I wonder whether anyone can ever run away or lie or cheat or kill—even in the name of freedom—without feeling pangs of remorse and guilt in the process.

Further, as a Christian, Onesimus must have realized that his act of "freeing" himself had to have had a reverse effect on Philemon. Onesimus's grab for equity inevitably would have created an adversary alignment and made Philemon "the enemy," who now had been put down, cheated, robbed of a valuable possession he undoubtedly had acquired in all honesty. No, there were all sorts of things about Onesimus's new freedom which just could not be right.

So, with Paul's help (although certainly not at his *demand*), Onesimus *freely* chose another method of liberation—that of voluntary, Christian self-subordination. He decided to *go back,* to exercise his freedom by giving it up, to save his life by losing it.

Think what this action had to mean for Onesimus. Here was a runaway slave—guilty from every legal standpoint—offering to put himself at the mercy of his offended master. His only defense is a scrap of paper signed with what he hopes is the magic name, "Paul." It is hardly likely that Onesimus stood afar off and sent Tychicus in with the note, awaiting Philemon's response before deciding which way to move. Hardly. Onesimus must have himself handed that note to Philemon, putting not just his hard-won freedom but his very life into jeopardy and ready to accept whatever might result—fully convinced that, whatever did result, this was the only way to true freedom.

Consider, then, that Onesimus's original running away had not been a truly free action—it was too much motivated by self-interest, too much driven by self-serving needs and desires. It was rather his going back, his *voluntary* subordination, his willingness to lose his life for Christ's sake and the gospel—only this was free in a way no other action could be.

Onesimus's earlier running away had not been a freeing action, either. We already have imagined the side-effects that led him to want to undo that one. We can be certain, however, that his going back *did* create all sorts of freedom. We can say that even without knowing how Philemon responded—and bear in mind that we don't know. All we have is the note; Scripture gives us not one word as to how it was received. And this is how it should be. Onesimus's action was *right,* no matter what the consequences. My belief is that Onesimus would have *wanted* to go back—would have felt himself freed in going back—even if he had known ahead of time that he would be returning to slavery, torture, and execution. Yet, even at that extremity, consider the freedoms that would have ensued.

Through his act of repentance, reconciliation, restitution, and asking forgiveness, Onesimus would have freed himself from the guilt of his previous action. He would have freed his relationship to Philemon of all its animosity, ill will, and adversarial conflict. And although it does not figure into our customary calculations, don't assume that a dead slave is for that reason unfree. Because he had acted as a child of God, Onesimus had guaranteed for himself the coming revelation of what his sponsor Paul called "the glorious liberty of the children of God." What Paul wrote to the Galatians he could as well have addressed to his Philemon-bound friend: "For freedom *Christ* has set us free; stand fast therefore, and do not submit again to a yoke of slavery [slavery to what the world calls 'freedom']." Most certainly, Onesimus is included when Paul says, "For he who was called in the Lord as a slave is a freeman of the Lord." We have all sorts of arky-liberated people running around who don't begin to know the sort of freedom experienced by the Christian slaveboy who may voluntarily have gone to his death.

Because the success of voluntary self-subordination is not measured by its outward results, the story of Onesimus is right—is the very model of Christian action—even though we don't know what consequences there may have been. Yet this, of course, is not to suggest that the outcome *had* to be that of enslavement and death. Indeed, the probability is quite otherwise. Paul, apparently, was a rather good judge of character; so, if he was reading his pal Philemon at all correctly, then Onesimus likely was soon on his way back to Ephesus with Tychicus. It would take a pretty tough nut to resist the blandishments and loving arguments of Paul's most crucial effort in salesmanship. I don't think there's a chance in the world that Philemon could have held out against it. And finally—and to my mind most conclusive—is the fact that the letter survived.

Think about it: If anything had happened to Onesimus other than his being freed and sent on his way to Paul, who would have wanted to save the letter? It was saved, obviously. So who would have wanted it? Well, it belonged to Philemon, and he undoubtedly valued it. Yet my guess is that (except for his Christian inhibitions) Onesimus would have knocked him down and taken it, if Philemon had shown reluctance about giving it up. After all, to Philemon it was a nice letter from a friend; to Onesimus, however, it was his reprieve from death and charter of freedom. In any case, that note was preserved for some period of years until it could be incorporated as a one-of-a-kind entry in the New Testament.

Is that the story? Well, maybe so and maybe not. New Testament scholar John Knox is the one who ferreted out what may be its continuation. We have to go clear beyond the New Testament now, but there is more.

Fifty to sixty years after the most probable time of Paul's writing, there was, in Syria, a Bishop Ignatius who was apprehended by the Romans and escorted overland to Rome, where, eventually, he was tried and executed. Because Ignatius was a prominent figure in the church, as his party came to (or even close to) any Christian locales, the congregations sent out representatives to visit and offer him hospitality. After he arrived in Rome, then, Ignatius sent "thank you notes" to a number of the churches that had hosted him. These letters—dated about A.D. 110—have been preserved (not in the New Testament, obviously, but as some of the earliest Christian literature outside the New Testament). One of them is addressed to the church at Ephesus; therein, Ignatius waxes eloquent about the welcome he had received from the Ephesian delegation headed by their Bishop Onesimus.

Hold on! Don't go jumping to conclusions until I tell you; then we can all jump to the conclusion at once. There is nothing in the way of positive proof, and Onesimus is not a completely rare name. Yet the place and timing are right. If our slaveboy went back to help Paul in Ephesus, he could have worked his way up in the congregation and been a seventy-some-year-old bishop at the time Ignatius came through.

Moreover, in the first six paragraphs of his letter, Ignatius names Bishop Onesimus three times and refers to him eleven other times. And it is in this same section of the letter (and not elsewhere) that scholars also pick up subtle echoes of the language of Paul's letter to Philemon—including one play on the word "benefit" that is almost identical to Paul's. Apparently, Ignatius knows the Philemon letter and is teasing its language into his compliments of Bishop Onesimus. You can decide how conclusive that is in proving that Ignatius knows which Onesimus the Ephesian bishop is, but I am ready to jump. Now!

Here, we must move beyond Ignatius, but the plot continues to thicken. Scholars are pretty well convinced that the letters of Paul did not come into the New Testament one by one, from here and there. The greater likelihood is that someone became interested in Paul at an early date and made inquiries among his congregations as to whether they had any of his letters and would be willing to share copies. It would have been, then, this earlier Pauline collection that was introduced into the New Testament as a unit.

Where would such collecting most likely have taken place? Among the Pauline congregations, Ephesus is as well situated and thus as good a guess as any. And who is most likely to have been the moving spirit behind such a project? Why not Bishop Onesimus?—he has as good a reason for remembering and loving Paul as anybody (and a whole lot better reason than most). But with this suggestion, now, we get a real nice answer to one of the most troublesome questions regarding the epistle to Philemon. Within the Bible, it is a unique specimen—a brief personal note addressed to a private individual on a matter involving neither the life of a congregation nor the teaching of the faith. So why should it be in the New Testament? And how did it get there in the first place?

Without recourse to "Bishop Onesimus," I don't see that those questions are answerable. With "Bishop Onesimus," they become easy. If Onesimus is the collector of the Pauline *corpus,* he would, of course, be eager that "his" letter be part of it. Likewise, the Ephesian congregation would very much want *this* letter included, as a gesture of respect and gratitude—and a matter of record— regarding their own slaveboy bishop. The very presence of the letter within the New Testament canon may be the strongest proof that the Ephesian bishop of A.D. 110 is indeed the very same person as Philemon's slave.

Earlier—under the possibility that Onesimus actually was returned to slavery and executed—we portrayed the *minimum* of freedom, liberation, and justice that might have resulted from his going back. Now—whether or not it is the *maximum*—we have portrayed just how incredibly far God may have taken that slaveboy's Christlike decision to take up his cross and go back. And Onesimus's personal rise in equity from slave to bishop is only a starter. The Ephesian congregation seems to have received the godly leadership that not only made it a strong church but may even have spelled its survival into the second century (it is not evident that all of Paul's congregations lasted so long). Most of all, it may be that God used Onesimus's going back to give us the Pauline one-fourth of our New Testament and so preserve an understanding of the faith that has been of untold value in the life and history of the church to the present day. When God is in the picture, who's to say how "useful" one "Onesimus" can be?

But more! I am ready to say that—in a proleptic, representative way—the example of Onesimus marks the truer freeing of more slaves than all the emancipation proclamations ever proclaimed and all the class warfare ever warred. In this case God sounds the death knell of slavery (all sorts of slavery) for the whole of creation for all time. There is not the slightest doubt that the Christian church—the Onesimian church—went on to become the greatest force for freeing slaves the world has ever seen. And it strikes me that the Onesimian method of ending slavery is the only sure method of doing so. The secular way of "revolutionary arky contest" may be quicker and more spectacular, but it is also far less dependable, carrying all sorts of negative side effects. Emancipation proclamations and civil wars may create a degree of justice and eliminate some aspects of slavery. But they also create all sorts of animosities and hatreds, leave battlefields strewn with corpses, and take us out of slavery only to put us into Jim Crow.

The Onesimian approach is much the more powerful. It may take a while, but no slaveholder can forever hold out against the loving persuasions of a Paul, the loving self-sacrifice of an Onesimus, or the loving Spirit of an Almighty God. That owner actually has a much better chance of resisting political pressure and the violence of class warfare. Moreover, the Onesimian way, rather than demanding the denunciation and destruction of the moral dignity of the slaveholder, offers him a gracious way out. Onesimus was liberated without Philemon's having to be demeaned in the process. Best of all, of course, to go Onesimian leaves everyone involved—

slave, owner, and apostle—as brothers in Christ. The side effects are all positive, without a trace of contention's negativity.

Yet the most essential distinction, I suggest, is this: The political struggle for liberation is posited wholly on human wisdom, idealism, and moral ability. It thinks there is only one way. . . . It operates in a closed system that neither seeks nor expects anything more than its human methodology can be calculated to achieve—though seldom do the final results come to even that much. Human beings (and especially well-intentioned doers of good) are noted for overestimating the power of their own piety.

With Onesimus, things are quite otherwise. Because his was a theological action taken at the behest of *God*, in the service of *God*, through the Spirit of *God*, with the enablement of *God*, and to the glory of *God*—this action invited God in and urged him to make of it what he would. The results? Completely incalculable—even to the preserving of the Pauline gospel for the ages. There is absolutely no telling how much good, how much social change, how much freeing of slaves, how much gospel, how much kingdom, might follow from an Onesimian laying down of one's life for God.

Finally, then, consider how totally Onesimus's was "another way"—an anarchical way bearing no likeness at all to the accepted arky method of skinning cats. Not one of the characteristics of arky faith is to be found.

To be sure, slaves are freed and the classless society is formed. Yet, throughout, each of the principals (slave, owner, and attendant theologian of liberation) acts and is acted toward simply as the human individual he is—brothers three, only that and nothing more. No one (least of all the theologian directing the action) tries to use Onesimus as symbol of the "oppressed but righteous poor" whose consciousness of injustice must be raised to the point that he will join the class struggle. Paul, rather, convinces him to quit "fighting it" and go back—even into slavery. No one (least of all the theologian directing the action) tries, conversely, to use Philemon as a symbol of "the evil, oppressing, slaveholding class," exposing his injustice as a means of recruiting class warriors to fight against him. No one (least of all the theologian directing the action) has any interest in anybody's fighting anybody, in even seeing the matter as an adversary alignment.

The problem of human slavery is, of course, a *political* one. But our "theologian of liberation," being truly a *theologian*, says, "There just has to be more than the one *political* way of skinning this cat (i.e., the way that is limited to human probabilities and possibilities). Let us act *theologically* (i.e., in a way that both obeys God and, at the same time, invites him into the action). Let's try it that way—and see where God chooses to take it."

So they did. And so He did. And just see how far it went. You know, it's true: There *is* more than one way. . . .

Chapter Eleven

JUSTICE, FREEDOM, AND GRACE
The Fruits of Anarchy

Justice, Freedom, Grace—these three—and, biblically, the greatest of these is Grace. Necessarily is this the case because, biblically, both Justice and Freedom are actually gifts (or creations) of God's Grace. And thus, though our arky-faith theologies of liberation are so very strong on Justice and Freedom, even in this they are biblically flawed, for the fact that they do not have (and cannot admit) the reality of Grace to serve as source and context.

Biblically, "justice" is the end result of *God's* making things right according to his definition of "right"—and "freedom" is Paul's "For freedom *Christ* has set us free." It follows that both biblical justice and biblical freedom, from the outset, are assumed to be consequences, or end products, of God's work of grace. Apart from grace, justice and freedom are impossible goals.

For a starter, then, we need to work at the concept of "grace." At several different points, Paul calls grace a "gift." And that's fine; grace always is a gift and, by definition, cannot be anything else—such as a reward. Yet we should be careful not to turn the phrase around to say that any and all of God's gifts are of the character of grace. To do so weakens grace by broadening it out over too much territory.

When we think of God's "gifts," for instance, or say a table "grace" (a poor word for what it identifies), most often we proceed to thank him for the blessings of this good earth (for health and strength and daily food), for family, friends, etc. Now those are all certainly fine gifts; they *are* your many blessings that should be counted one by one. Yet, if we stop with those, we have not yet touched what Scripture intends by grace. To avoid confusion, we would do well to identify those things as "blessings"—the fruits of

God's "beneficence"—and reserve "grace" for that gift of God which goes a whole level deeper and represents a radically different quality from these.

My *Dictionary of New Testament Theology* tells me that, clear back with the Old Testament, the Hebrew word for grace identified not simply "nice gifts for nice people," but rather the rescue operation of pulling out those who were far gone—even if they had created the predicament for themselves, even if they had rejected the Lifeguard's advice and been insulting to him in the process.

In Romans 5:12-18, the apostle Paul gets the New Testament concept of grace even more closely defined. There he suggests that grace is God's restoring us to life after we have committed suicide—made ourselves *dead*—with our sin; our defiance of God; our unwillingness to accept his love, help, and guidance.

Obviously, Paul cannot be thinking simply of physical death when he includes himself and his alive and breathing readers in the words "so death spread to all men because all men sinned." His thought, certainly, is that all of us are already dead. I take him to mean, therefore, that—as far as having any chance of making it on our own, of being able to avert the degeneration of ourselves and our society, of having the capacity to get ourselves alive again through self-invented means of artificial respiration—by any of these indications we are as much as *dead*. Unless there should come the grace of God, *we're dead*.

In that situation, we have no grounds at all for *expecting* that such grace will be forthcoming. In dying as we all have done, we simply have been getting what we asked for. After we have treated him so badly, God is under no obligation at all to jump in and rescue us, no obligation at all to give life to those who have already refused it from him in preferring their own brand of death.

I—along with Paul and Henry F. Lyte—am ready to affirm that "change and decay in all around I see." From where I stand (and from the newspapers I read) it seems plain that we live (if you can call it that) in the midst of a dead (or at least far from "living") humanity. Indeed, who can dispute the strong note of Scripture that, were it not for innumerable past rescue operations of God's grace, the human race would not have survived as long as it has? No, Paul is right: *In Adam*—that is, on our own, on the basis sheerly of our own inherent piety and power—none of us, either individually or corporately, shows the ghost of a chance of making it. We are the dead and the dying.

Thus, in an earlier chapter, we examined arky faith's *modus operandi* which sees history in terms of progressive human moral accomplishment—and, over against that, the anarchical *modus operandi* which sees it in terms of death and resurrection. Implicit in that analysis is also a social justice that could be both defined and established *without* recourse to any concept of God's grace over against one that can't come otherwise than through God's grace. We implied that *resurrection* is perhaps the one word in the dictionary that can be spelled in no way other than g-r-a-c-e.

Similarly, in our previous chapter, Onesimus's first try at freedom (through the arky method of rebelling and running away, the freedom that proved so much less than satisfactory)—this freedom did not call upon or make any use of grace. Yet, of course, in his second try at freedom (in the completely unarkycal action of voluntarily going back) Onesimus was doing nothing other than throwing himself upon the grace of God. Clearly, only that *freedom* founded upon *grace* proved real.

Both arky faith and Christian Anarchy are committed to "justice," but only anarchy understands that justice needs grace. Both arky faith and Christian Anarchy are dedicated to "freedom," but only anarchy understands that freedom, also, needs grace. Paul, then, gives us another presentation of grace that may explain why, in our arky faith, we so often find grace unwelcome and even threatening.

In 2 Corinthians 12, Paul talks about the overwhelmingly wonderful "visions and revelations of the Lord" he had received. But, he recognizes, these very blessings easily could make him feel self-important and think too highly of himself. So he says, "To keep me from being too elated by the abundance of revelations, a thorn was given me in the flesh, a messenger of Satan, to harass me, to keep me from being too elated. Three times I besought the Lord about this, that it should leave me; but he said to me, 'My grace is sufficient for you, for my power is made perfect in weakness.' I will all the more gladly boast of my weaknesses, that the power of Christ may rest upon me."

Two points here are plain: (1) "Grace" is an utterly *theological* concept. Ultimately, of course, "the power of Christ" is the power of resurrecting the dead, the power of bringing back those who are far gone. No more than Paul could manage the taking of the "thorn" from his own flesh can the world devise its own equivalent of grace that would effect a "de-thorning" of itself. No, grace comes from God or it isn't grace at all.

(2) The only possible receptor of divine grace is human weakness. As long as anyone is feeling elated about himself, self-confident and self-sufficient, there is no way he will even consider the possibility of grace—even if God be perfectly ready to proffer it. One simply cannot know the grace of being rescued, of being resurrected from the dead, if he hasn't been willing to admit that he's out of his depth, that he's in trouble, that realistically he's *dead*. No, human weakness is the one true counterpart, the only possible receptor, for divine grace.

Arky faith, we now will see, is actually prohibitive of grace on both these counts. Earlier we made the distinction between *the political* (that which operates entirely in terms of human possibilities and probabilities) and *the theological* (that which operates solely from the premise that there is a God whose presence makes a decisive difference even in public affairs and the course of history). Arky faith (by definition, the belief that the outcome of history is determined by the victory of good human arkys over the bad ones) is essentially *political* in nature. So arky faith can't manage any real concept of "grace," because grace can have no source other than God and arky faith is ultimately a faith in human possibility rather than in a gracious God.

Yet Paul's second point is even more directly relevant. Because arky faith presupposes struggle and contest as the given means of the good's victory in history, the arky vehicles of that good as much as always must operate out of strength. Weakness (or sin) is the last thing a contending arky can afford to confess of itself. Yet self-defensiveness, the strong assertion of one's own righteous deserving, is the hallmark of our age, whether on the level of the individual or of our corporate arkys. Because either "justice" or "freedom" (as we are wont to define them) lies precisely in "fighting for your rights," gaining what you or your befriended constituents *deserve,* the requisite action must be that of establishing at all costs the moral strength and superiority of your own good arky over against the guilt and moral weakness of the opposing bad arky. Obviously, in such a setup, even the idea of grace will be a threat to the very possibility of justice. For me to admit in myself any sort of weakness, defect, or sin calling for the ministrations of God's grace would also, in effect, be giving ammunition to my enemy. To admit that I am dead and that this death is what I truly deserved would be to put me out of the contest completely. Arky faith simply cannot afford the idea of grace.

This "gracelessness" shows up on another level as well. God's grace toward us (what we shall call "vertical grace") clearly is meant to spin off as graciousness among ourselves (what shall be called "horizontal grace"). Of course, horizontal grace is not at all the same phenomenon as vertical grace: we humans have neither the power nor the will that can rescue or redeem another, and certainly nothing that can actually resurrect the dead. Indeed, we might do well to identify the horizontal variety simply as *graciousness* and reserve the term *grace* for the vertical variety alone.

Nevertheless, there is a likeness and a relationship. "Graciousness" is the awareness of our own weakness that makes us willing to go easy on the weaknesses of others, the awareness of logs in our own eyes that makes us lenient regarding specks in other people's. Graciously, we are ready, now, to be patient with them, understanding of them, nonjudgmental toward them, forgiving of them, willing to overlook what we otherwise would be inclined to make a big fuss about. And there is a second side of graciousness that is just as important. It is the readiness to recognize and appreciate all the graciousness that has been shown me—perhaps even by some of my enemies.

The connection between divine grace and human graciousness is a direct one. Finding the idea of grace subversive of our efforts toward justice, we have never truly been open to the experience of God's grace toward us. And never having really known grace there, we don't know what it calls for or feels like on the horizontal plane, either. Living in a social dogfight in which everyone is out to get the bone to which he knows he's entitled, we find horizontal graciousness to be just as inappropriate as the vertical sort. We live in a world that has no room for grace.

Of course, when it means being gracious to people we like, there's no problem. Yet grace is truly grace, not where it comes easily, but only where it comes very hard indeed. (And don't suppose that we are such nice people that God must find it easy to be gracious toward us.) But I must say I have been frightened at times to discover how mean and just plain graceless good Christians can be toward the bad people they have come to designate as "enemy."

One small example will show what I have in mind. Some time ago now, President Reagan spoke before a conference of professional women and, obviously in an effort to be friendly and complimentary, said something to the effect that women are to be credited with having civilized the race, getting the poor, barbaric males out of the cave and into some decent clothes. Whether the president's remark was a boo-boo or not, it was received any way but graciously. Rather than being willing to overlook anything, those women plainly were intent to pick up on anything they could make a scene over—which they proceeded to do.

Had the speaker been a woman and made the remark, the likelihood is that it would have been greeted with laughter and applause. Had it been made by almost anyone other than President Reagan, even if the wording were perceived as being a bit awkward and insensitive, it would have been graciously overlooked. No, plainly it was not the remark but the identity of the speaker that brought forth viciousness where there should have been grace.

You see, long before the president entered the room, these women (whether rightly or wrongly) had him identified as a "bad guy," "the enemy." And according to the rules of arky contest, when you spot a weakness in the enemy, the thing to do is latch on to it, dramatize it, and exploit it to his humiliation and loss. Otherwise, to practice graciousness—overlooking and forgiving an adversary's weakness—would be to miss a good chance for casting the first stone, passing up a made-to-order opportunity for exposing his wickedness and advancing one's own righteous cause. Is it not true that today's enthusiastic fight for justice and liberation actually brings with it a loss of felt need for God's vertical grace, at the same time introducing an ugly gracelessness that poisons our horizontal relationships?

However, in contradistinction, my earlier book, again (*Towering Babble*, chaps. 6–7), includes a detailed study of the biblical traditions of justice and, by implication, freedom. "Justice," there, turns out to be nothing like our fight for equality and human rights, our good arkys gaining power over and demolishing the evil ones. No, that concept of justice is seen to be an inheritance from our secular juridical tradition—which is not to deny that it may well be the highest concept of justice of which *political* thought is capable. But, biblically and *theologically*, "justice" is the situation created when the one true "Judge Jehovah" renders a "judgment" that has the effect of "justifying" and making right whoever and whatever needs "justification." The biblical concept does not presuppose an adversary alignment and nowhere has in view this business of one set of "just" people breaking the power of another "unjust" set. In consequence, directly contrary to the political concepts of justice and freedom, the theological ones find grace not to be *excluded* but deliberately and necessarily *included*.

Just a couple of the texts cited in that study can be taken as typical and used to make the point here. Isaiah 1:21-27 is pointed and powerful:

> How the faithful city
>   has become a harlot,
>   she that was full of justice!
> Righteousness lodged in her,
>   but now murderers.
>
> Your princes are rebels
>   and companions of thieves.
> Everyone loves a bribe
>   and runs after gifts.
> They do not defend the fatherless,
>   and the widow's cause does not come to them.
>
> Therefore the Lord says,
>
> I will turn my hand against you
>   and will smelt away your dross as with lye
>   and remove all your alloy.
> And I will restore your judges as at the first,
>   and your counselors as at the beginning.
> Afterward you shall be called the city of righteousness,
>   the faithful city.
>
> Zion shall be redeemed by justice.

Notice that, with the rebellious princes on the one hand and the fatherless and widows on the other, we have the makings of an oppressing-versus-oppressed class distinction. Unfortunately, there being on hand no "theologian of liberation" to spot it, to raise the class consciousness and instigate the class warfare, nothing of the sort develops. Even more unfortunately, Judge Jehovah's moral standard being what it is, *everyone* is found guilty and there is not left the makings of a holy arky, a Justice and Freedom Party he could elect to contest the arky of evil. With no help to be had from any of us good people, God sees no alternative but to create justice in his own theological, anarchical way.

It is plain that that way does involve punishment, retribution, and the breaking of the power of the evil arky. However, because that evil arky is universal in membership, God's is an entirely different action from one human arky taking it upon itself to wreak righteous judgment upon another. It is precisely in this regard that Markus Barth once explained why the New Testament forbids *us* to act as judges toward one another, demanding rather that we leave all vengeance to God.

Even Isaiah's "punishment language" makes clear that the ultimate intention behind it is *cleansing;* and the progress of the passage then moves to a redemption that could as well be called "resurrection." What Barth pointed out is simply that, in our justice-making zeal, we humans rate among the best in passing out righteous condemnation, damnation, and punishment. However, when it comes to the justifying finale of redemption and resurrection, we just do not have the wherewithal (haven't the remotest beginning of a wherewithal). So, if there is no chance of our seeing the justice-process through to its justifying conclusion, we would better let God do it his way from the outset.

However, the major point to be made is that, where *political* justice necessarily is prohibitive of grace, *theological* justice, God's justice, is as much as synonymous with grace. God's justice is not a program that has the party of the innocent-oppressed contending to get what they *deserve;* it is a program that has every party involved being justified (made right) quite apart from anyone's *deserving* anything. "God's justifying of *whoever* and *what all* will accept it": call that "justice," call that "freedom," call that "grace," call that "resurrection," it all comes to the same thing. Admittedly, the Isaiah passage opens with a justice of God that *damns* Zion. Yet that in itself leads to and concludes in the line proclaiming that justice shall also *redeem* Zion. If I may say so, such "grace-justice that redeems"—that is indeed one rare justice—one hardly to be found among us or even our holy arkys, one obviously to be found only in the God who invented and controls both justice and grace.

A second citation—this one from Isaiah 45:19-23—will make the concept of "grace-justice" even more explicit. Biblical talk of justice always has reference to "Judge Jehovah" as the one whose "judgment" eventuates in the "justification" of the guilty defendant. Accordingly, the mental imagery which may be in the background of all biblical justice talk (and which moves into the foreground with some frequency) is that of a trial transpiring in Judge Jehovah's courtroom. And that is a *Hebrew* courtroom, we need to bear in mind, not a Graeco-Roman or Western one—there's a difference. The following picture is one of the Bible's best—one that Paul brings over into Philippians 2.

I the Lord speak the truth,
I declare what is right.

Assemble yourselves and come,
    draw near together,
    you survivors of the nations!
They have no knowledge
    who carry about their wooden idols,
and keep on praying to a god
    that cannot save.

Declare and present your case;
    let them take counsel together!
Who told this long ago?
    Who declared it of old?
Was it not I, the Lord?
    And there is no other god besides me,
a righteous God and a Savior;
    there is none besides me.

Turn to me and be saved,
    all the ends of the earth!
For I am God, and there is no other.
By myself I have sworn,
    from my mouth has gone forth in righteousness
    a word that shall not return:
"To me every knee shall bow,
    every tongue shall swear."

There is enough juridical terminology scattered throughout
this passage to make it certain that the courtroom metaphor is meant
to control the whole. There is only One who is qualified to serve as
Judge of all the earth, who not only can *say* what justice is but also
is capable of bringing it to be the actual state of affairs. The defendant in this instance is not God's own city, his own people unfortunately gone wrong, as was the case in our previous text. No, here
the defendant is that truly no-good outfit of "the nations," "the
Gentiles"—the absolutely evil arky that had regularly oppressed innocent Israel, that Israel continually had to be fighting, whose damnation and destruction Israel sought as "justice."

The Judge knows very well that this defendant is as guilty as
can be—guilty of the number 1 sin and ultimate injustice of trying
to evade the Judge by setting up wooden idols and praying to gods
that cannot save. Apparently this defendant has already taken some
punishment in consequence; he is identified as the "*survivors* of the
nations." Even so, completely contrary to Israel's own sense of arky

justice (passages like this one just cannot be explained as creations of Israelite culture), the Judge introduces himself not simply as "Judge (righteous God)" but as the Judge who is likewise "Savior." Who can say whether "justice" or "grace" is the more prominent theme here, when the two are, in effect, congruent?

But the courtroom—indubitably the place of judgment—is here presented as also being the place of grace and salvation. It is the place where not merely the "oppressed" can hope to find justice, but where the ends of the earth (including, of course, the "oppressors") can be saved by turning to the Judge (who, we are quick to grant, was, in the same trial, also their condemner). That Judge's final, sworn decree is that his courtroom will stay open until every knee bows in recognition of the fact that he is the Judge whose grace-justice not only can but *will* and *has* saved and justified to the uttermost.

"There's no denying that what you've just shown us from Isaiah is a wonderful theological vision. The trouble is that it is so theologically idealistic as to be entirely irrelevant to the real political world in which we live and in which we must do our seeking of justice. The evil, oppressing arkys against which we must contend are themselves so totally impervious to anything like 'grace' that, in the struggle, it would be sheer foolishness for us to try anything like a gracious approach to them. Really, it's too bad; yet the fact of the matter is that the world is so locked into the ways of power-justice that we have no alternative. Isaiah's will have to remain what it is, a wonderful theological *vision*."

I disagree. The above objection actually sells God short. In rebuttal, allow me to present another "trial" story—this one under the title "The Grace of the U.S. Government." And if the pairing of "grace" with "the wicked, oppressing arky of the U.S. government" strikes you as the height of outrage and ludicrousness—well, that only shows you need to keep reading.

Of course, what immediately must be said is that *grace* is the wrong word and that what I actually have in mind is "The *Graciousness* of the U.S. Government." As a Christian anarchist, I am under no illusion that *any* human arky (including the church) can so nearly approximate God as to communicate anything remotely resembling justifying, redeeming, resurrecting *grace*. Obviously I have in mind only the spin-off of horizontal, human-level *graciousness*—though goodness knows, even this much is an entirely rare commodity in the setting of arky contention for justice. Specifically, then, my story is meant to show how the practice of true Christian Anarchy can lend an air of graciousness even to political arky confrontations normally marked by contention, accusation, and ill-will. Christian Anarchy seeks justice in a spirit entirely different from that of arky faith.

I actually have better reason than most to think very ungraciously of the U.S. Government. I've been under its gun. Actually, it was son Enten rather than I personally who was under the gun, but I was standing close enough to be mighty uncomfortable. We are speaking, of course, of the government that indicted him for following his conscience in declining to register for its military conscription. It then put him through a full-fledged (and highly publicized) federal trial where, before the world, he was found guilty and convicted as a felon.

I was in the courtroom as a witness for the defense and was closely informed regarding all the action outside the courtroom. I can speak for one who has been done to as a designated "enemy" of the U.S. Government. All the official papers bore the heading: THE UNITED STATES OF AMERICA *versus* ENTEN VERNARD ELLER. This was the setup for a power struggle in which all the power was on one side—and in which all the right to define and enforce justice was on one side, too. As an arky contest, this one didn't promise to be a very fair matchup. At least with David against Goliath, the kid wasn't pacifistically inhibited from slinging pebbles (or mud).

Let it be clear that, as I now proceed to speak of the graciousness of the U.S. Government, I am in no way legitimizing that arky as being of God, am in no way suggesting that it is above criticism. Shortly following the trial itself, I published an article in which I made my witness-protest, speaking to the points at which I felt the government to be dead wrong—such things as the calling of a registration that is of no practical military value; calling a registration in the absence of any perceived emergency; enacting legislation that does not recognize or make any provision for religious conscience; and, in a way completely disproportionate to much more serious crimes, making nonregistration a felony punishable by five years in prison and a $10,000 fine.

Yet that is only half the story—and sheer honesty (quite apart from any graciousness on my part) demands that the other half be told as well.

(I am choosing, now, not to name anyone by name—except Enten, of course. It is not that I am reluctant to give credit where credit is due, but that I very much *do* want to give credit where it is due. Thus, it is not so much that we are dealing with a number of exceptionally nice individuals who should be credited by name. I will be quick to confess that neither Enten nor his father belongs in that category. Rather, we are dealing with an exceptionally nice God who ought at all times be named by us; to that end, I am keeping the human names in the background.)

First, it must be said that, all the way through, Enten spoke and acted toward the government in an entirely gracious manner. His nonregistration was totally a *theological* act of obedience to what he understood to be the will of God—and not at all the *political* "civil disobedience" of mounting a power protest against the wickedness of the state. He made no effort to call attention to his "just cause" or to try to make the government's cause look bad. We are grateful that Enten was enabled to act so and thank God for making such conduct possible.

Enten knew, of course, that his Bible forbids him from going to law. So, not having perfect freedom in that matter, he did the next best thing and prohibited his attorneys from mounting, on his behalf, any sort of legal challenges to the law or the actions of the government. His idea was that the trial should deal exclusively with his act of nonregistration and the rationale behind it—and not be turned into contention with the state. As is quite understandable, the attorneys were not a little frustrated—and so opened their case by complaining a bit to the judge and explaining that the defenselessness of the defense would be owing entirely to Enten's Christianity and not to any lack of adversarial will or skill on their part.

However, the judge figured a way to get around Enten's peccadillos (and thus show that it was *he,* and not Enten, who was running this trial). At the conclusion, in announcing his findings of fact, His Honor also took opportunity to educate Enten's attorneys and everyone present by listing the challenges and arguments he thought might be effective with a judge if *he* were a defense attorney (and if Enten were to let him mount them). It could be that the judge was a little jealous, thinking that in this particular case it would have been more fun to be on the defense than to have to be the judge. He did speak of the "agony" of judging this one—though I didn't feel too sorry for him, knowing that many other of the participants were undergoing agonies of their own.

However, at no point did government representatives show anything but respect and honor toward Enten. At no point did the government try to strengthen its case by accusing him of malice or by trying to blacken his reputation. Now, the government knows how to do that, of course—knows how to play "adversarial put-down" just as well as the peace movement does. The government could have done that. The fact that it did not can be credited only as horizontal grace.

I think I am correct that never in the course of the entire case was Enten confronted by an armed officer of the law. He was never arrested, handcuffed, or held in any sort of custody. Such, of course, is hardly accepted procedure with accused felons. It was indeed gracious of the government to recognize that a show of force was not appropriate in Enten's situation.

The closest thing to an officer of the law would have to have been the FBI agent in charge of the case. He was the witness for the prosecution in proving that Enten had not registered (although the trial time could have been cut in half simply by asking Enten whether he had). During the agent's cross-examination by the defense, the attorney asked him whether he had met Enten personally, and could he identify the defendant in the courtroom as being the nonregistrant. In answering, the agent let drop the fact that he had a daughter who was a student at Bridgewater College along with Enten. (He didn't say whether he had used her as a spy and informant to report on Enten's wickednesses.) He then went on to support his identification of the defendant in this way: The agent, it turns out, is an elder in the Presbyterian church where he resides. One Sunday he was at church when the Bridgewater touring choir gave its concert. He noticed Enten's name on the program, figured out (I guess) who was the most criminal-looking kid of the bunch, and went up and introduced himself during the picnic that followed.

This whole story came from the witness employed by the government to show Enten to be as guilty as possible. When I related it to a colleague who teaches in our University Law School, he opined that to voluntarily introduce this sort of information before the court and the press was indication enough that the government wasn't all that serious about nailing Enten to the wall—which is indeed a graciousness.

There were two prosecuting attorneys in the trial, both of whom had earlier interviewed Enten, politely and caringly warning him of what could happen if he continued to turn down extended offers for him to register. At one point the judge asked Enten whether he hadn't even made friends with the prosecutors. Enten would almost admit "friends" but wasn't quite ready to go to "bosom buddies." However, one of those prosecutors opened the trial by averring that the government was not in any way questioning the sincerity of Enten's conscientious objection, the legitimacy of his religious views, the right of any group to advocate pacifism, or, in particular, the integrity of the Church of the Brethren and its position.

The other prosecutor closed the government's case with these words:

> Everyone in this courtroom by now knows that the young man has not registered, and that his decision was made over a long period of time. I gather that everyone is persuaded that his decision was made intelligently, it was made by him carefully, and it was made with a considerable amount of counseling. The government does not today, and has not, challenged the sincerity of this young man's convictions. We do not claim or believe for one minute that the beliefs he has presented are a sham. We are persuaded he does indeed hold them.

Now, when, in any trial, the job of the prosecution is to *prosecute*—to put the defendant in the poorest possible light and make him out to be as guilty as it can—this sort of testimony comes through as high-level graciousness. Indeed, at some point in the proceedings, a journalist friend of Enten's who was seated in the press section (which took up the whole of the jury box and half the gallery) overheard the veteran Associated Press correspondent whisper, "This is the strangest trial I've ever seen."

The high-water mark of prosecution graciousness came in its cross-examination of the defendant. Instead of trying to score points against him, the prosecutor spent the time handing points to him. He began by expressing appreciation for the candor and openness Enten had shown all the way through and got from Enten the agreement that the prosecution had been "up front" in its turn. It was he, the prosecutor (and not the defense) who put it into the record that, even before Enten had been indicted or was under any sort of legal obligation, he had provided the prosecutors with his summer itinerary so he could be found without difficulty.

Although both in the press and from the public Enten had been accused of being a publicity seeker, it was the prosecutor (and not the defense) who revealed to the court that, early on, there had been a telephone conversation in which the defendant and the prosecution agreed that neither would seek media attention in making a public issue of the case. He then volunteered that Enten had fulfilled that pledge and received Enten's confirmation that the government had, too. Here, I suggest, the government was recognizing an all-important distinction between Enten's Christian Anarchy and the holy-arky "civil disobedience" with which it must regularly contend. The arky effort *needs* media coverage as the *empowerment* of its challenge to government wickedness; Enten wasn't challenging anyone, so neither needed nor wanted any help from the media.

Then, the judge—as much a representative of the U.S. Government as anyone else, recall: Almost as soon as the defense had its turn, while I was on the witness stand, the judge interrupted with a comment indicating that he saw the case as I was interpreting it—as having nothing to do with how good or bad Enten might be, but as a conflict between religion and the law.

Later, in the process of supposedly "examining" Enten, the judge got turned around actually to initiate an argument and help the defendant formulate it, namely, that Enten didn't even have an opinion as to whether God willed anyone else to join him in not registering, and that, in effect, he was not representing any power bloc and wanted no part of any. Here again, as I understand it, the government was pushing a second all-important distinction. "Civil disobedience," of course, is eager to recruit participants and amass supporters as a show of *power*. Yet, not even being in a power game, Christian Anarchy says only, "I must be obedient to what God wants from me—quite apart from what anyone else thinks or does."

In the formal announcement of his conclusions, the judge—as a finding of *fact*—said this: "I find further that, as of this time, he cannot conscientiously register with the Selective Service System." Of course, Enten had been catching all sorts of flak about being unpatriotic, a traitor to his country, and whatever. It may have been with this in mind, then, that, during the sentencing, the judge made a point of saying: "It seems to the court that this is a classic clash between your religious beliefs and the law of the land. I'm sure you love your country. I'm positive of that fact. I'm sure you love the people of this country." And his final words in the courtroom that day were these: "I think the defenses you have raised—or the defenses you haven't raised and so forth—have made you certainly an honorable person within the eyes of this court. And I think that your appearance here underscores that."

There is more graciousness in the trial that could be reported.

But when the person customarily addressed as "Your Honor" in effect bestows that title also upon the defendant he has just found guilty, that's grace (or at least a high level of human graciousness). There's nothing requiring a judge to undercut his own verdict by explaining it away, saying in effect: "I have to find you guilty of a felony, Enten; but I am ready to say loud and clear that I don't consider you a felon in any sense of the word." You tell me whether, in that trial, Enten was convicted or acquitted.

In his decree, the judge set as one of the terms of Enten's probation that, within ninety days, he must "comply with the registration requirements." For this part of the story you need to know that both of Enten's attorneys had, over the years, had close associations with the judge. Also in the picture is a man we shall call "the Shadow"—a good friend of mine, a Brethren attorney who had also been a longtime friend of the judge and who consequently was in touch with him throughout the case.

As Enten's time for compliance was running out, through the Shadow the judge leaked to Enten that it was 99 percent certain he would go to prison. However, when Enten did not comply, at the hearing the judge simply changed the terms of probation to two years of public service work. In a press interview given on that occasion, he was quoted as saying: "I wasn't going to give him a prison sentence. He's just different. He's a very special person."

Now Enten's attorneys had expressed their opinion that the judge really thought Enten would break down and register. However, the Shadow says flatly that the judge was certain Enten would not. And the Shadow knows. I'm sure of one thing: that particular judge would have a hard time living with himself if he knew he was responsible for *powering* Enten into acting contrary to what he felt was the direct leading of God. That judge would have leaked his threat only in the confidence it would not be heeded. What was going on throughout was "Christian graciousness."

Then, just as Enten was getting well started on his work project in Virginia, his sister was to be married in California and wanted him as a member of the wedding. He arranged with his employer for an absolute minimum of leave, missing only a Thursday and Friday at work. When, then, Enten applied to his probation officer for legal permission to make the trip, Mike said, "Well, if you're going so far, why don't you stay longer?" You can be sure Enten took him up on his graciousness; he was home for a full week.

At one point in the trial, from the stand the defendant thanked the judge for the "ease" he had felt in his courtroom. Rather than "ease," he could as well have said "freedom." Ellul started us out in this book by suggesting that Christian Anarchy is dedicated to our finding "freedom" by wresting it from the powers, "shaking an edifice, producing a fissure, a gap in the structure." I have no quarrel with that; in most of our exercise of anarchy the story will probably end there. However, when, into that fissure, that gap, there comes *the grace of God*—when divine grace spins off into human graciousness—there is no telling how far the freeing-up can go.

Enten found freedom in the very process of being convicted—praise the Lord! But wonder of wonders, if that damnable old arky of the U.S. Government (which, always remember, likewise consists of human individuals, just as much as Enten does) didn't experience some rather impressive freeing-up of its own—praise the Lord!

There was found the freedom for every person in that courtroom to be treated with the dignity and respect (and, yes, even love) due human individuals. There was found freedom from the necessity of conducting the trial as the arky contest: The United States of America *versus* Enten Vernard Eller. (As Enten told the press, the question as to who had won didn't make sense, because there hadn't been a fight.) There was found the freedom of the government to drop all the niceties of legal protocol ("the strangest trial I've ever seen") and play it simply as a group of concerned individuals addressing a common problem. There was found the freedom for the prosecution once to try its hand at producing evidence for the defense. There was found the freedom for the court to arrive at a conviction without creating wrath anywhere.

There was found grace. There was found freedom. And there was found justice—justice of a quality that the defendant could say to the judge: "I want to assure you that I would not condemn you if you were to convict me. . . . That is a choice that you have to make; and I admit that I am comfortable with you making it, because of what I have heard of you. And it is said that you are a just man. So I rest secure that, whether I am convicted or acquitted, you believe that justice has been served. And I'm comfortable with that."

All this, bear in mind, took its start from an *anarchical* action of refusing to obey the Big Arky's law. Nothing was found here that represents a legitimizing of the state, a recognizing of holy obligation toward it, any suggestion that it is above criticism. As I said, I even took the occasion to publish an article—done, I hope, in the rational persuasions of speaking the truth in love—which was my witness and protest against the evils and injustices of the draft registration law.

So, finding grace, freedom, and justice here manifest within the arky workings of the U.S. Government does in no way indicate that it is, in fact, a holy arky elect of God. Yet neither is there any counter-indication, that it is a demonic arky elect of Satan. No, all the indications are that it is simply a *human* arky—sometimes good, sometimes bad, and most times in-between (even as you and I— and probably in about the same proportions). Yet, even as in us God can sometimes find a fissure through which to introduce a bit of grace that frees us to be gracious (and even loving) toward that arky—so can he sometimes find a fissure through which to make it gracious in response.

Granted, Enten's U.S. Government trial and Isaiah's Judge Jehovah trial are not at all the same thing—yet they aren't totally dissimilar, either. My explanation of the similarity is not that the U.S. Government is like God, but that, ultimately, it was the same Judge conducting both trials—praise the Lord!

It is, of course, the presence in the trial of "human graciousness" that we have been arguing—and not necessarily that of the divine grace of God himself. Yet, at the same time, I certainly don't want to be guilty of *denying* that latter possibility. My reluctance is explained by the leeriness I feel around those who are so quick and self-confident in identifying what are manifestations of God's grace and what not; we humans are no more infallible in that regard than in any other. Yet in the trial, it must be said, God's grace was given every opportunity. Enten and company had a prayer meeting on the steps of the Federal Building before going in. When we got in, word came from the judge that he would be a little late. Enten's attorney (who well knows the judge) said, "He's probably in prayer with his pastor." That judge, it turns out, is basically a Sunday-school teacher for whom Sunday Classroom or Weekday Courtroom are all the same—he runs both the same way. In fact, I have reason to believe that considerable silent praying went on *right in the courtroom itself* (that's not unconstitutional, is it?). Granted, in Enten's trial we didn't do too good a job at maintaining our vaunted "separation of church and state"—but the point is that, although "human graciousness" is no proof, it *can be* a direct product of "God's grace."

Well then, we have portrayed justice, freedom, and grace as fruits of Christian Anarchy. Recently, two events coincided in time to impress me with the arky-faith equivalents. The first was the Republican Convention with its disgusting rush of conservative, evangelical Christians to ordain the Reagan Administration as holy government in holy tandem with holy church. Yet that is sheerly the zealotism of foot-kissing, collaborationist legitimizing, with nothing of truly Christian justice, freedom, or grace to be found in it or expected from it. For sure, the U.S. Government isn't *that* good— or the church, either, if it comes to that.

About the same time, there appeared an issue of *Sojourners,* a magazine of radical discipleship, with this headline on the cover, in large, colored, block lettering:

RONALD REAGAN IS LYING ABOUT NICARAGUA.

IF THE U.S. INVADES NICARAGUA,
thousands of U.S. citizens
are promising massive public resistance.

If that is discipleship, it is the following of a Lord different from the one I ever heard speak; it represents a type of offense-causing entirely different from his. This is sheerly the turned-up volume of zealotism and revolutionist class warfare with nothing of truly Christian justice, freedom, and grace about it or to be expected from it. For sure, the U.S. Government isn't *that* bad, either—so bad that it now becomes "speaking the truth in love" to accuse and damn it for sins not yet committed.

It's enough to make one grateful to be a Christian anarchist, free to give God what belongs to God rather than having to choose between the holy-arky alternatives.